Fixing Global Finance

Fixing Global Finance

How to Curb Financial Crises in the 21st Century

● ●

MARTIN WOLF

Yale University Press

NEW HAVEN AND LONDON

For information about this and other Yale University Press publications, please contact:
U.S. Office: sales.press@yale.edu   www.yalebooks.com
Europe Office: sales@yaleup.co.uk   www.yalebooks.co.uk

Printed in Great Britain by TJ International Ltd, Padstow, Cornwall

Library of Congress Cataloging-in-Publication Data

Wolf, Martin, 1946–
  Fixing global finance / Martin Wolf.
    p. cm.—(Forum on constructive capitalism)
  Includes bibliographical references and index.
  ISBN: 978-0-300-14277-8 (ci: alk. paper)
  1. International finance. I. Title.
    HG3881.W65 2008
    332′.042—dc22

                                                                    2008011089

A catalogue record for this book is available from the British Library.

10 9 8 7 6 5 4 3 2 1

To Daniel, beloved brother and dearest friend

Contents

Preface

Much has been written about panics and manias, much more than with the most outstretched intellect we are able to follow or conceive; but one thing is certain, that at particular times a great deal of stupid people have a great deal of stupid money. . . . At intervals, . . . the money of these people—the blind capital, as we call it, of the country—is particularly large and craving; it seeks for someone to devour it, and there is a "plethora"; it finds someone, and there is "speculation"; it is devoured, and there is "panic."

WALTER BAGEHOT

WHEN I STUDIED ECONOMICS at Oxford University between 1967 and 1971, as an undergraduate at Corpus Christi College and then as a post-graduate at Nuffield College, the return of an era of financial crises seemed inconceivable. The Great Depression of the 1930s had scarred my parents' generation. For my father—a Jewish playwright who had lived in Vienna until the imminent threat of the Third Reich persuaded him to depart for England in 1937—the economic disaster had been frightening enough. But its political effect was even worse. In the early 1930s, the rapid rise in German unemployment that left a quarter of the labor force out of work had brought Adolf Hitler to power. The response of almost everybody in western Europe after World War II was *never again*. The managed capitalism of my childhood was the result.

Financial crises had been largely absent in the "golden age" of the 1950s and 1960s, an era that shone particularly brightly in western Europe and Japan. Capital markets had remained caged, both domestically and internationally, since the 1930s. Most countries, including the United Kingdom, imposed tight controls on foreign exchange transactions—not just on capital account, but even on current account. Under Harold Wilson's Labour government people were, at one point, not allowed to take more than £50 out of the country for an overseas vacation. Governments not only curbed foreign transactions, they also constrained domestic finance: banks and providers of mortgage finance ("building societies," as they are called in the United Kingdom; "savings and loans" or "thrifts," as they are known in the United States) were the dominant suppliers of funds to companies and households. The activities of such institutions were closely regulated. Even the relatively free-market United States had ceilings on interest rates, while the United Kingdom controlled credit growth directly. Few imagined that financial crises would return. Like London's outbreaks of cholera in the nineteenth century or the Great Plague of the seventeenth century, such events were presumed to be of merely historical interest.

The past is indeed a foreign country. The publication in 2006 of the late Andrew Glyn's book on the restoration of capitalism and the unleashing of finance reminded me of how distant that world is now.[1] Glyn, an economics fellow at Corpus Christi College, had, while still a graduate student at Nuffield College, taught me macroeconomics. A man of the left, he was then beginning to identify a looming crisis of capitalism, as a triumphant working class pushed up real wages at a faster rate than productivity growth, thus squeezing corporate profits and lowering the share of profits in gross domestic product. But, as he admits in his book, those on his side of the political argument failed to foresee that the crisis which befell post–World War II managed capitalism in the 1970s would result not in its replacement by the socialist economy they desired but in the restoration of a free-market version in the West and even "in the planned economies of the USSR and the rest of the formerly communist world."[2] Those opposed to socialism were for the most part just as surprised by this outcome, if more pleased.

This astonishing turnaround remains, as Glyn's thought-provoking book makes plain, the central political and economic story of our era, not just in the rich countries of which he writes, but in the world as a whole, as I pointed out in my own book on globalization, published in 2004.[3]

When I was a student, all this still lay far in the future. In international economics, the dominant concern remained old-fashioned foreign-currency crises—situations in which large trade deficits and a shortfall of official holdings of foreign-currency reserves forced governments to accept devaluations. The pound sterling had been chronically weak during the first three decades after World War II. A devaluation was forced upon a reluctant Labour government in 1967, after three years of fruitless defense.

More importantly, economists were already becoming aware of the "dollar problem," as the rising U.S. trade deficits—themselves needed, as the Belgian economist Robert Triffin had argued, to create global liquidity—threatened the key currency of the global economy.[4] Peter Oppenheimer of Christ Church, who taught me international economics when I was an undergraduate and had worked at the Bank for International Settlements in

Basle, supported the idea of raising the price of gold to increase global liquidity. That is, of course, not what happened: gold was demonetized altogether, though its value in the market did indeed soar well above the official price of $35 an ounce. In 1971 President Richard Nixon imposed a temporary import surcharge to force a devaluation of the dollar against the currencies of his country's reluctant trading partners. This loss of an anchor for monetary policy turned out to be one step on the path to a decade of inflationary turmoil. That surcharge may also be a precedent for the current situation, as the United States confronts today's vastly bigger trade deficits.

The abandonment of the Bretton Woods system of fixed, but adjustable, exchange rates in the 1970s marked the beginning of a new global economy.[5] It was the start of an era of unstable exchange rates among the world's most important currencies. Other events followed: two oil shocks and the great inflation of the 1970s and the subsequent restoration of monetary stability under Paul Volcker's chairmanship of the Federal Reserve; the "recycling" of petrodollars to emerging market economies and the consequent public sector debt crises of the 1980s; Deng Xiaoping's reforms in China since 1978; the liberalization of exchange controls by Margaret Thatcher's new Conservative government in 1979 and the privatizations of nationalized industries; the election of Ronald Reagan in 1980; the fall of the Soviet empire between 1989 and 1991; the liberalization of India's economy after the crisis of 1991; and the completion of the Uruguay Round and the subsequent creation of the World Trade Organization in 1996.

These developments led to the emergence of the new market-oriented world economy—sometimes known as the "second globalization" since the industrial revolution, to distinguish it from the "first globalization" of the late nineteenth and early twentieth centuries. It was a time of great promise, but also of substantial disappointment. Above all, these turned out to be what Robert Aliber of the University of Chicago's Graduate School of Business, in his posthumous edition of Charles Kindleberger's classic work, calls "the most tumultuous decades ever" for financial manias and panics.[6]

Economists have made progress in recent decades in understanding how financial markets work and what can go wrong with them. Progress in financial theory also created vast new markets in financial products known as derivatives. Meanwhile, events forced economists to confront the impact of the financial sector on macroeconomic performance. As the chief editorial writer for economics of the *Financial Times* from 1987 to 1996 and its chief economics commentator since then, I have had a ringside seat. All too often, the policymaking world was struggling to understand what was happening. Now the underlying economic forces are becoming a bit clearer. Unfortunately they are also rather depressing. It is hard, it turns out, to generate a sustained and stable net transfer of resources to emerging market economies. Every time this has happened, a severe crisis has resulted. The U.S. current account deficits of today are, I have concluded, the direct consequence of that failure. The United States has become the world's spender and borrower of last resort, precisely because the world of globalized finance has proved so unstable.

This is the story I have been telling in my columns for the *Financial Times*. But it is one that needs elaboration. My book on globalization contained a discussion of the finance of emerging market economies with which I am happy, so far as it went.[7] But I was aware, even at the time of writing, that it needed to go much further. For this reason, I was particularly grateful to Francis Fukuyama for the invitation to present three lectures to the Bernard L. Schwartz Forum on Constructive Capitalism at the Paul H. Nitze School of Advanced International Studies (SAIS) of the Johns Hopkins University in the spring of 2006.[8] I am also grateful to Bernard Schwartz for his generous sponsorship of that series. The SAIS lectures built on the Richard Snape Lecture, which I gave in Melbourne in November 2005.[9] Richard was a renowned international economist and an admired friend. It gave me great pleasure to deliver one of the lectures in what has become a distinguished series.

Presenting these lectures was not only an honor but also a great opportunity. It gave me the chance, for the first time, to tell the story of international finance of the past three decades and, in particular, of the move from emerging market crises to global imbalances. I argued that the rise of U.S. borrowing is a solution, but an unsatisfactory one, to the failures of the global financial system of the past three decades. I wanted to explain how close has become the link between the microeconomics of finance and the macroeconomics of exchange rates and the balance of payments. It is in the area of finance that microeconomics and macroeconomics merge most completely. It is in this area, too, that the domestic and the global meet most intimately and with the greatest potential for calamity. These were the themes of my lectures. They remain the themes of this book, which builds upon those lectures.

No one completes a book without a great deal of help. This one has been no exception. I thank five people in particular, apart from those already mentioned: Max Corden, who awoke my interest in the international economy when I was a postgraduate student in economics at Nuffield College and who has written such illuminating pieces on international macroeconomics; Lionel Barber, editor of the *Financial Times,* who tolerated the two long summer breaks during which the lectures were turned into this book; Felicity Bryan, my devoted and perennially enthusiastic agent; Keith Fray, who obtained the data for so many of the figures; and, not least, my wife, Alison, who read and commented on all the chapters and encouraged me to keep going when I was convinced I should abandon the job of writing on so fast-changing a subject. I am deeply grateful to them all.

Fixing Global Finance

CHAPTER 1

Learning Lessons

The people who benefit from roiling the world currency markets are speculators, and as far as I'm concerned, they provide not much useful value.

PAUL O'NEILL, FORMER U.S. TREASURY SECRETARY

FINANCE IS THE BRAIN OF THE MARKET ECONOMY. Unfortunately, as the world has been reminded too frequently over the past three decades— not least in the credit squeeze that began in the summer of 2007—this brain is susceptible to a variety of infirmities. In particular, it is prone to wild swings of mood, from euphoria to panic. The history of global finance since 1980 has, as a result, been one of frighteningly expensive financial crises—expensive not just in terms of the costs to the taxpayer or of output forgone, but in terms of the shattered lives of innocent victims.

Waves of Crises

These disasters have turned global finance into the biggest economic challenge for those who support the integration of the world economy, a process now almost universally known as globalization. It is far from the only such challenge: international conflict, terrorism, and environmental catastrophe may ultimately prove far more important. But these challenges are not for economic policy alone. The workings of the financial system fall squarely within the economist's domain. If global finance does little more than bring catastrophe in its wake, it becomes almost impossible to defend existing, let alone increased, levels of financial integration.

Pointing to these waves of crises, some eminent economists have condemned financial integration outright. Among them have been the Nobel laureate Joseph Stiglitz of Columbia and Manchester universities and Jagdish Bhagwati, also of Columbia, the most distinguished contemporary proponent of liberal trade.[1] These two economists agree on few things, but they do agree on this. While almost all economists concur on the benefits of free trade, the same is decidedly not true for liberal finance. On this topic, opinions in the profession are far more evenly divided. George Soros, the contemporary world's best example of a financial poacher turned would-be gamekeeper, has also been a persistent critic of the financial markets.[2] The financial disasters have also had direct and dire consequences on the politics of emerging economies. Because of a wave of devastating financial crises, the public mood in Latin America has swung sharply against what is widely condemned as "neoliberalism" on that continent.

I am not quite so pessimistic. There are potential advantages to liberal financial markets. But exploiting those advantages, while minimizing the risks, poses an enormous challenge. The experience of the past three decades has demonstrated that conclusively. Even in the mid-1980s, few economists understood the potential for disaster in the interplay between liberalized finance, global financial integration, and the international monetary system. A notable exception was the late Carlos Díaz-Alejandro, wisest of all Latin American economists, in a prescient article published in 1985.[3] We all know better now, but only after a long series of brutal lessons.

If we are to do better, however, we need to understand both the advantages and the dangers of liberal global finance. Even today, a harvest failure or a huge shift in the price of a particular commodity may have a significant impact on a developing country. The price of oil is an obvious example. Yet in high-income countries and in most of the larger developing countries as well, no single productive sector has an economy-wide effect. But a financial crisis can have a huge impact on an entire economy. Indeed, it can have a serious impact on many economies at once. To understand the nature of these risks and the policy challenges they pose, we need to understand both the microeconomics of finance and the macroeconomics of exchange rates, public finance, and monetary policy. It is in finance that microeconomics and macroeconomics meet. It has always been so.

Financial crises are most significant when they are international. A purely domestic financial crisis is not inconceivable. Of the significant crises of the past three decades, the Japanese crisis of the 1990s comes closest to being such a predominantly domestic event. While the crisis had both international causes and international consequences, Japan was (and remains) a creditor country. For this reason, it was relatively easy for the authorities to manage the crisis without drastic consequences for the rest of the world. Indeed, they should have been able to resolve that crisis far more swiftly and effectively. It was, above all, quite easy for them to raise the resources they needed by borrowing from their own people.

Crises that involve foreign suppliers of capital—and, by definition, globalization means that financial systems include foreigners—have tended to be far costlier and more difficult to manage. Foreigners, by and large, do not place much trust in the governments of other countries, particularly of less-developed countries. More important, the domestic authorities of the country in crisis cannot dragoon foreigners. Above all, crises involving foreign capital usually result in exchange rate crises and so quite often in a "twin crisis," in which the interaction between a collapsing exchange rate and large net foreign-currency liabilities ensures mass insolvency in the private sector, including a bankrupt financial system. In this situation, the domestic authorities frequently lose their access to world financial markets and are then unable to rescue their financial systems without foreign assistance.

Fixing What Has Gone Wrong

This book argues that the failure to make international finance work tolerably well has had consequences, for both the affected countries and the world economy as a whole. It has created a number of large global economic shocks. The "subprime crisis" that began in the United States in 2007 was itself a direct result of those shocks. This history raises two fundamental questions: What has gone wrong? And how is it to be fixed?

In the 1970s, 1980s, and 1990s financial crises always followed periods of large-scale net capital flows into emerging market economies. Subsequently most of the latter decided (or were compelled by the markets) to cease being net importers of capital. Many even became substantial capital exporters. In the 2000s, the desire of private investors to invest once again in many of these countries has led the emerging market economies to engage in large-scale foreign-currency intervention and accumulation of foreign-currency reserves. Emerging market economies "smoke, but do not inhale" in global capital markets. The majority are prepared to engage in capital markets, but do not accept—indeed have worked hard to avoid accepting—net capital inflows into their economies. This is astonishingly —and disturbingly—different from the experience with financial globalization in the late nineteenth and early twentieth centuries.

Happily, as late as fall 2007, no sizable emerging market crises had occurred after 2001 (when Argentina defaulted), while the last global wave of crises to affect emerging economies occurred between 1997 and early 1999. This may suggest that the world economy has attained stability. That would be a premature judgment. Since emerging market economies are unable or unwilling to absorb surplus savings generated in the world economy and, on the contrary, are generating surpluses themselves, some high-income countries must instead absorb those funds. Thus the net flows of capital were from the rest of the world to a few creditworthy high-income countries and, above all, to the United States, which has become the superpower of global borrowing. The emergence of America as an enormous borrower did indeed generate a welcome degree of economic and financial stability. Having the largest economy and the world's most important currency, the United States is far better able to borrow abroad on a large scale than any other economy or even group of economies. But even there the domestic counterpart of the external borrowing generated what ultimately proved to be unsustainable increases in household indebtedness. These led to the "subprime" crisis—a wider crisis that had its roots in U.S. mortgage lending practices—and to a financial shock that began to ripple across the high-income countries in 2007. The U.S. external deficit then started shrinking, as demand weakened and the dollar tumbled.

We have not reached the end of financial history. The events described above raised two questions: Was this pattern of global net capital flows sustainable? And is the flow of capital from poor to rich countries desirable? The former question is the more controversial. While the course on which U.S. external liabilities were launched looked unsustainable in the long term, because it implied an explosive rise in the country's net liability position, it might have endured for a long time. But the domestic counterparts of that external borrowing became problematic far sooner.

The undesirability of this reaction to the prior instability of capital flows to emerging market economies is evident. A large-scale flow of capital from poor countries to the world's richest nations is perverse. What makes it even more perverse is that strong political forces within the beneficiary country, the United States, resent the generosity of their creditors. Adding to this incendiary situation is the likelihood that the suppliers of finance will ultimately suffer large losses when the United States is called upon to repay—or at least to service—the capital it has received. Indeed, many are already experiencing such losses as the dollar tumbles.

The macroeconomic question is how adjustment of the global balance of payments might occur. A key issue is the time horizon, since that is likely to have an important impact on the needed changes in real (and nominal) exchange rates: the slower the adjustment, the smaller these changes will need to be. But a deeper set of questions must be addressed: whether there exist a set of policy changes and developments that would allow a liberal global financial system to transfer capital to emerging market economies without precipitating large-scale crises. For only under these conditions can one imagine an outcome that would be both sustainable and satisfactory.

This book argues that such changes are indeed feasible. But they will require substantial reforms, particularly in emerging market economies, and, first and foremost, greater congruence between the currency system and the pattern of international finance. In a multicurrency world, we must have multicurrency finance. Countries must borrow in their own currencies, accept capital in the form of equity, or help their domestic private sectors find some other way of hedging long-term currency risks. These changes should occur naturally if emerging market economies are prepared to accept the full disciplines—both micro- and macroeconomic—of running internationally open financial systems. But they will take some time. Meanwhile, the international financial institutions might be able to help, largely through improved pooling of foreign-currency reserves. The less pooling there is, the more tightly emerging market economies must regulate their financial systems, the more determined they must be to eliminate significant currency mismatches within their economies, and the more they must insure themselves against externally generated financial crises.

A Prescription for Change

What is special about finance? Why is it so important, and why can it so easily go wrong, particularly in emerging market economies? Chapter 2 attempts to answer these questions. Finance rests on promises—which, by their nature, can be broken. Above all, the recipients of the promises know they can be broken. This makes the financial system vulnerable to changes in expectations about an inherently uncertain future. Uncertainty is likely to be particularly significant when promises are made across frontiers, and even more so when they are made to foreigners. Governments are always essential players in any set of financial promises, even if they themselves have not made them. They provide the institutions that help make certain that promises are kept, and they can intervene to ensure that they cannot be kept. The debts they incur and the money they issue are the basis for any set of financial contracts. Trust in foreign governments is often limited, since outsiders know that such a government is not accountable to them. It is particularly limited in the governments of emerging market economies, which tend to be more corrupt, more inefficient, and often more populist than those of the high-income countries.

The discussion turns, in Chapter 3, not just to what can go wrong but to what has gone wrong in global finance. The chapter recounts the crises of the past three decades and describes their huge costs. In most cases, the largest costs arise when devaluations occur in emerging market countries that have had significant current account deficits and, almost inevitably, substantial mismatches in currency denomination between liabilities and assets. These crises, in turn, imposed heavy costs, particularly on the tax-payers of affected economies and on those who lost their incomes in the crises. These painful outcomes have led to a swing away from borrowing by emerging economies and to determined efforts to keep exchange rates down, sustain strong current account positions, and accumulate official re-serves. This is particularly true in East Asia, where the scars of the 1997–98 crisis ran deep, not just in the victims but also among the bystanders. China is far and away the most important of such bystanders.

If there exist some countries with sizable structural current account surpluses and thus surpluses of savings over investment or income over ex-penditure, others must show the opposite behavior. Chapter 4 discusses the result—the arrival of the so-called global imbalances in the late 1990s and 2000s, partly as a legacy of financial crises past and partly as a result of the considerable rise in oil prices since 2003. I argue that Ben Bernanke, currently chairman of the U.S. Federal Reserve, was fundamentally right when he stated that these imbalances were the consequence of a "global saving glut," so long as this glut is understood as a surplus of savings over investment in the rest of the world—that is, the world apart from the United States. In recent years, that surplus has been about a sixth of the savings of the rest of the world. The result has been a tendency toward low real interest rates, even at a time of rapid economic growth, and pressure on the United States to run very large current account deficits.

The fact that real interest rates were so low strongly suggests that U.S. deficits were not crowding out investment elsewhere. Instead low spend-ing elsewhere was crowding in U.S. spending and external deficits. These outcomes were not the result of decisions by the private sector alone. The exchange rates and associated macroeconomic policies of much of Asia—above all, the targeting of the U.S. dollar and the sterilization of the con-sequent reserve accumulations—helped create the surpluses that the United States has been absorbing.[4] If the United States had been unwilling to im-plement expansionary fiscal and monetary policies capable of absorbing the surpluses and so refused to accept a huge and growing current account deficit, the U.S. economy would have been stuck in recession, and the rest of the world would have suffered economically as well.

In Chapter 5 I suggest that the period of global financial calm may prove misleading. I begin by asking whether the current "solution" to the instability of the global financial system is either desirable or sustainable. It had obvious advantages for the creditor and debtor countries and indeed for the rest of the world. So long as the United States was the dominant borrower in the system, the chances of another series of crises were much reduced. But the path on which the U.S. economy was launched was unsustainable in the long run. The problem was not only the accumulation of external liabilities but also the need for either the U.S. government, the U.S. private sector (in practice, the household sector), or both to go ever more deeply into debt. These trends could continue for some time, but not forever.

Meanwhile, the creditor countries gained real advantages from the currency link to the United States, but their vast accumulated claims on that country made little sense. Not only was there likely to be a protectionist backlash in the United States, but they were likely to lose a great deal of money when adjustment finally occurred. (Indeed, the evidence suggests that some creditor countries have already lost a great deal of money.) Above all, these countries should be able to find higher-return uses for surplus funds at home, such as in additional public or private consumption. Thus the "solution" to global financial instability afforded by U.S. external borrowing, and the associated current account deficits, itself caused significant problems.

This takes the discussion to the questions of global adjustment and reform. There is a tendency among creditor nations to argue that so-called imbalances are caused by U.S. profligacy alone and to recommend smaller U.S. fiscal deficits or a higher level of private-sector savings. But, as emphasized in Chapter 6, the outcome is the result of policies in both the surplus and the deficit countries. Adjustment requires changes across the globe in levels of spending and in incentives to consume and produce tradable goods and services. Yet a durable solution to the problem of financial crises and the associated pattern of current account surpluses and deficits cannot be offered by macroeconomic policy alone. Such an outcome also requires domestic and international reforms.

On the domestic front, reforms must address exchange rate, monetary, and fiscal regimes; the regulation of the financial sector; legal institutions; and protection of property rights. The aim is to create a combination of micro- and macroeconomic conditions in which large flows of capital from abroad become relatively safe. Governments of emerging market economies must find ways to bind themselves to treating creditors well. External regimes, such as membership of the European Union, help. But in practice the best way is for a government to become credible in the eyes of its own citizens. Foreign creditors can then piggyback on the resulting confidence with relative ease. If a country cannot borrow easily from its own citizens in its own currency, foreigners lend to it, in any currency, at their great peril!

Chapter 7 considers global reform. This is less important than domestic changes, but there are important issues here as well. There is a case to be made for a global currency. But in practice the aim should be to make a floating-rate regime work as well as possible. The implications for the nature of the flows and the distribution of risk must be thoroughly understood. In particular, currency risk needs to be borne by creditors rather than debtors, who find it far more difficult to hedge. An important question is whether there is a need for greater pooling of reserves than the International Monetary Fund (IMF) is now capable of. China's foreign-currency reserves alone are five times the IMF's resources. One possibility would be to develop a system of prequalified access to resources on a large scale in the event of a crisis. But this would require an ability to easily distinguish safe from risky countries. Such prequalification would also have to be done proactively, since countries fear the signal they send by asking for access to such credit lines.

The case for liquidity for countries that are affected by sudden cessation of capital inflows remains strong. There has also been much discussion of a global bankruptcy regime for countries. The need for this is not obvious. Debtor countries are in a good position—too good, one might argue—to impose solutions on creditors, as Argentina's restructuring of its debt after 2001 demonstrated. More importantly, international regimes to which countries could subscribe—thereby demonstrating the quality of their domestic financial systems, legal institutions, and treatment of the rights of creditors—could be extremely valuable. A start has been made in these directions with the implementation of various standards and codes. Further steps are needed.

In bringing together the previous discussions, Chapter 8 offers two main conclusions: First, it is impossible to separate reform of the macroeconomic regime—exchange rate systems, monetary and fiscal policies, and the role of the IMF—from that of the microeconomic regime—in particular, regulation of the financial system. The two must be driven in tandem. Second, a better-balanced global flow of funds will occur only if the emerging economies feel that it is safe to accept large net inflows of foreign capital. Their massive accumulations of foreign-currency reserves are an important step in that direction. But they will probably need to do more before they shift course. This is likely to be particularly true for the giant among the holders of external surpluses—China, whose role as the world's largest surplus country has become pivotal to any resolution of the global imbalances.

The failures of the past have led to the so-called imbalances of the present. The United States, issuer of the world's most important currency, has become the world's borrower of last resort. This has been far from the worst result of the experiment that is global financial liberalization. But it is, in the long run, neither sustainable nor desirable. It is the outcome of obvious failures:

- the failure to understand properly the inherent risks of all liberalized financial markets, where decisions are made by competing market-oriented institutions;
- the failure to appreciate the greater risks when finance crosses frontiers, particularly for fragile emerging market economies;
- the failure of debtor countries to understand the risks inherent in borrowing in foreign currencies and the consequent need for greater fiscal and monetary discipline;
- the failure to understand exchange rate risk by both creditors and debtors and, in particular, the vulnerability of adjustable peg exchange rates in a world of liberalized capital movements;
- more broadly, the failure to understand what it means to live with the exchange rate instability of today's multicurrency world, instead of the high predictability of the gold standard of the late nineteenth and early twentieth centuries; and
- the failure to modernize global institutions in time.

The huge deficits that the United States willingly incurred gave the world breathing space. But that could not last forever. Adjustment in the global balance of payments is now taking place. If it is to occur smoothly, we must move toward a world in which sizable net flows of capital to emerging market economies can occur without crises. Few would dispute that such an outcome is desirable. The question is how best to achieve it.

CHAPTER 2

Blessings and Perils of Liberal Finance

The emergence of today's global financial markets can be likened to the invention of the jet airplane. We can go where we want to go much more quickly, we can get there more comfortably, more cheaply and most of the time more safely—but the crashes when they occur are that much more spectacular.

LAWRENCE SUMMERS, FORMER U.S. TREASURY SECRETARY

EVERYBODY LOVES TO HATE FINANCE. The "speculator," or worse, the bloodsucking usurer, is a perennial villain. Not for nothing was Shylock—marked as an outsider by being both a Jew and a moneylender—the villain of Shakespeare's *Merchant of Venice*. But finance is also the engine of a sophisticated, open, and dynamic market economy. Finance allows people to set up businesses with other people's money, to participate in the profits from other people's ideas, to smooth expenditure over a lifetime, and to insure both lives and property. Finance gives individuals freedom and security and economies dynamism and flexibility.

At its most basic, finance provides a mechanism for shifting resources from those who own them but cannot use them productively to those who can use them but do not own them. It is, therefore, the engine of a decentralized market economy. Ideas without finance are sterile. The more flexible and responsive the financial system, the better any economy will work, for the larger will be the ranges of demands that will be financed and of ideas that will be exploited. The absence of finance is crippling. But when finance goes wrong, the consequences can be devastating.

This chapter explains what finance is for, why it is both important and crisis-prone, particularly when it crosses borders. It starts by looking at the central feature of the financial system: it is a pyramid of promises—often promises of long or even indefinite duration. This makes it remarkable that sophisticated financial systems exist. (They are certainly relatively modern inventions, by which I mean inventions of the past few hundred years.) Promises may not be kept. Indeed, it is often in the direct interest of those who make the promises not to keep them. To give people confidence in this complex structure, one needs strong and credible institutions, including an honest, effective government constrained by the rule of law. When things work well, the financial system brings significant benefits. But when it goes wrong, it can wreak havoc. The same is also true when finance goes global: again, large benefits accrue but sizable risks are run. The aim of policy is to create conditions under which gains are maximized and risks managed. That, alas, is far from what has happened.

Pyramids of Promises

At the end of 2005, the households and nonprofit organizations of the United States—the world's largest market economy—owned assets worth $64.4 trillion (or $64 trillion, rounded to the nearest $1,000 billion), a little over five times the country's gross domestic product (GDP), and owed $11.9 trillion, which gave them an aggregate net worth of $52.5 trillion.[1] Of these assets some $25.6 trillion were tangible—principally residential property. The rest, worth $38.7 trillion, consisted of financial assets—claims on other households, on the rest of the U.S. economy, and on the rest of the world. The financial assets of U.S. nonfarm, nonfinancial corporate business amounted to another $10.9 trillion and those of nonfarm, noncorporate business, to $2.3 trillion. The total financial assets owned by the U.S. private sector thus amounted to some $52 trillion in 2005.

According to the McKinsey Global Institute, total financial assets of the Eurozone in 2005 were some $30 trillion; of Japan, $19.5 trillion; and of the United Kingdom, a further $8 trillion.[2] These four economies held no less than 80 percent of the world total of $140 trillion. This colossal sum was, in turn, equal to 316 percent of world output, up from just 109 percent in 1980 and 218 percent in 1995. The rise in financial intermediation has been quite general: between 1995 and 2005, the ratio of financial assets to GDP rose from 303 percent to 405 percent in the United States, from 278 percent to 359 percent in the United Kingdom, and from 180 percent to 303 percent in the Eurozone.

Moreover, of the global stock of financial assets in 2005, as much as $44 trillion were equities, $35 trillion were private debt securities, $23 trillion were government debt securities, and $38 trillion were bank deposits. The share of the latter fell from 42 percent in 1980 to 27 percent in 2005, as the world shifted to more indirect forms of intermediation. This sophistication is shown even more clearly in the composition of the financial assets of U.S. households and nonprofit organizations in 2005: deposits, $6.1 trillion; credit market instruments, $3.1 trillion; directly held corporate equity, $5.7 trillion; indirectly held equity, $8.9 trillion (via life insurance companies, $1.1 trillion; claims on pension funds, $3.0 trillion; claims on government retirement funds, $1.9 trillion; and mutual funds, $2.9 trillion); and all other claims, $14.8 trillion.

This huge and rapidly growing mountain of financial assets represents promises of future, often contingent, receipts in return for current payment. Bonds promise a fixed payment at regular intervals; equity promises a share in future corporate profits; pensions promise a stream of income in retirement; a life insurance policy promises a payout after some fixed date or in the event of death; and an accident or health insurance policy promises a payout if some event occurs. As the financial system grows more complex, it piles promises upon promises. A mutual fund promises to return to its investors the proceeds from the mutual fund's purchases of promises from corporations; an option is a promise to hand over a claim to a certain promise under specified conditions. The bulk of these claims are now held in electronic form, as bits in computer memories.

All these promises ultimately rest upon title to real assets in one form or another. This is obvious of corporate equity. But it is also true of housing loans or, for that matter, corporate bonds: it is only possible to lend to a company if one has reason to believe it owns what it claims to own and earns what it claims to earn.

The financial claims held by Americans do not merely help the economy. They *are* the economy. If they vanished, the economy would be based solely on cash. But the willingness to buy and hold these promises—and so the ability to sell them—depends on confidence or, in short, trust. Instead of keeping gold in strongboxes or banknotes in mattresses, people must be willing to lend money at low interest rates for long periods or to invest money in companies over which they have little direct control. They must be prepared to hand over their purchasing power to those who, they believe, are able to make better use of it. Thus the promises rest on trust not just in people's probity, but in a well-entrenched and reliable system for defining and protecting property rights.

Sophisticated and dynamic modern economies depend on pyramids of promises far more impressive and complex than those of stone constructed by the pharaohs almost five thousand years ago. Yet the confidence that sustains them could all too easily prove misplaced. People would then end up with promises not worth the paper they are no longer printed on. For the financial promise is subject not just to calculable risks— to "known unknowns," in the famous words of Donald Rumsfeld, former

defense secretary to President George W. Bush—but to fundamental uncertainty—to "unknown unknowns." These are what the brilliant analyst
Nassim Taleb has called "black swans"—events that are highly improbable
and have huge impact, and, after the fact, we would like to believe were
more predictable than was the case.[3] Nevertheless, U.S. households were
willing to hold the stupefying total of $39 trillion worth of promises in
2005; Americans as a whole, a total of $52 trillion; and all of humanity, a
grand total of $140 trillion.

What is even more extraordinary, in light of human history, is that
Americans are largely right to do as they do. Even in the midst of the "subprime crisis" most Americans continue to trust most of the financial promises made to them. Historically, however, this degree of trust has been extraordinarily rare. It is rare today, across the globe. That is at least part of
the reason why financial crises have been so frequent and so dangerous.

Keeping Promises

It is important to understand more precisely what can go wrong with
financial promises and, more important, how the various perils can be
avoided or at least mitigated. Thus the promise may not be kept because
the person making it *does not wish* to keep it. The promise may not be kept
because the person making it *is unable* to keep it. Finally, there is the inescapable uncertainty about whether the promise can or will be kept or
what it might be worth if it is. Worse, these difficulties are an inherent aspect of finance. As Raghuram Rajan (formerly the chief economist of the
IMF) and Luigi Zingales of the Graduate School of Business at the University of Chicago argue, "chance, ignorance, or knavery—in the jargon, uncertainty, adverse selection, or moral hazard—can intervene to prevent financing from being repaid."[4]

Consider that the purchasers of promises will know that the sellers
normally know much more than they do about their prospects. The name
for this is "asymmetric information." They will also know that those who
have no intention of keeping their word will always make more attractive
promises than those who do not. This is "adverse selection." They will
know that even those who are inclined to be honest may be tempted, under some circumstances, not to keep their promises. The source of this is
"moral hazard." The answer to adverse selection and moral hazard, it
may appear, is to collect more information. But this too has a drawback:
"free-riding." If all information is present in the market, those who have
made no investment in collecting it can benefit from the costly efforts of
those who have done so. That will, in turn, reduce the incentive to invest

in such information, thereby making markets subject to the vagaries of "rational ignorance." If the ignorant follow those they deem to be better informed, there will be "herding." Finally, where uncertainty is pervasive and inescapable—who, for example, knows the chances of nuclear terrorism or the economic impact of the internet?—the herds are likely both to blow and ultimately to burst "bubbles."

Finance is a jungle inhabited by wild beasts. How then are they to be made at least tolerably tame? The simplest of all techniques is restricting one's dealings to those one has good reason to trust—such as members of one's family, of one's religious community, or of some other group of people with whom one can expect a long and valuable series of economic and social exchanges. The drawback of this solution is that it restricts access to finance to those with valuable connections.[5] What has come to be called "crony capitalism" is the market economy's most familiar and durable form. To stick to relationships with those one knows well is normal; to trust those one does not know is abnormal. While the latter approach opens up the field of entrepreneurship more widely, it is worth noting that even in advanced economies the majority of small businesses are family owned and run.

An alternative and slightly more sophisticated solution is the holding of hostages—in this context, happily, not people but things. This is collateral. At its simplest, it can be seen in the almost universal practice of pawnbroking. The taking of collateral is the basis for home finance: the financing of home purchases through mortgages. But the drawback of this solution is that it benefits only those who already have wealth. Moreover, even collateral will only work if there are sound and effective laws of property. Only if creditors can be confident of possessing their collateral in the event of default will it provide adequate security. Shylock understood this principle. In India, according to the World Bank's *Doing Business,* it can take ten years to resolve a bankruptcy case.[6] Collateral will not be worth much under such circumstances!

Under either of these solutions, the circle of finance is tightly restricted and the benefits of finance are correspondingly limited. Too many people will have to finance themselves out of their own savings—in other words, they will have to "self-finance"—with unhappy consequences for their current levels of consumption. It is possible, however, to widen the options. The microfinance model pioneered in Bangladesh by the Grameen Bank—a system of very small loans among households known to one another—extended the notion of finance within a circle of personal relationships. But, as Rajan and Zingales point out, "the poor tend not to have rich friends or relatives. So, again, it is typically the rich who have the right connections to obtain financing."[7]

How then can this host of obstacles to effective finance be removed? Extensive screening of applicants, close monitoring of the behavior of borrowers, and compilation of detailed credit records not only direct credit to reasonably honest and responsible borrowers, but should encourage them to stay that way. Insistence that borrowers hold equity stakes of their own or that the insured make significant co-payments (or receive repayment only after deductions) are further ways to limit opportunistic behavior (though this also screens out honest, but poor, people). Beyond this, there need to be precise definition and effective enforcement of property rights, reliable accounting, ways of policing management, and accurate and reliable records. In the United States, all this exists to an advanced (though certainly incomplete) degree. U.S. households mostly trust the organizations they deal with, the security of the systems those organizations use, the accuracy of published accounts, and even, for the most part, the probity of lawyers and accountants and the effectiveness of the legal system. Had they not done so, the country's present level of financial development would have been impossible. The U.S. financial system rests on a sophisticated institutional base. It also—and perhaps more importantly—rests on the social behavior and values that sustain those institutions.

As Frederic Mishkin, a governor of the Federal Reserve System and formerly a professor at Columbia University, points out in his book on global finance, financial intermediaries—above all, banks—are uniquely able to deal with the variety of difficulties listed above.[8] Their relationship with their customers provides them with a wealth of information about them and with effective means of monitoring and policing them. Banks also provide something everybody wants: safe, liquid assets and a simple and flexible means of payment. Banks are, therefore, the foundation of any modern financial system. In developing countries they are nearly the whole of the financial system. Even when, as is the case in advanced economies, the financial system develops beyond overwhelming reliance on credit from (and deposits in) banks, they remain the core of the financial system.

While banks, as intermediaries between the providers and users of finance, remove some of the dangers inherent in any financial system, they do so, in part, by shifting those perils elsewhere. Banks usually have a small amount of equity—even a well-capitalized bank today has capital equal to only some 10 percent of its risk-weighted assets. An inherent feature of the banking business is "maturity transformation." The vast bulk of banking assets are financed by short-term loans from money markets or liquid deposits, which the banks' customers think of as equivalent to cash. But a large portion of the banks' assets are long term and, if banks are engaged in standard lending practices, illiquid. In addition to these inescapable maturity and liquidity risks, banks are also exposed to market, credit, currency, and wider economic and political risks. Market risk consists of the danger of falling asset prices, perhaps because of rising long-term interest rates; credit risk covers the potential bankruptcy of borrowers; currency risk derives from a mismatch between the denomination of liabilities and assets; and economic and political risks relate to such untoward events as a global crisis, a war, or a revolution.

While banks are indeed indispensable financial institutions, they are also perilous. This is because intermediation makes them rickety financial structures. That is also why banks typically have impressive premises. "Look," these buildings proclaim, "our institution is as solid as a mountain of stone or a castle of steel and glass." Nothing could be further from the truth. The insolvency not just of individual banks but of entire banking systems has, as will be discussed in Chapter 3, been a disturbingly frequent event over the past three decades.

Because depositors find it impossible to discover the true value of their bank's assets, there is, at times of doubt, the risk of a "run" or a widespread desire to take their money out, as happened so dramatically with the United Kingdom's specialized mortgage lender Northern Rock in the autumn of 2007. If a number of apparently better-informed customers withdraw their cash, others may well take this as a signal to do the same. Since the value of a bank's liabilities does not adjust under these circumstances, the run may continue until the cash is exhausted. The bank will then be forced to liquidate its illiquid, long-term assets, but at a discount. In this way, a panic may turn a solvent but illiquid bank into an insolvent one. The panic is then likely to spread throughout the banking system, partly because the insolvency of one bank directly threatens that of others, but also because the same uncertainty about the true value of one bank's assets also applies to those of the others. Thus the problem of asymmetric information that banks exist to solve is created by their own opacity.

The Role of Government

The essential role of government is to supply the institutions that create and sustain trust in financial promises. Governments are responsible for the establishment and protection of property rights. Although it is possible for private agents to go some way in this direction—for example, by creating informal systems of arbitration or taking advantage of communal or close commercial ties—the obstacles to effective cooperation are considerable. Private enforcement is a poor alternative to that by the state. It can too easily collapse into gangsterism or outright civil war. The role of the state as protector of the people and so as creator and enforcer of the law is a natural territorial monopoly and continues to provide the rationale for the existence of the state.

Governments were also responsible for creating the most important of all financial markets—that in government debt. The creation of a safe market in government debt was the foundation on which all other debt markets were erected. Similarly, the first important joint stock company in the history of European capitalism was a government creation—the Dutch East India Company, on which the English East India Company was modeled. The modern company and stock market owe their origin to this innovation in the Netherlands during its seventeenth-century golden age. If—and only if—the government succeeds in maintaining the quality of its credit over time will a sophisticated financial market be sustained. If it does not—as the experience of Argentina has repeatedly shown, most recently after 2001—governments have an irresistible temptation to loot banks and subvert property rights, thereby impairing, if not ruining, financial stability.

Equally important, it is only when governments are solvent that money —the unit of account, the ultimate means of payment and, in the absence of inflation, the safest store of value—will remain trustworthy. A government that has exhausted its credit has an overwhelming incentive to debauch the currency, inflate the price level, and, in this way, quietly default on its debt. With metallic currencies, inflation involves the relatively difficult process of debasing the coinage. In the modern age of fiat money— money created by governmental decree—it requires only use of the printing press or a book entry with the central bank.

The state has long had a role in the provision of money. Initially this was limited to certifying a certain weight and purity of precious metals in coinage (and exploiting that role when tempted to debase the coinage). In the course of the past three centuries the monetary system evolved into a pyramid of notes convertible into metal at fixed prices—the gold exchange system. In the course of the Great Depression of the 1930s, most currencies ceased to be convertible into gold. After World War II the dollar was the only significant currency still convertible into gold at a fixed price, and even then only at the request of other governments. Finally, after the collapse of the Bretton Woods exchange rate system in 1971, the world moved to a system of pure fiat (or government-created) currencies. This is a novel world, very different from that of the earlier period of globalization in the late nineteenth and early twentieth centuries, when the gold exchange standard created what was, in effect, a single world money. This shift has powerful implications for both domestic monetary policy and the global monetary system, to which I will return below. It is, unquestionably, a source of substantial vulnerability.

The view that the quality of public institutions is the single most important determinant of economic growth is now widely (though not universally) accepted.[9] That institutions play a central role is certain.[10] The question is why governments should promote institutions that make their citizens prosper. One possible answer is that the state does so when that is the only way for the state itself to become rich. If it is able to extract valuable resources directly, it will be relatively uninterested in development of the economy. If, however, it depends largely on revenue from commerce, it may—if it is both intelligent and far-sighted (neither characteristic being certain, given the vagaries of human character)—see its own interest in promoting commercial development.

This distinction is powerful, both historically and to this day. It explains, for example, why the Russian and Chinese states of today, both highly centralized and both legally unaccountable, should take such different approaches to economic development: the former extracts rents from resources, while the latter extracts resources from commerce.[11] Thus the Chinese state has a direct and immediate interest in economic development that is lacking in Russia. Yet reliance on an absolute state to behave well over a long period is always dangerous. The state may change its behavior opportunistically. This is particularly likely as a regime reaches its end, as was shown clearly in the looting that accompanied the declining years of the Suharto regime in Indonesia. Such temptations make an enduring bureaucratic despotism, such as China's, a better long-term bet for domestic and foreign investors than a personal autocracy, such as Indonesia's.

What is needed is an eternal regime that represents the interests of the mass of property owners who are not strong enough individually to protect their interests, but who are strong enough collectively to insist that the state do so. That regime is democracy, though possibly limited-suffrage democracy.[12] This is a regime of citizens, rather than subjects. In modern Europe, such a regime began in some of the Italian city-states and then evolved on a larger scale in the Netherlands and England of the seventeenth century. By wresting political power from the crown, English property owners created a regime accountable to themselves, with remarkable results for the safety of property, as Adam Smith himself noted a century later when he pointed out that "in Great Britain industry is perfectly secure; and though it is far from perfectly free, it is free or freer than in any other part of Europe."[13]

The creation of a government accountable to a the large mass of property owners has, argues former investment banker James Macdonald in a fascinating recent book, had an even more direct impact on the development of financial markets than on property rights. It made governments creditworthy because it put government into the hands of its creditors and so secured the growth of a large, stable, and reliable market in public debt.[14] Indeed, so great was the creditworthiness of the British state that it was able to float large quantities of irredeemable securities at interest rates as low as 2.5 percent. The ability to borrow from its citizens on a huge scale at low cost was the decisive advantage of the British state in its successive wars against continental autocracies.

Macdonald points out, however, that "the argument holds good only for domestic borrowing—when the lenders are citizens. The argument does not apply to external borrowing."[15] The significance of this distinction will become evident below. The argument will also not apply to domestic borrowing if the majority of voters are not creditors but rather dependents of the government. Thus a universal-suffrage democracy in a country with mass poverty or, even more important, a high degree of inequality may also be uninterested in preserving the credit of the government. Such a country's government is likely to be default prone and so suffer from chronically poor credit. Indeed, because it is deemed likely to default it may, in difficult times, be forced to do so—another point that will emerge more clearly below. For precisely the same reason, such a country is likely to suffer chronic bouts of inflation. This has been the history of much of Latin America. But if a government is, instead, run in the interests of a large class of domestic creditors, property is likely to be secure and credit sound. This, in turn, will create the conditions for a flourishing financial system.

Good government is then the foundation of any sophisticated financial system—the base on which the pyramid of promises ultimately stands. Good government is also most likely to be produced by a property-owning democracy. But what about the positive role of government? What policies does a sound government need to pursue to limit the defects inherent in any financial system—asymmetric information, adverse selection, moral hazard, herding, and panic—without restricting its benefits to a small circle of well-connected insiders?

The earliest such challenge was, as mentioned above, the impact of panic on the stability of a fractional-reserve banking system, one in which the vast majority of banking liabilities are short-term deposits, redeemable more or less immediately at par, while assets are predominantly long term and illiquid and, above all, holdings of cash are very small. The historic solution, elucidated by the brilliant Victorian economic journalist Walter Bagehot, has been the central bank's role as lender of last resort.[16] But once the central bank offers insurance of this kind, it has to ensure that the moral hazard it creates is not exploited by the commercial banks. The subsequent invention of deposit insurance—designed to remove the incentive for large-scale withdrawals by small depositors—further increases the need for wide-ranging and intrusive prudential regulation. In many cases, governments have gone much further: they have given absolute guarantees of banking liabilities, with predictably dangerous consequences. In effect, this policy turns deposits into implicit or contingent public sector debt. When banks are badly enough run or crises big enough, taxpayers end up bearing huge costs.

Suppose there were no lenders of last resort, no government deposit insurance, no government regulation of financial intermediaries, and no government bailouts. Would the financial world be more or less dangerous than it is? The answer to this question is not at all obvious. While the perils to which financial systems are vulnerable, as listed above, are genuine, it is far from clear that government intervention makes things any better. What is certain is that without any prospect of intervention, financial systems would look quite different: banks would be far better capitalized; maturity mismatches would be reduced, with greater reliance on securities or on long-term and more illiquid deposits in banks; and deposits would be better matched by highly liquid securities. Given the frequency of banking crises, this might be a big improvement. Whether one believes government intervention has improved things depends on how one balances the failings of the financial system on the one hand against the defects of government intervention on the other.[17] Unfortunately, in many cases, as we shall see, government policies seem to have made things worse.

The Benefits of Finance

The development of a large and sophisticated financial system, such as that of the contemporary United States, is evidently a social achievement of a high order. The ability to take its daily functioning for granted is proof of its extraordinarily effective infrastructure. But is having such a system worth it? In particular, should emerging economies endeavor to imitate what the world's most advanced economy has achieved? The answer is: yes. The late Mancur Olson once argued that the wealth of a society depended on its ability to make long-term investment commitments.[18] Why should that matter? Consider, for a moment, what a successful financial system achieves. It allows the creation of vast enterprises out of the combined capital, supplied at modest cost, of thousands or even millions of people; it permits a wide range of outsiders to start new businesses and so undermines the position of incumbents; it repackages and so reallocates risk; it allows people to time their spending decisions over their lifetimes; and it insures individuals against the big risks of life. What is more, as Rajan and Zingales make plain, developments in financial theory have allowed huge further progress in these directions.[19] Such progress, in turn, has further improved the management of risk and so allowed greater economic development. All this, they rightly argue, also increases individual economic freedom.

This may all seem somewhat theoretical. It is not. By now, a substantial body of research links economic development to the financial system. Mishkin has summarized this literature in his book on financial globalization.[20] A study by Robert King and Ross Levine published in 1993 used a sample of eighty countries to show that those with larger financial sectors in 1960 achieved greater economic growth in the subsequent three decades.[21] Another paper, by Ross Levine, Norman Loayza, and Thorsten Beck, suggested that a doubling of the size of private credit in an average developing country is associated with a 2-percentage-point annual increase in the rate of economic growth.[22] This, as Mishkin notes, implies a doubling of GDP, relative to what it would otherwise be, over thirty-five years. Industries and companies that are more dependent on external financing will grow faster in countries with deeper financial systems. Similarly, notes Mishkin, "more new firms are created in countries with better-developed financial systems."[23] Evidence also suggests that the impact of financial development is felt, above all, through improvements in the efficiency of capital, rather than through increased investment levels. Thus the financial system plays an important disciplining role, forcing companies to use resources relatively efficiently.[24] This argument fits well with the remarkable recent productivity performance of the United States.

The Risks of Finance

The principal risk of finance is crisis. Crises occur when the pyramid of promises starts to collapse and all begins to look frighteningly unstable. In such situations, investors run for cash, lowering the price of all risky or illiquid securities and forcing the contraction of the balance sheets of institutions engaged in maturity transformation.

Financial crises are as old as capitalism itself.[25] There are two polar views on these crises: either they are always and entirely the result of irresponsible behavior in the markets, or they are always and entirely the result of incompetent government intervention. The former view points to the habitual human propensity to swing between an excess of greed and an excess of fear: in the first period, there is excess; in the second, there is panic. The latter view points to the distortions introduced by government guarantees to risk taking. These create an overwhelming incentive to privatize gains and socialize losses. In the absence of subtle and comprehensive government regulation, the result will be excessive risk taking and often huge losses. When these emerge, the result may be panic, particularly if it appears likely that the government is unable to meet its commitments.

The plausible conclusion is that both views are correct: financial markets are indeed risky, because of the challenge of managing their inherent difficulties—asymmetric information, adverse selection, moral hazard, herding, and so forth—but the interventions of government often make them less safe, not more so. Particularly dangerous is the combination of poor fiscal discipline with lack of monetary discipline. When inflation is high and variable, finance becomes short term, maturity transformation more deeply embedded, and the financial system correspondingly less stable. Furthermore, mistakes in exchange rate policy can also greatly increase the fragility of the financial system.

Huge and costly crises have occurred, as we shall see in Chapter 3, in countries that liberalized financial systems into which governments had introduced large distortions. This allowed the markets to "game the government," with predictably expensive results. Thus the trick—immensely difficult to pull off—is for governments to intervene in ways that increase stability, rather than its opposite. Governments should not provide open-ended guarantees to private risk taking. They should insist on transparency. They should preclude related-party lending by institutions to which they provide deposit or liquidity insurance. They should ensure that the management and shareholders of failed institutions bear heavy losses. Since neither markets nor governments can ever be perfect, crises will not be eliminated. But the wave of crises of the past three decades was exceptional, by any standards, and must not be repeated.

The Benefits of Financial Globalization

How might the pyramid of promises work when finance goes global? Is the impact of globalization on finance beneficial or perilous? The answer seems to be quite clear: it is both. Consider first the benefits and then the dangers.

Globalization creates a more competitive environment, driving down profits and forcing companies to seek outside finance. This will improve monitoring of companies. It will also encourage companies to lobby for a more efficient, flexible, and accessible financial system. Opening up to foreign financial institutions will increase competition in the financial sector and improve access to the most efficient and advanced players in world financial markets. As the World Bank has noted, in the late 1990s two-thirds of all developing countries had banking sectors with assets of $10 billion or less, and a third had banking sectors with assets of less than $1 billion. Yet in 2000 the world's fiftieth largest bank had assets of $83 billion. As this comparison suggests, in many emerging market economies the domestic economy is too small to support a number of domestically oriented institutions that are large enough to master the full range of modern technologies and management systems. That is a powerful argument for allowing the presence of foreign banks, including banks from other emerging market economies. But, as Mishkin adds, the benefits of foreign entry depend on competition. There is little benefit in asking a foreigner in to participate in the excess profits of an entrenched cartel.

A more open and competitive financial system can also have a significant impact on the quality of domestic regulation and law.[26] In such an environment, there will be pressure for improved accounting standards, a better legal system (including a more effective system for handling bankruptcy), and more effective financial regulation. In addition, foreign financial institutions should act as a lobby for improved transparency, since they will lack the access to insider information of entrenched domestic institutions.

Also potentially valuable is the flow of finance itself (and not just the entry of foreign institutions). Domestic citizens can diversify their assets and, in so doing, constrain the activity of predatory governments. This is an important aspect of the wider notion of "regulatory competition": bad governments or governments that pursue misguided policies (inflationary finance or excessive taxation) find that capital leaks out. Access to foreign finance should also permit diversification of risk across frontiers, both for individuals and for countries as a whole. But hitherto only advanced countries, with sophisticated financial systems, have been able to take advantage of this potentially important opportunity.[27]

At the same time, the supply of foreign capital can lower the cost of capital to the domestic economy. Foreign institutions with very large resources will tend, under normal circumstances, to increase the liquidity of the financial system. Moreover, Peter Henry of Stanford University has argued that opening up stock markets has lowered dividend yields by 2.4 percentage points and increased the growth of investment by 1.1 percentage points and the growth of output per worker by 2.3 percentage points. He concludes that "the facts cast doubt on the view that capital-account liberalization brings no real benefits."[28]

A subsequent analysis of the microeconomic impact of capital controls by Kristin Forbes of the Massachusetts Institute of Technology concludes that

First, capital controls tend to reduce the supply of capital, raise the cost of financing, and increase financial constraints—especially for smaller firms, firms without access to international capital markets and firms without access to preferential lending. Second, capital controls can reduce market discipline in financial markets and the government, leading to a more inefficient allocation of capital and resources. Third, capital controls significantly distort decision-making by firms and individuals, as they attempt to minimize the costs of the controls or even evade them outright. Fourth, the effects of capital controls can vary across different types of firms and countries, reflecting different pre-existing economic distortions. Finally, capital controls can be difficult and costly to enforce, even in countries with sound institutions and low levels of corruption. The microeconomic evidence on capital controls suggests that they have pervasive effects and often generate unexpected costs. Capital controls are no free lunch.[29]

The United Kingdom has been one of the countries most open to foreign investment in the financial sector. It has certainly drawn huge benefits from their involvement. Yet at the macroeconomic level, the evidence on the benefits of financial globalization are less persuasive, at least for the emerging market economies, as three important surveys from the IMF demonstrate.[30] The great majority of the empirical studies fail to find robust evidence on the impact of capital account liberalization on growth—although admittedly this is true for most of the likely determinants of growth. There appear to be thresholds of institutional quality above which financial liberalization is conducive to growth and below which it is harmful. Moreover, those benefits from financial integration are due far more to various collateral gains—development of the financial system, better governance, and macroeconomic discipline—than to the direct effects of the capital inflows themselves. Because the gains come in this indirect way, it is inevitably hard—if not impossible—to isolate the impact of financial globalization on growth. Moreover, "premature opening of the capital account in the absence of some basic supporting conditions can delay the realization of those benefits, while making a country more vulnerable to sudden stops of capital flows."[31] Some developing countries are already across these thresholds, even if most are not.

In a kind of Catch-22, financial globalization can contribute to a country's economic development, but, if the country's institutions have not reached a certain level, liberalization is likely to generate crises that are themselves bad for economic development. It is advisable, therefore, to attain that level of development *before* liberalizing, even though liberalizing ought to help a country attain such development.

Yet there are, suggest the IMF staff, some reasons for greater optimism about the contribution of financial liberalization in the future. First, foreign direct investment and other non-debt-creating forms of capital flow account for a higher share of external financing. These seem to be substantially more beneficial and substantially less crisis prone than debt flows. Second, policy and institutions have generally improved, partly because of the painful experience to be documented in Chapter 3. This should push more countries above the threshold at which financial flows are beneficial. Finally, the painful lessons of the 1980s and 1990s have led everybody to agree on the "'integrated approach' which envisages a gradual and orderly sequencing of external financial liberalization and emphasizes the desirability of complementary reforms in the macroeconomic framework and the domestic financial system as essential components of a successful liberalization strategy."[32]

The Risks of Financial Globalization

The late Charles Kindleberger recognized that "a few crises are purely national . . . . [and] some countries may not be affected by international crises that impact neighboring countries . . . . For the most part, however, financial crises ricochet from one country to another."[33] It is obvious why they should:

- first, markets are directly connected to one another, both for commodities and for financial instruments;
- second, perception of an unexpected weakness in one country will increase concern about conditions in other, apparently similar, countries;
- third, failures of important governments to respond to crises in expected ways in one case will, again, increase doubts about their willingness to act elsewhere;
- fourth, a heightened perception of risk caused by one crisis is likely, once more, to spread to other markets; and
- finally, a higher price of risk or, more important, the rationing of credit to risky borrowers—on the principle that borrowers who make promises to pay through the nose have little intention of keeping them— can turn what had previously been mere vulnerability into crisis (a point to which I will return at greater length in Chapter 3).

Such "sudden stops," argues Guillermo Calvo of the University of Maryland, explain the severity of many of the crises that have afflicted emerging economies over the past two decades.[34] At its most basic, panic is the cause of flight to safety by investors who know they do not know the riskiness of the assets they own. In this situation, the value of a very wide range of risky assets will be impaired and international flows of capital interrupted, with potentially devastating results. Many economists (though not all) would now accept that shifting expectations can create multiple self-fulfilling equilibria—in which bad or good outcomes are the result of expectations alone.

A more important question is whether there is something in international transactions that makes them inherently more crisis prone. The answer is: yes. At its most fundamental, trust in promises made by foreigners is likely to be weaker than trust in promises made by fellow citizens. This is partly because people know and understand their own economy and the behavior of the people in it better than they know the economies of foreign countries—and the more foreign or "different" are those countries, the more that will be the case. This natural tendency is often offset by another and even more powerful tendency of the wealthy citizens of developing countries: to place greater trust in the behavior and institutions of the advanced countries than in those of their own economies. They expect their governments to deceive and their institutions to fail—and they are not often disappointed. The populism and authoritarianism that are characteristic of the politics of emerging economies are both a cause and a consequence of these suspicions.

Governments are always partners—hidden or open—in international financial transactions. They decide a country's exchange rate or macroeconomic policies. They determine the country's fiscal and monetary policies. They determine whether the country should have exchange controls. Even if foreigners have good reason to trust the citizens of a foreign country, they are bound to have relatively little reason to trust its government, since the latter does not normally depend on foreigners for its hold on power. A default-prone government is even more likely to facilitate a default to foreigners—or expropriation of their assets—than to its own citizens. Argentina has given a superb demonstration of these proclivities over the past decade.

The repeated failure of government to provide currencies with reasonably stable purchasing power, almost always as a by-product of imprudent public finance, makes international finance less secure. In a country with an unreliable currency, people insist on holding foreign currencies instead. Foreign-currency deposits force even domestic financial institutions to make foreign-currency loans. That, as Calvo emphasizes, makes the economy extremely vulnerable to shifts in exchange rates.[35] Similar dangers can follow from large discrepancies between interest rates on domestic and foreign loans in the context of an apparently pegged exchange rate (an exchange rate that the government has fixed against some other currency or basket of currencies). Many borrowers effectively speculate that the pegged rate will endure, thereby creating a huge vulnerability to devaluation. That tendency proved very important in the Asian financial crisis of 1997–98.

Perhaps even more important, governments cannot act as lenders of last resort in foreign currencies. A domestic crisis can, if necessary, be met by resort to the printing press—admittedly with concomitant risks of higher inflation. Yet, without international rescue, a crisis over foreign lending is likely to generate an outright default, not just by government but (if only as a result of the default by government) by private borrowers as well. Defaults by government or by large parts of the private sector—or, worst of all, by both—normally have a much more devastating impact on the credibility of property rights, particularly when bankruptcy regimes are undeveloped, than a bout of inflation.

Surprisingly, existing empirical studies do not support the view that greater financial integration increases the likelihood of crises.[36] But this is almost certainly because the countries least prone to crises—the advanced countries—are also those that are most financially open. It appears that among those countries with open financial accounts, those that have had relatively poor policies and institutions are also, as one would expect, more prone to crises. Threshold effects are at work here, too: an open Switzerland was not crisis prone; an open South Korea was. The most plausible explanation for the frequency of financial crises in the 1980s and 1990s was the number of countries with poor policies and institutions that decided upon—or, worse, were cajoled or even forced into—financial globalization.

The conclusion is simple: as former U.S. Treasury Secretary Lawrence Summers remarked (when still deputy secretary), international finance brings big benefits and big risks. The latter are, in essence, a concentration and magnification of the risks inherent in any financial system. They are particularly severe when finance enters emerging market economies that are, by definition, relatively poorly managed, with weaker public finances, less transparency, more corruption, more related-party lending, weaker legal systems, worse protection of property rights, greater reliance on banks, and thus, in short, greater levels of moral hazard, adverse selection, and all the rest. If one combines all this with the ignorance of foreign investors and their normal tendency to reach first for yield and then for safety, the dangers are obvious. As we shall see in Chapter 3, what one might have expected to happen did happen. The age of financial liberalization became the age of crisis, with consequences that still mark the world economy.

Financial Crises in the Era of Globalization

The free market system has failed and failed disastrously.
MAHATHIR MOHAMAD, PRIME MINISTER OF MALAYSIA

OURS HAS BEEN AN ERA OF FINANCIAL TURMOIL. The fifth edition of
the late Charles Kindleberger's classic book on crises, edited by Robert Aliber of the Graduate School of Business of the University of Chicago, goes
even further:

> The inference from the changes in asset prices, the changes in currency
> values, and the number and severity of banking crises since the mid-
> 1960s is that the lessons of history have been forgotten or slighted.
> These decades have been the most tumultuous in international mone-
> tary history in terms of the number, scope, and severity of financial
> crises, More national banking systems collapsed than at any previous
> comparable period; the loan losses of the banks in Japan, in Sweden,
> and Norway and Finland, in Thailand and Malaysia and Indonesia, and
> in Mexico (twice) and Brazil and Argentina ranged from 20 to 50 per-
> cent of their assets. In some countries the costs to the taxpayers of pro-
> viding the money to fulfill the implicit and explicit deposit guarantees
> amounted to 15 to 20 percent of their GDPs. The loan losses in most of
> these countries were much greater than in the United States in the Great
> Depression of the 1930s.[1]

The fundamental point is simple: liberalization of the inward-looking
and repressed financial systems of the 1950s and 1960s led to excess and
often to severe crises. Furthermore, those crises have been hugely exacer-

bated by the interplay between the financial system and central features of macroeconomic policy, particularly exchange rate regimes and monetary and fiscal policies. Most of the biggest crises and all of those which proved least manageable by the domestic authorities have occurred in emerging economies—unmanageable principally because they involved large foreign-currency liabilities.

This chapter discusses what went wrong, particularly in the finance of emerging economies. It begins by listing twelve fundamental mistakes made in the course of liberalization. It then examines the frequency and cost of the crises, and how they happened. (Fortunately, we now have a clearer idea than we did at the time.) Finally it glances at the legacy of the crises. The chapter is the precursor to Chapter 4, which will examine how the crises in emerging market economies started the shift into our present world—the world of "global imbalances."

A Catalogue of Errors

Why have these crises occurred on so vast a scale? Here are twelve unhappy features of the world of the so-called second globalization that help explain the plague of crises:

1. Liberalization put financial institutions, investors, and regulators into an almost entirely unfamiliar environment, even in such relatively sophisticated and advanced countries as Japan, Sweden, or the United States. This unfamiliarity invited them to make mistakes—as they duly did.
2. Policy makers and investors failed to understand how limited was the capacity of institutions to assume responsibility for decisions previously made by finance ministries or central banks. This was true not only of public sector banks but also of many supposedly private institutions.
3. In many countries financial systems continued to operate under a host of explicitly or tacitly unprofitable or risky obligations.
4. In many countries legal systems remained inadequate, property rights ineffective, and bankruptcy procedures almost nonexistent.
5. Implicit and explicit government guarantees to the financial sector were effectively unlimited in many countries.
6. It was almost impossible for investors (or regulators) to police behavior, since doing so required an understanding of what was happening to the financial system (including off-balance-sheet and offshore transactions), official reserves (including forward transactions), public fi-

nances (including contingent liabilities), and the balance sheets of the nonfinancial corporate sector (including foreign-currency exposures).

7. The supply of foreign capital encouraged governments, businesses, and households—once again especially in emerging market economies —to rely on outside capital, particularly borrowing, to a much greater degree than before and to take substantially greater risks than before.

8. Lack of trust in the probity of public finances in emerging market economies and in the stability of their currencies' purchasing power generated heavy reliance on index-linked finance or, even worse, lending and borrowing in foreign currencies. Foreigners were almost entirely unwilling to lend in the currencies of emerging market economies —a phenomenon some economists label "original sin."[2] This reluctance generated huge mismatches in balance sheets and consequent extreme vulnerability to large movements in exchange rates.[3]

9. Excess borrowing showed up at the level of entire economies as large current account deficits, fiscal deficits, or debt-financed private sector investment booms, which greatly exacerbated vulnerability to swings in investor confidence and so to changes in the supply of finance.

10. While most emerging market economies and many small advanced economies, particularly in western Europe, remained reluctant to accept a freely floating exchange rate, the commitment to pegging was also weak—an almost inevitable outcome when movements among the world's major currencies were very large. The pegs lent the illusion of safety to foreign-currency lending and borrowing—but not the reality.

11. All these risks, almost inevitably, proved most significant in emerging market economies, where institutions were undeveloped, experience with liberalized financial markets scant, the supply of skilled and experienced people limited, the effectiveness of government modest, and corruption, suborning of regulators, insider dealing, related-party transactions, and similar behavior pervasive. These are, after all, the defining features of an "emerging" economy.

12. Finally, all these features of the liberalizing global financial system exacerbated enormously the scale and adverse impact of the customary tendency of financial markets to experience cycles of greed and fear, as inherent uncertainty manifests itself in excesses of confidence or anxiety.

In essence, therefore, the newly liberalized and globalized financial systems were accidents waiting to happen—and happen they did, again and again and again. And when they did, the crises proved shockingly expensive, in terms of both lost output and the fiscal costs of a cleanup.

Incidence and Cost of the Crises

In 2001 the World Bank estimated that there had been 112 systemic banking crises in 93 countries between the late 1970s and the end of the twentieth century.[4] To have had one crisis may have been a misfortune; to have had 112 was surely the result of extreme carelessness. Indeed, it is evident from the data that some countries were careless enough to have had more than one. The reader may not be surprised to learn that Argentina is one of those countries: it is currently emerging from its third banking crisis within the past twenty-five years—admittedly an extreme case. The banking industry is evidently a disaster not merely waiting to happen, but in fact happening all the time, and all around us.

Another study, by Barry Eichengreen of the University of California at Berkeley and Michael Bordo of Rutgers University, counted ninety-five crises in emerging market economies and another forty-four in high-income countries between 1973 and 1997.[5] Seventeen of the crises in emerging market economies were banking crises, fifty-seven were currency crises, and twenty-one were "twin crises," that is, a combination of currency and banking crises. Nine of the crises in the high-income countries were banking crises, twenty-nine were currency crises, and six were twin crises. In all, there were twenty-six banking crises, eighty-six currency crises, and twenty-seven twin crises in this short period of twenty-four years. The authors argued that "relative to the pre-1914 era of financial globalization, crises are twice as prevalent today," though they also concluded that they are not, in general, more severe.[6]

Most discouraging is the contrast between the decades immediately following World War II and more recent decades. Between 1945 and 1971, there had been only thirty-eight crises in all, with just seven twin crises. Emerging market economies experienced no banking crises, sixteen currency crises, and just one twin crisis in this period. Then, between 1973 and 1997, there were 139 crises in all.[7]

The age of financial liberalization was, in short, an age of crises. Moreover, it would be wrong to think that only "unimportant" countries were on the list of those affected. The United States is on the list by virtue of the savings and loan (S&L) crisis of the 1980s. Japan is also included, owing to its far more significant banking crisis in the 1990s. But these two giants were easily able to manage their crises themselves because of the creditworthiness of their governments.

These developments took the economics profession by surprise. Most of the macroeconomists who were used to thinking about exchange rates and macroeconomic policies did not appreciate the trouble a liberalized financial system could get itself into, particularly when borrowing in foreign currency. They also did not appreciate how foreign-currency borrowing by the nonfinancial private sector could generate mass bankruptcy, including bankruptcy of the financial system itself. They did not appreciate the diabolical interaction between the exchange rate and the solvency of the private sector under these circumstances. Above all, they did not appreciate how far these interactions would compromise governments' freedom of maneuver in monetary policy. When their currencies started to fall, governments faced a choice between two dreadful alternatives: either raise interest rates—hoping to keep the exchange rate up, thereby helping those with large foreign-currency liabilities while damaging those with high leverage in domestic currency—or else lower interest rates, allowing the currency to fall, thereby helping those with large domestic-currency debt but damning those with foreign-currency debt.

Prior to the late 1990s, most economists who were interested in international macroeconomics thought relatively little about finance, while most economists who were interested in finance knew little about international macroeconomics. The IMF itself was much stronger in macroeconomics than in finance. This lacuna is not surprising: until the 1990s private sector financial crises were not a significant element of exchange rate or public debt crises in emerging market economies. An exception was the crisis in Chile in the early 1980s, which had most of the features that were to become familiar in the 1990s—an unregulated financial system, a large current account deficit, huge foreign-currency borrowing, and, finally, a collapsing exchange rate that forced much of the heavily indebted private sector into bankruptcy. Moreover, domestic financial crises had been rare before the era of liberalization, which began in the 1980s, because finance was so heavily regulated. When I studied banking in the 1960s, not only was the underlying financial economics primitive by contemporary standards, but the possibility of a sector-wide insolvency was barely even considered.

The costs of crises are considerable—and taxpayers foot the bill. Indeed, one of the lessons of experience is that the liabilities of the banking system are in fact contingent public debt: the banking industry privatizes its gains and socializes its losses as soon as those losses become large enough to wipe out its equity, and sometimes even before. According to a superb database put together by researchers at the World Bank in 2003, there had been 117 systemic banking crises (in which much or all of the capital of the system was exhausted) in ninety-three countries since the late 1970s.[8] As Figure 3.1 shows, twenty-seven of these crises imposed fiscal costs equal to or exceeding 10 percent of GDP. In other words, they involved a jump in public debt equal to 10 percent of GDP. Often the cost was much more. The most expensive crises were those in Indonesia after

Figure 3.1 Fiscal Cost of Financial Crises

Percent of GDP

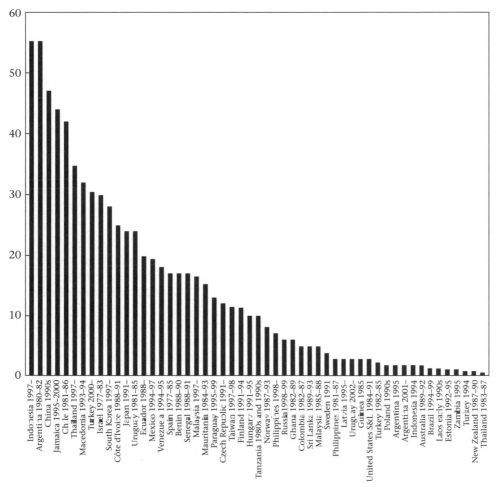

Source: Caprio and Klingebiel (2003).
Note: Listed are those crises in which costs exceeded 10 percent of GDP.

1997 and in Argentina in the early 1980s, both of which cost taxpayers 55 percent of GDP. To put these numbers in the context of the United States, an increase corresponding to 10 percent of GDP would mean a jump of $1.2 trillion in the country's fiscal debt. These are staggering losses. Yet not all crises have been so expensive. The S&L crisis in the United States cost "only" 3 percent of GDP, for example. Moreover, not all were international crises. But a great many countries did experience very expensive financial crises in the 1980s and 1990s.

The costs these countries suffered were not just fiscal. There was almost always, in addition, a large cumulative loss of output. According to the World Bank database, forty-seven countries suffered cumulative losses of 10 percent of GDP or more as a result of financial crises. Even in accordance with the conservative methodology employed by the researchers, some of these losses were huge. In the years listed in the figure, Japan suffered a cumulative loss of 48 percent of GDP; Chile's loss was 46 percent; Thailand's, 40 percent; Indonesia's, 39 percent; Malaysia's, 33 percent; the Philippines', 26 percent; Denmark's, 24 percent; Finland's, 21 percent; and South Korea's, 17 percent.[9]

The Path to Crises

So why and how did all these costly crises happen?[10] In his book on financial globalization, Frederic Mishkin argues that they have normally been the product of at least one and often two fundamental errors: mismanaged liberalization (including mismanaged globalization) and fiscal indiscipline (usually leading to inflation).[11]

The S&L crisis in the United States was a good example of mismanaged domestic liberalization. More often globalization has also been involved to some degree, not least because the integration of a new financial system into the world economy offers novel opportunities for mistakes to be made by both the residents of that country and foreigners. Fiscal indiscipline is a prime cause of financial distress, not least because insolvent governments face an irresistible temptation to stuff their banks with unpayable debt: Argentina in 2001 was a superb example of this harmful practice.[12] Fiscal indiscipline is also the most important reason for chronic inflation, which is in turn the most common impetus for the widespread use of foreign currencies ("dollarization" and "euroization") in place of increasingly worthless domestic paper. This defense mechanism, although understandable, accounts for the deadly nature of twin crises.

Mishkin describes four stages on the road to the twin crises that have been so devastating for emerging economies: liberalization, the run-up to the currency crisis, the currency crisis, and finally the general financial crisis. Let us look at each of these stages in turn.

The first stage is that of financial liberalization (or maybe just fiscal indiscipline). What happens if one liberalizes a rotten banking system? One sees the following progression, as the Gadarene swine rush over the cliff:

excessive risk taking by inexperienced financial institutions or, worse, ones with dangerously close relations with their borrowers;[13] ineffective regulation by naive, inadequate, underpaid, or corrupt regulators; moral hazard generated by government guarantees;[14] and rapid growth of credit, fueled by easy access to foreign funds. Then there are also mounting losses, leading to cutbacks on lending; bank failures, with contagious effects on even healthy banks via the interbank market or via the insolvency of large customers; further contraction of bank lending; and finally regulatory forbearance, which allows yet more risk taking by banks "gambling for resurrection" at the taxpayers' expense.

A fascinating example is provided by South Korea, which in many ways had an excellent economy.[15] Its 1997–98 crisis shows just how dangerous financial failings can be when a financial system is liberalized. By the 1990s, the big government-backed Korean conglomerates—the chaebols—were no longer making profits. But that did not stop them from borrowing. On the contrary, the government insisted that they continue to grow. So they had to borrow and expand, even if they were not making any money. The question was, where could they borrow? The answer was: abroad. South Korea was also liberalizing its exchange controls at the time. Indeed, this had been a condition for its gaining membership in the Organisation for Economic Co-operation and Development (OECD). (Joining the OECD has become something of a leading indicator for a financial crisis: think of Mexico or the Czech Republic.) So South Korean companies and banks started to borrow abroad. Everybody knew that South Korea was a terrific economic success: it had had one of the most dynamic economies in the world over the previous three decades. Why not lend to it? And so they did—with the painful results the world saw in 1997 and 1998.

In the second stage, there is a run-up to the currency crisis: higher interest rates abroad undermine credit quality; this produces a decline in cash flow and a simultaneous fall in investment and economic activity; this then leads to a greater need to borrow precisely when doing so has become more expensive. Banks reduce lending even to good companies, no longer confident that the latter will invest the funds wisely. The failure of companies or political turmoil leads to greater uncertainty or even panic. Declining asset prices undermine the solvency of even good risks, particularly in the property sector, since property companies borrow heavily against the value of the land and buildings they own.

As economic conditions decline, moral hazard and adverse selection worsen. The smaller a company's equity cushion, the greater the incentive to take risks, with less left to lose and more to gain. Financial institutions face a clamor of requests for loans from companies that know they may not have to repay. This then is adverse selection: those who make the most expensive promises are precisely those least likely to keep them. For these reasons, rational banks will cut back lending as economic conditions grow harder. Of course, guaranteed banks, those with little or no equity of their own, may not do so. But that is how huge nonperforming loans are racked up, ultimately at the expense of the hapless taxpayer.

The third stage is the currency crises. Residents and foreign speculators start to sell the currency, lenders stop lending, and short-term lenders (principally the commercial banks) pull out their money. This is what economists call a "sudden stop." Governments then face Hobson's Choice: if they raise interest rates to support the currency, they undermine corporate solvency and worsen the crisis; if they do not raise interest rates then the currency may collapse, wiping out companies (including banks) with large net liabilities in foreign currency (of whom there are often many). Speculators face a "sure thing," because currencies can move in only one direction. Large fiscal deficits also undermine banks, as default nears, and cause speculators to run for the exit.

Finally, in stage four comes the full financial crisis, triggered by the currency crisis. In countries with histories of inflation and default, loans tend to be short term and denominated in foreign currency. Often the equity cushion in companies is also small, because of family ownership and a history of poor treatment of outside shareholders. Then when interest rates shoot up and the currency tumbles, a costly crisis emerges. Companies that produce nontradables but have contracted debt denominated in foreign currency are frequently wiped out. Export-oriented companies are in potentially much better shape, which is one reason why South Korea recovered so quickly from its crisis. But the insolvency of many companies spreads to previously creditworthy companies and banks. Multiple bankruptcies hit countries that often have inadequate bankruptcy procedures. The result is a host of zombie companies. Nobody rational wants to lend to insolvent companies. Domestic credit seizes up. Inflation surges as the currency tumbles. The economy falls into a deep recession. Worried foreign investors begin to shun other borrowing countries, which they consider to be in similar situations.

Capital Flows and Systemic Financial Crises

That then is the broad story. How has it played out over the past two decades? The erratic behavior of global capital markets is a central element in the story.[16] For this is not just a story of individual countries that fell into trouble, but of global waves of capital. I emphasize this by focusing on three major events: the Latin American debt crisis of the early 1980s, the so-called Tequila Crisis, which started in Mexico in 1994–95 and spread elsewhere in Latin America; and, most important of all, the rolling crisis that started in Thailand in June 1997 and spread elsewhere in East Asia, and to Russia and Brazil, in 1998 and early 1999. What made these systemic crises so important were their longer-term effects, partly because they were so unexpected at the time.[17] The Argentine crisis of 2001, in contrast, was expected and, for that reason, had little global effect. The Turkish crisis of 2001 was also seen as a unique event, with little global importance.

The most important point for the story in this book is that emerging market financial crises have large macroeconomic effects. In particular, when foreign finance flows inward, countries can run large current account deficits. But when it flows out again, they must shift into current account balance, or even surplus, often very quickly. These shifts are economically costly. If the current account deficit is to improve, domestic spending must decline relative to output. This is true by definition, since the current account is equal to the difference between aggregate spending and output. This is intuitively obvious: if a collection of people spend more than their income on goods and services, they must be receiving loans or investment from elsewhere, to finance the excess of their imports over their exports.[18]

When domestic spending falls, so automatically will output of non-tradables. The service sector and construction will suffer particularly badly. To offset the impact of this painful shrinkage in the output of nontradables on levels of activity and employment, and to improve the current account at the same time, output of tradables—particularly exports—needs to rise. What is needed is a bigger incentive to produce tradables. A rise in the price of tradables relative to nontradables will achieve this. The price of tradables relative to nontradables is the real exchange rate. So what is needed is a depreciation in the real exchange rate. These effects on the overall economy—the recession and the moves in relative prices—are painful. Unfortunately pain is—as will be seen—precisely what financial crises generate.[19]

In Figure 3.2, from the Washington-based Institute for International Finance, the picture of the overall balance of payments of the emerging market economies is clear.[20] Current account balances have gone through two huge cycles, ending up in substantial surplus in the 2000s. The emerging market economies, in the aggregate, have become suppliers, not importers, of capital. As we shall see, they have had good reason to do this. But this has had large consequences for the global balance of payments.

In the early 1980s, the emerging market economies had large current account deficits in relation to GDP: they were, all together, able to spend substantially more than their incomes. The "recycling" of oil surpluses at that time made this possible. The deficits were particularly large in Latin

Figure 3.2 Current Account Balances

Share of GDP

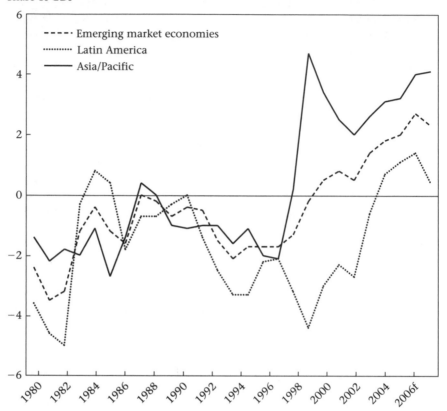

Source: Institute for International Finance.
Note: f, Forecast.

America, whose emerging market economies ran an aggregate current account deficit of 5 percent of GDP in 1982. For emerging market economies
as a whole, the deficit was 3.2 percent of GDP in that year. For Asian emerging economies, however, it was only about 2 percent.

Then came the debt crisis of the 1980s, which began when Mexico an-
nounced its imminent default in August 1982. By 1983, the Latin American deficit had shrunk to 0.3 percent of GDP and that of emerging market
economies as a whole to 1.2 percent. In 1984 Latin American emerging
countries ran a surplus of 0.8 percent of GDP. To put this in the context of
the United States, the shift between 1982 and 1984 was equivalent to an

improvement of almost $700 billion in today's U.S. deficit, in just two years. Such a swing in the U.S. current account would certainly be accompanied by a deep recession. So it was in Latin America. In 1982 the GDP of the Latin American emerging market economies shrank by 1.1 percent, followed by a decline of another 2.5 percent in 1983. Between 1981 and 1983, the total absorption of resources—a measure of total expenditures— fell by almost 8 percent, as the current account shifted toward surplus by just over 4 percent of GDP and GDP itself fell by a cumulative total of 3.5 percent.[21]

Between 1983 and 1991, the emerging market economies as a whole were close to balance. Then came a second episode of generous market financing of emerging market economies. This time, moreover, the Asians were heavily involved. By 1996 the aggregate current account deficit of the emerging market economies reached 1.7 percent of GDP. The deficits of the Latin American and Asian countries were both 2.1 percent of GDP. Then came the East Asian crisis. By 1998 the aggregate current account of the Asian countries was in surplus by 4.7 percent of GDP—an astonishing shift of 6.8 percentage points in two years. At the same time, the aggregate GDP growth of Asian emerging countries, which had been 8 percent in 1996, fell to 5.8 percent in 1997 and just 0.2 percent in 1998, before recovery. Meanwhile, Latin America was going deeper into deficit. But this trend also peaked in 1998, when the deficit reached 4.4 percent of GDP, before the current account shifted rapidly into surplus (and growth plunged from 5.2 percent in 1997 to zero in 1999). Overall the emerging market economies ran current account surpluses from 1999 onward. These reached close to 3 percent of GDP in 2005, when the Asian surplus reached 4 percent of GDP.

So the world has witnessed two big waves of current account deficits in the emerging market economies. The first, in the late 1970s and early 1980s, led to a significant crisis. The second and even bigger wave, in the mid-1990s, led to a still bigger crisis. And then the emerging economies effectively said "enough." Ever since, in the aggregate, they have been running current account surpluses.

The proximate cause of these swings in the availability of finance has been the immense volatility of funding from the private sector (Figure 3.3).[22] The private sector has had extended periods of optimism about emerging market economies, followed by something that looks very much like panic. Aggregate net private flows to emerging economies rose from next to zero in the late 1980s to $324 billion in 1996, before falling to $135 billion in 1998 and $112 billion in 2002 and then jumping to over $500 billion in 2005 and 2006. Net private flows to the Asian emerging economies rose from $43 billion in 1991 to $180 billion in 1996 before they fell to

Figure 3.3 Private Net Capital Flows

Billions of US$

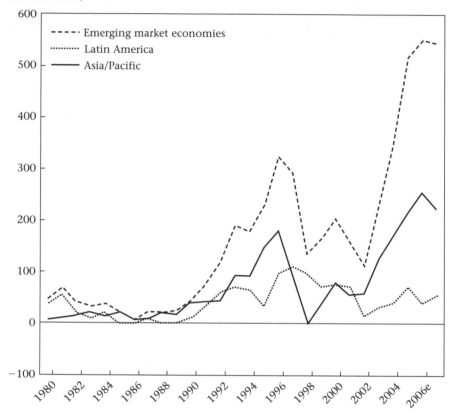

Source: Institute for International Finance.
Note: Inflow positive. e, Estimated.

–$0.2 billion in 1998. Then they started rising again, to reach $166 billion in 2004 and $254 billion in 2006. But, as will be shown further below, the response of the emerging market economies has been quite different this time: *they have refused to accept the money.* They have sent it more or less right back where it came from, while retaining their current account surpluses. Emerging market economies are resisting the logical corollary of large capital inflows—current account deficits. And they are resisting them for a good and understandable reason: current account deficits have come to mean crisis.

Now look at the composition of the net capital flows to emerging market economies as a whole (Figure 3.4). This illustration brings out three central elements of the picture:

1. Private flows are both the dominant source of finance and highly unstable;
2. Net flows from residents are often a good leading indicator of a coming crisis, since residents know much more about what is going wrong than foreign investors; and
3. The governments of the emerging market economies are now well aware of the risks and are putting the money their countries are receiving from both capital inflows and the current account into foreign exchange reserves on a staggering scale of around $600 billion a year (a negative sign in the figure represents a reserve accumulation).

Emerging market economies have been accumulating reserves since the late 1980s. Obviously they did not share the euphoria of foreign private investors—and, as it turned out, they were right not do so. But in recent years they have refused to allow substantial private net capital inflows to shift them from their determination to run very large current account surpluses. It is their combination of enormous net private capital inflows with enormous reserve accumulations that has become so significant for the world economy (Figure 3.5). In essence, this is government recycling of money earned through the current account and money received from private sector capital flows: the emerging market economies are, as I have remarked, smoking capital, but not inhaling.

How do the various forms of private capital behave? Which is the most nervous? The answer, shown in Figure 3.6, is bank credit. Foreign direct investment started to become significant in the 1990s. It has remained, on the whole, positive and remarkably stable. Portfolio equity investment has been less significant and less stable. But it has remained positive throughout. Nonbank credit has also remained positive but considerably less stable than either form of equity flow. But bank credit is the fount of instability. The collapse in bank credit was the proximate cause of the Latin American debt crisis in the early 1980s. It was not important in the Tequila Crisis of the mid-1990s because the Mexican government had come to rely on short-term, nonbank, dollar-denominated credits, called "tesobonos." But the shift in bank credit from a net inflow of $119 billion in 1996 to a net outflow of $60 billion in 1998 was the proximate cause of the Asian financial crisis.

Commercial bankers are dangerous: they offer short-term credit and are in a poor position to sustain large losses. So when they perceive heightened risk, they take their money out, with devastating effect on the econ-

Figure 3.4 Composition of Net Capital Flows to
Emerging Market Economies

Billions of US$

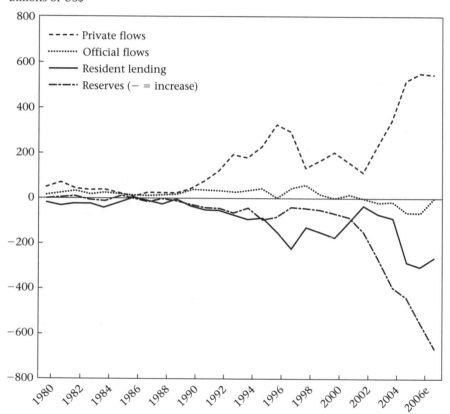

Source: Institute for International Finance.
Note: e, Estimated.

Figure 3.5 Emerging Market Current Accounts, Net Private
Capital Inflow, and Reserve Accumulations

Billions of US$

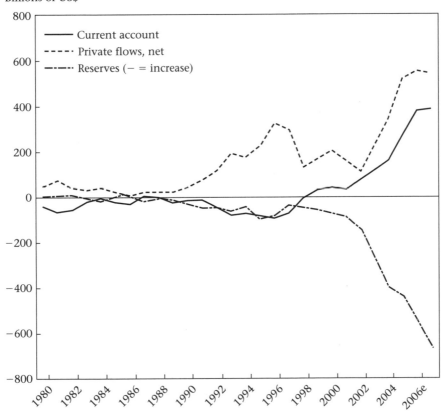

Source: Institute for International Finance.
Note: e, Estimated.

Figure 3.6 Composition of Private Net Capital Flows to Emerging Market Economies

Billions of US$

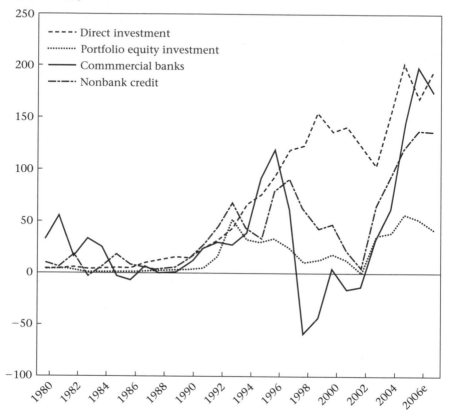

Source: Institute for International Finance.
Note: e, Estimated.

omy to which they have been lending. After the behavior of residents, that of commercial banks is the most sensitive indicator of a looming storm. Net commercial bank lending to the emerging market economies exploded upward once again in the second half of the 2000s to reach $200 billion a year in 2006. Such lending has previously been the harbinger of another crisis. Will it be different this time?

When crises happen, people who were confident about lending to developing countries and who were sure everything was fine realize that they were wrong. Look at the credit spreads over U.S. Treasury rates for emerging market government borrowers shown in Figure 3.7. In late 1997 the spreads were low. They tripled within about six months. Such violent swings in spreads are quite common—consider Turkey in 2000 and 2001 or Brazil in 2002. When interest rates become this high, credit markets dry up for fear of adverse selection: the only borrower prepared to borrow at rates like those confronting Brazil in 2002, or so the markets believe, is one prepared to default. They are right: real rates of interest over 20 percent are indeed unmanageable. So this degree of risk aversion generates a "sudden stop" in lending.

By March 2006, after all these crises, lenders to the emerging market economies of developing countries were more confident than they had ever been. Spreads were very low. But that was partly because the countries concerned were no longer net borrowers: they were running current account surpluses, not deficits, as was shown in Figure 3.5.

Finally, let us look at the capital flow picture for the two most important regions—Latin America and East Asia. Figure 3.8 shows the remarkable instability of private capital flows to Latin America—the rise in the early 1980s, then the collapse, then the big rise in the 1990s, then another collapse in the late 1990s, culminating in the Argentine default of 2001, before yet another modest rise. Also evident is the sensitivity of resident lending: foreign private capital repeatedly invested in Latin America while the domestic private sector was selling the countries short. One lesson is that one should always look to the Latin American private sector if one wants to know what is really happening.

Now consider the flows to Asian emerging economies (Figure 3.9). Here again, private flows were overwhelmingly dominant but inherently unstable, rising sharply in the 1990s, then collapsing between 1996 and 1998, before recovering strongly, particularly in the 2000s. But the gigantic reserve accumulations of the 2000s more than offset the increased capital inflows.

Dynamics of the Crises

So how then did the big crises unfold? The answer is that the sudden cessation of capital flows forced the current account deficit to fall, the currency to collapse, and credit to shrink. Deep recessions followed. In emerging economies hit by crises, devaluations frequently cause the economy to contract, not expand—the reverse of what has happened in many high-income countries. One reason for this difference is the low credibility of monetary policy in many emerging economies. A devaluation is viewed as a harbinger of inflation. Monetary policy then has to tighten, not loosen.[23]

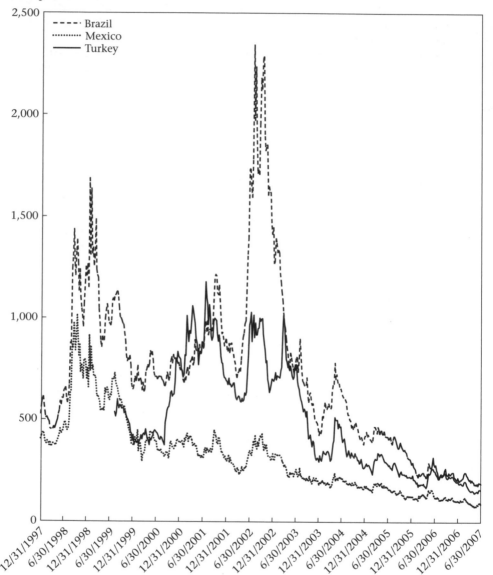

Figure 3.7 Spreads on Emerging Market Currency Loans

Basis points

Source: Thomson Datastream.
Note: Spreads over U.S. Treasuries, JPMorgan EMBI index.

Figure 3.8 Composition of Net Capital Flows to Latin American
Emerging Market Economies

Billions of US$

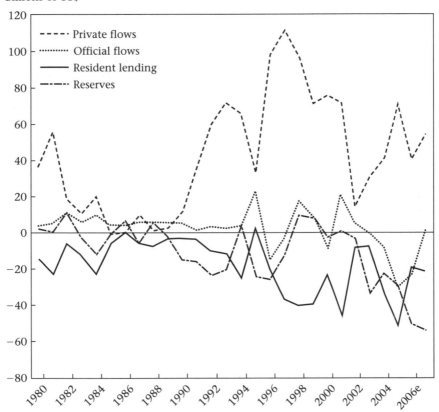

Source: Institute for International Finance.
Note: e, Estimated.

Figure 3.9 Composition of Net Capital Flows to Asian
Emerging Market Economies

Billions of US$

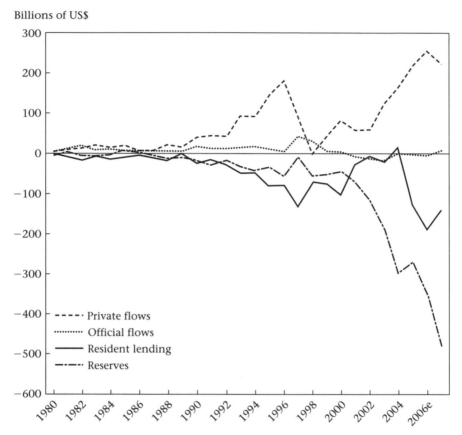

Source: Institute for International Finance.
Note: e, Estimated. Values for 2007 are forecast.

Another and more important reason is the prevalence of currency mismatches in the economy. The fall of the currency directly threatens insolvency for any borrower with foreign-currency-denominated liabilities
that have been used to finance domestic assets. When a foreign-currency
loan is used to invest in production of tradables, the danger is smaller, since
the price of the output will rise as the currency devalues. But when someone borrows foreign currency to build, say, a supermarket, the danger is evident. Moreover, even a bank that itself has a perfectly matched position
will be badly damaged if its clients have large currency mismatches.

What matters is the overall national balance sheet. As Morris Gold-stein of the Institute for International Economics and Philip Turner of the Bank for International Settlements argue:

> large negative currency mismatches either lead or are contemporaneous with currency and banking crises. . . . In this connection, we draw attention to the large negative foreign-currency positions in Mexico in 1994–96, the Asian-crisis countries (Korea, Indonesia, Malaysia, the Philippines, and Thailand) in 1997–98, Russia in 1998, Argentina in 2001–02, Brazil in 2002, and Turkey in 2000–02. In terms of dollar values, the largest negative foreign-currency position by far was Argentina's imbalance in 2001–02 (at around $100 billion); next in line were Brazil ($76 billion), Mexico ($64 billion), Korea ($58 billion), Turkey ($46 billion), Russia ($34 billion), Thailand ($33 billion), and Indonesia ($28 billion).[24]

Given these mismatches, take a look at what happened to the currencies and economies of countries hit by crises. The big Latin American cases are shown in Figure 3.10. Russia is included, because its pattern is similar and—as a resource-rich, corruption-ridden, dollarized emerging economy—it bore some similarities to Argentina and Mexico.

It is not very difficult to understand that when a currency loses more than 60 percent of its initial value against the currency in which much of its debt is denominated, there will be distress and a large impact on economic activity. This, interestingly, is not apparent for Russia, largely because of the limited foreign-currency indebtedness of the private sector. But it was true for Mexico and Argentina (the latter twice) (Figure 3.11).

The pattern for East Asia was similar: the currencies experienced deep devaluations (Figure 3.12). The Indonesian rupiah lost 80 percent of its value almost overnight. That this collapse should have had a devastating effect on an economy with large quantities of foreign-currency-denominated debt is hardly surprising. The currency collapse also explains the scale of Indonesia's fiscal losses (see Figure 3.1). It is a horrifying story for a country that had had no history of serious inflation.

The devaluations were again associated with deep recessions (Figure 3.13). Indonesia's GDP fell by about 15 percent in the first year and by 2001 it had failed to reach precrisis GDP levels. The country that recovered quickly, even though it lost a sizable amount of GDP in the year after the crisis, was South Korea. The speed of the South Korean policy response, the flexibility of the economy, and the ability to expand exports from the competitive manufacturing sector all led to a satisfactory outcome. The bounce-back was also quite good in Malaysia. But it was poor in Thailand, which also suffered long-term consequence of the crisis.

Moreover, not only was a great deal of the borrowing in foreign currency, but a huge proportion was also for a short term (less than a year), as Barry Eichengreen points out in discussing the data shown in Figure 3.14.[25]

Figure 3.10 Value against the U.S. Dollar: Latin America and Russia

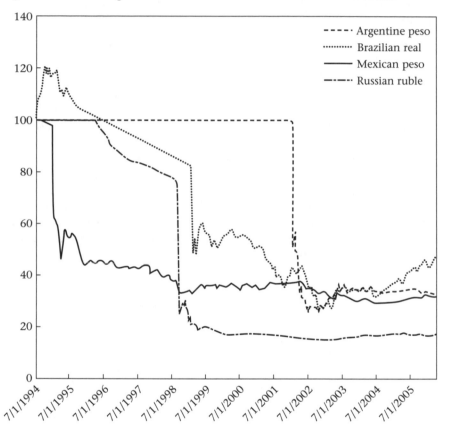

Source: Thomson Datastream.
Note: Starting at 100.

Figure 3.11 Macroeconomic Consequences of the Latin American and Russian Crises

Index (year 2 = 100)

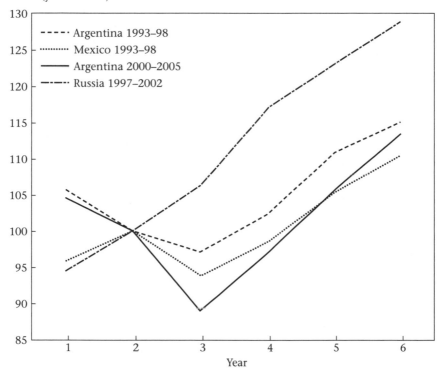

Year

Source: Thomson Datastream.
Note: GDP in the year before the crisis and in the four subsequent years.

Figure 3.12 Value against the U.S. Dollar: East Asia

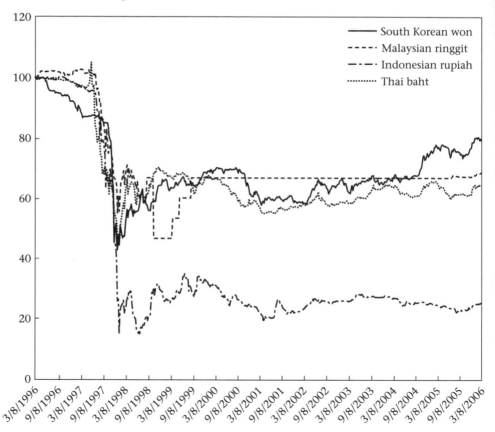

Source: Thomson Datastream.
Note: January 1996 = 100.

Figure 3.13 Macroeconomic Consequences of the Asian Crisis

Index (year 2 = 100)

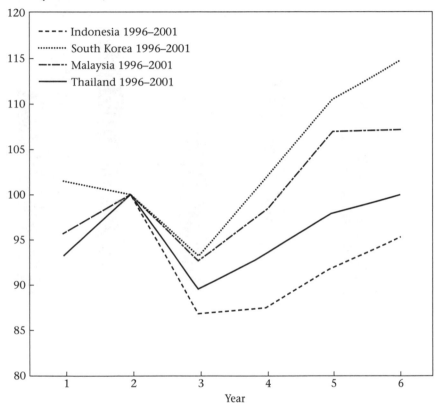

Source: Thomson Datastream.
Note: GDP in the year before the crisis and in the four subsequent years.

Figure 3.14 Share of Short-Term Borrowing in Foreign-Currency Borrowing of Asian Crisis Countries

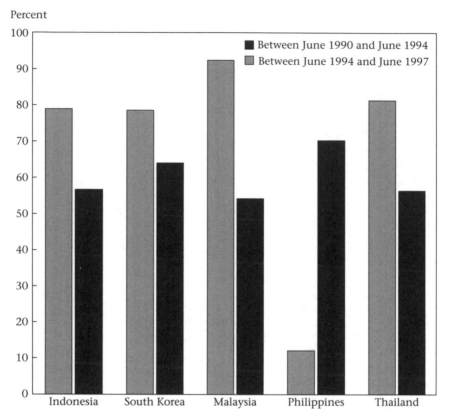

Source: Eichengreen (2004).

This meant, as he notes, that the countries had both a flow problem—a need to keep borrowing to finance the current account deficit—and a stock problem—a need to roll over the debt as it came due.

Finally, recall that, in addition to the significant recessions, these countries also had to bear significant fiscal costs to bail out their bankrupt financial systems (Figure 3.15). These costs varied between 55 percent of GDP in Indonesia and a relatively modest 6–7 percent in Russia. Emerging economies that suffered significant twin crises—currency and financial—have all incurred large fiscal costs. In the end, taxpayers bore much of the brunt, along with workers, farmers, and other ordinary people. The foreign bankers who made the decisions to lend—and so bear at least some of the

Figure 3.15 Fiscal Cost of Significant Emerging Market Crises

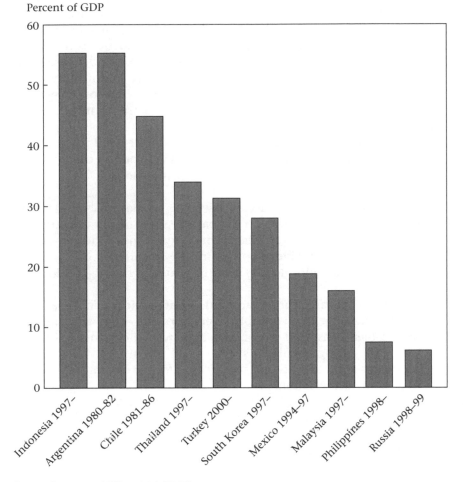

Percent of GDP

Source: Caprio and Klingebiel (2003).

blame for the disasters—often escaped unscathed. The citizens of the countries they fled did not.

Legacy of the Crises

After twenty-five years of being beaten over the head, people have now realized that there is danger in capital flows. The interaction between irresponsible lenders and equally foolish borrowers can generate enormous costs when the tide of capital flow goes out. From this outcome policy makers in emerging market economies have taken two lessons: they must improve their financial systems, and they must make themselves less vulnerable to reversals of capital inflows. The benign consequence is that financial systems have improved. The malign consequence is that many policy makers are frightened of running current account deficits. So we now see the phenomenon of capital markets trying to put money into emerging economies even as the governments of these economies, with even greater determination, recycle the funds in the form of foreign-currency reserves.

Why is there so much fear of current account deficits? After all, it is perfectly possible to have currency mismatches in a country that has a current account balance. There are several powerful reasons:

1. Most important, a current account deficit is, in the end, bound to generate a currency mismatch on the balance sheet of any country both dependent on borrowing (rather than on equity inflow) to cover its external deficit and unable to borrow in its own currency.[26]
2. Large current account deficits seem to be one of the triggers for capital outflow.
3. Correction of a large current account deficit requires a depreciation of the real exchange rate—possibly a very large one—that will cause serious problems inside the economy if there is a currency mismatch within the aggregate balance sheet.
4. Awareness of that fact is one good reason for the capital outflow that triggers the depreciation.
5. Awareness is also likely to force the borrowing to become increasingly and riskily short term, as creditors try to increase the liquidity of their position.
6. Finally, swift correction of a current account deficit is always painful and to be avoided if possible.

In addition, as a number of economists have noted, there is fear of floating. This is partly because of the disruption caused by big changes in relative prices. But it is also a result of concern over the damage done by currency mismatches. If one has a fear of floating, the answer is to maintain an undervalued exchange rate and a strong current account position. An attempt to force an *appreciation* of a currency in this position can always be resisted by buying more foreign currency. But if one tries to prevent a depreciation of a currency under pressure to devalue, one will sooner or later run out of reserves and have to resort to high interest rates, thereby imposing recession and still risking failure.

Quite apart from the prudential reasons for avoiding current account deficits, there has been another explanation for the strong current account positions of many East Asian emerging market economies: the desire to return to the tested route of export-led growth. This has proved a successful path to development in the past, one that reduces risks and accelerates the acquisition of industrial capabilities.

So the lesson learned by many emerging economies—both those directly affected by the crises and those who have been onlookers—is not to tolerate current account deficits. This strategy has another and perhaps even more important political advantage: if one's current account position is strong and the pressure on the currency is upward, there is no risk of the IMF intervening and making politically unpalatable demands. That fear is not limited to those who have suffered crises. The Chinese government certainly looked at what happened to its neighbors in 1997–98 and concluded that it would never allow anything similar to happen in China.

All this has had a good side—the risk of another wave of emerging market crises has lessened—and one that is less so—the U.S. current account deficit has increased enormously. For if there are countries that wish to provide capital and few that are prepared to take it, those that do accept it will end up with large deficits. The U.S. government knows it will never suffer from currency mismatches or unpleasant visits from the IMF. That is what it means to be the global hegemon. By the mid-2000s, the United States was running three-quarters of the current account deficits in the world. How this happened, and its consequences for the world economy, are the theme of Chapter 4.

From Crises to Imbalances

> Over the past decade a combination of diverse forces has created a significant increase in the global supply of saving—a global saving glut—which helps to explain both the increase in the U.S. current account deficit and the relatively low level of long-term real interest rates in the world today.
>
> BEN BERNANKE, GOVERNOR OF THE FEDERAL RESERVE

> Long-term rates have moved lower virtually everywhere.
>
> ALAN GREENSPAN, CHAIRMAN OF THE FEDERAL RESERVE

IN THE MIDDLE OF THE FIRST DECADE of the third millennium, the then-chairman of the Federal Reserve, Alan Greenspan, commented on the surprisingly low level of interest rates. Soon afterward, then-governor Ben Bernanke, who was shortly to succeed Greenspan as chairman, pointed to a "global saving glut" as an explanation for the persistent U.S. current account deficit. Both observations were correct. More importantly, the phenomena they describe are closely related: the high rates of net saving (savings less domestic investment) in much of the world explain both modest interest rates and the pattern of current account surpluses and deficits. Moreover, they are not an accident. They are, I argue, in important respects the consequence of deliberate policies of export-led growth and self-insurance against the risk of financial crises that result in the huge accumulations of foreign-currency reserves discussed in Chapter 3.

These relationships are the theme of this chapter. They explain why the United States, the world's most important market and the issuer of the world's most significant currency, has also become the superpower of international borrowing—the world's borrower and spender of last resort. This is an unprecedented situation: never before has the world's most advanced economy also been such a huge net recipient of capital. That this is so demonstrates just how far the reality of global capital account liberalization has diverged from what one might have expected. Capital now flows upstream, from the world's poor to the richest country of all.

A Pair of Puzzles

Let us start with the first of these two peculiarities of the world economy today: the low level not just of nominal interest rates (which is partly explained by low inflation) or of short-term interest rates (which reached very low levels in Japan, the United States, and the Eurozone in the aftermath of asset price bubbles in the early 2000s), but, far more important, of long-term real interest rates. Greenspan once called this a "conundrum." Let us call it a puzzle. What is puzzling is that this is an era of rapid productivity growth, at least in the United States, of catch-up in Asia, and of rapid growth in the world economy. At market exchange rates, the rate of growth of the world economy is expected by the IMF to average 3.7 percent between 2004 and 2007. These growth rates compare more than favorably with average growth of 2.5 percent a year between 1989 and 1998.[1] Yet eras of fast growth should normally have relatively high real rates of interest, not low ones.

As Figure 4.1 shows, a simple calculation of the world real interest rate by the staff of the IMF suggests that it had fallen to about 2 percent by 2004. This was not as low as it had been in the 1970s, when inflation soared, but it was lower than it had been since then.[2] This estimate is also consistent with the evidence on inflation-indexed government bonds in the United States, which yielded about 2 percent in real terms in 2004 and 2005. More recent calculations by the IMF show that the real interest rates in the United States, the Eurozone, and Japan were all below their post-1990 average in the mid-2000s, despite the strong growth of the world economy (Figure 4.2).

What makes this picture even more interesting is that the cyclically adjusted fiscal position of the high-income countries was so loose. According to the IMF's *World Economic Outlook* for April 2007, the fiscal deficit, thus defined, was 3.9 percent of GDP in 2002, 4.4 percent in 2003, 4.1 percent in 2004, 3.3 percent in 2005, and 2.7 percent in 2006. One would expect high cyclically adjusted fiscal deficits to lead to high real interest rates, not low ones. The plausible explanation is that the surplus of desired savings over investment in the private sector has induced—or been offset by—the fiscal loosening by governments. Whether by design or by accident, these fiscal policies supported demand.

Figure 4.1 World Long-Term Real Interest Rate

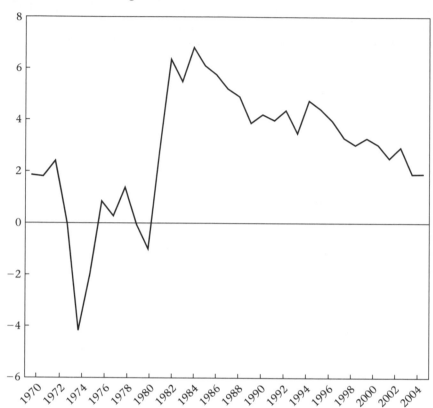

Source: International Monetary Fund, *World Economic Outlook,* April 2006.

Recent work from the IMF suggests that the current low real interest rates are not so anomalous when set against the long-term historical background, but only appear so when set against the very high real interest rates of the 1980s and early 1990s.[3] For example, between 1896 and 1913, during the heyday of the pre–World War I globalization, the global real interest rate is estimated to have been 2.2 percent, while GDP grew at 3.1 percent. Between 1919 and 1929 the real interest rate was 1.8 percent, against an economic growth rate of 3.4 percent. This looks not very different from today's picture: fast growth and low real interest rates. From this perspective, the conundrum may instead be the persistently low real returns on safe bonds. Moreover, the high real interest rates of the 1980s

Figure 4.2 Long-Term Real Interest Rates

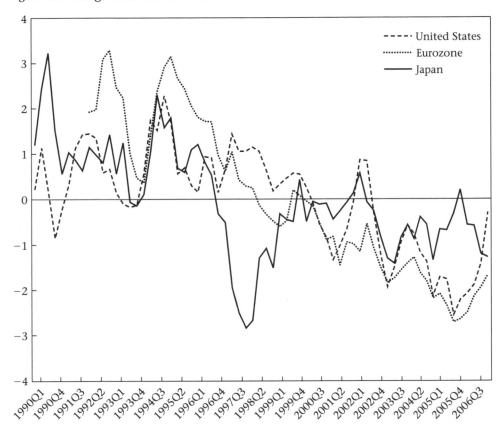

Source: International Monetary Fund, *World Economic Outlook,* April 2007.
Note: Rates are relative to the average.

and 1990s may be largely a response to the negative real rates during the great inflation of the 1970s.

Yet low real interest rates still remain a puzzle when one considers the second extraordinary phenomenon of our era: the explosive increase in the U.S. current account deficit, shown in Figure 4.3. From the 1920s through the 1970s, the United States was a creditor nation and ran a current account surplus. In the early 1980s, the current account moved into deficit by what then seemed an enormous amount, but one that now seems quite modest. This was the era of "benign neglect," with Donald Regan in charge of the

Figure 4.3 U.S. Current Account

Percent of GDP

Source: Thomson Datastream.

U.S. Treasury under President Ronald Reagan. Then in the mid-1980s came a fall in the dollar and a change in U.S. currency policy, marked by the Plaza Accord in September 1985, calling for the dollar to be depreciated in relation to the yen and the deutsche mark. The dollar fell steeply. U.S. trading partners also adopted expansionary monetary policies, partly because of direct U.S. pressure on them to do so and partly because the dollar's fall had a contractionary impact on their export-oriented economies. These loose monetary policies helped generate the Japanese bubble, which burst in 1990. But, together with the financing of the first Gulf War by U.S. allies, these adjustments in exchange rates and in the relative growth of demand eliminated the U.S. current account deficit by 1990. In the 1990s, the current account deficit exploded again, to hitherto unprecedented levels. Note, in addition, the acceleration of the deficit after 1998 and again after 2002.

Lawrence Summers, former U.S. treasury secretary, put the two points —the low real interest rates and the huge U.S. current account deficit— together sharply in a lecture in March 2006:

> There is one striking fact about the global economy that belies a dominantly American explanation for the pattern of global capital flows: real interest rates globally are low, not high. Whether one looks at index bond yields, measures of nominal interest rates relative to ongoing inflation, and yields on most assets, especially real estate or credit spreads, capital market pricing points to the supply of global capital tending to outstrip demand rather than vice versa. Real interest rates globally are low not high from a historical perspective. If the dominant impulse explaining global events was declining U.S. savings, one would expect abnormally high real interest rates, as with the twin deficits in the 1980s, not abnormally low real interest rates. America's consumption growth in substantial excess of income growth has been matched by substantial export led growth in the rest of the world.[4]

Why are real interest rates still so modest when the United States is running a current account deficit equal to perhaps a seventh of the rest of the world's gross savings? The answer is a global one: a large number of countries have been unable to absorb their savings at home, even at low real rates of interest. Because they cannot absorb their savings, they are exporting the excess, principally to the United States. The United States is thus running a huge current account deficit, which is, by definition, the mirror image of a huge surplus on the capital account. This "savings glut" hypothesis is not straightforward, since some of the most important excess "savings" are the consequence of government policies aimed at keeping exchange rates down, particularly in Asia. Furthermore, those policies have monetary consequences. How the savings glut hypothesis fits with the alternative view of a "money glut"—advanced by, among others,

Richard Duncan, author of the widely discussed *The Dollar Crisis*—is an important point to which the discussion will later return.[5]

The Global Savings Glut

How does one measure a savings glut? It is not something one can observe, at least not at the level of the world economy. By definition, measured global savings must equal global investment. There are three ways to identify such a glut: by measuring the level of real interest rates (which are, among other things, the price of savings, as discussed above), private sector balances of savings and investment, and the balances in individual countries or groups of countries. In the world of the mid-2000s, real interest rates are low, the private sectors in most important countries are running sizable savings surpluses (which are the counterpart of dis-savings by many governments), and many countries are running sizable surpluses of savings over investment, even at low real rates of interest.

So what has caused the excess savings condition of so many countries? One explanation was deliberate policies adopted by countries burned by the emerging market crises, both as victims and as onlookers. Another was the rise in the price of oil, which has shifted income to countries with high levels of savings, at least in the short run. The third was the aftermath of what we may now confidently call the global stock market bubble of 1999–2000. In most economically significant countries, corporations are very profitable but cautious about investing. So they also have positive cash flow: their retained earnings (their savings) exceed their investments.

The shift of income from labor to capital is an important phenomenon across the high-income economies.[6] Interestingly and significantly, the biggest shift from labor income has not been in the United States and other Anglo-Saxon countries, but in Japan and the Eurozone. Undistributed profits are the savings of the business sector. Unless they are offset by expanded investment in the sector (which has not happened), the result is a rise in savings that needs to be matched by offsetting reductions in the other three sectors of the economy (government, households, and foreigners). The corporate sectors of the high-income countries are now, in general, excess savers: undistributed profits exceed investment.[7] In any case, when the corporate sector is running a large financial surplus, either other domestic sectors must run offsetting deficits or the country as a whole must run a substantial savings surplus that will show up in the balance of payments. The corporate sector has been running a financial surplus in the United States as well, but there (and in a few other countries) the government and household sectors more than fully offset corporate excess savings.

If we look at the world as a whole and at many significant countries, we find the notion of a savings glut is not right. It might be better thought of as an investment dearth. This is true for the high-income countries in particular. The overall global picture is shown in Figures 4.4–4.6.[8] These figures emphasize five central features of the world:

1. Global savings rates have been falling, because of the decline in savings in the high-income countries.
2. The investment rates of the high-income countries have also been falling, particularly since the early 1990s.
3. The savings and investment rates of emerging economies and oil exporters have been rising over the same period, except for the sharp fall, particularly in investment rates, in the aftermath of the 1997–98 financial crises.
4. The high-income countries have become importers of savings, since their savings rates have fallen below their investment rates.
5. The savings rates of the emerging economies and oil exporters have risen above their investment rates, and so they have become capital exporters.

Figure 4.4 Global Savings and Investment

Percent of global output

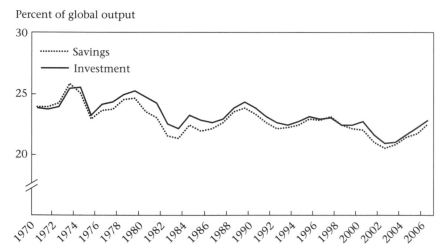

Source: International Monetary Fund, *World Economic Outlook*, April 2007.

Figure 4.5 Savings, Investment, and Current Account of
High-Income Countries

Percent of GDP

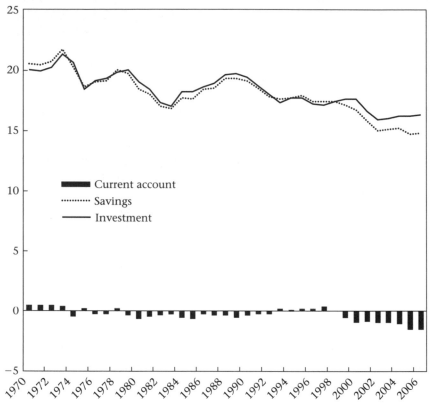

Source: International Monetary Fund, *World Economic Outlook,* April 2007.

It is easy to understand some of this. The decline in investment rates
in the high-income countries is partly the result of the maturity of the European and Japanese economies and, in particular, of their stagnant or
even declining populations (see Figure 4.5). These countries do not need
to invest as much as they did during their high-growth periods. The reverse should be happening in the high-growth emerging economies. But,
interestingly, their investment shares in global gross product did not return to 1997 levels until 2005.

Now look at the global distribution more narrowly. Figure 4.7 shows
savings rates and net lending (the difference between savings and invest-

Figure 4.6 Savings, Investment, and Current Account of
Emerging Market and Oil-Exporting Countries

Percent of GDP

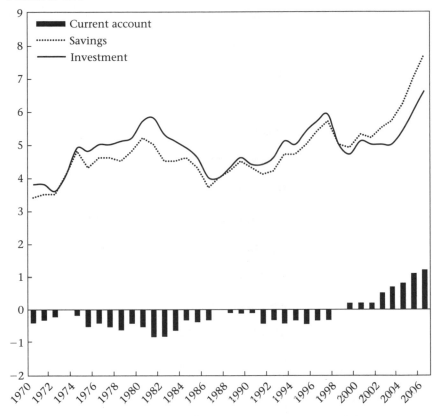

Source: International Monetary Fund, *World Economic Outlook,* April 2007.

ment) across the world, with economies ranked by savings rates, in 2006.
It shows, first, that countries with relatively low savings rates—such as the
United States, the United Kingdom, and central and eastern Europe—
imported capital, while those with relatively high savings rates—such as
Japan, the Commonwealth of Independent States, the newly industrialized
Asian economies, the fuel exporters, developing Asia (which includes both
China and India), and China—all exported capital. It shows, second, that
the highest-saving economies in the world are developing countries and
the lowest-saving ones, on this list, are the United States and the United
Kingdom, both members of the group of seven leading high-income coun-

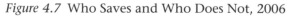

Figure 4.7 Who Saves and Who Does Not, 2006

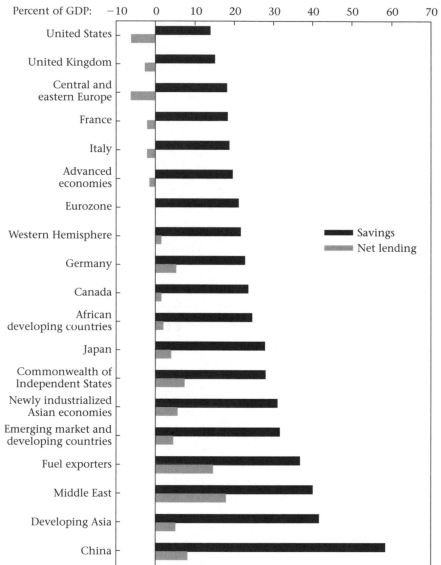

Source: International Monetary Fund, *World Economic Outlook,* April 2007.
Note: Values are savings and net international lending.

tries. It shows, third, how big the variations in national savings rates are, all the way from the low rate of 14 percent of GDP in the United States to the almost unbelievable rate of 59 percent in China. The latter must be the highest in any economy ever. It shows, finally, how dependent low-saving economies are on the supply of foreign finance: in the case of the United States, foreigners financed almost a third of investment in 2006.

Let us look more closely at the developing countries, whose high savings rates have been such a big part of the global picture and whose opportunities and challenges lie at the heart of this book (Figure 4.8). First are the East Asian developing countries, other than China. These are fairly high-saving countries, whose investment rates fell by about 10 percent of GDP between 1997 and 1998 (at the time of the crisis) and never subsequently recovered. As a direct result, they moved from an aggregate current account deficit to a substantial and persistent surplus.

Then there is the most remarkable picture of all, that of China, which is almost the precise opposite of that of the United States. The broad story is clear—incredibly high and rising investment rates matched by even higher savings rates (see Figure 4.9). Despite having the highest investment rate of any significant economy in history, China has a huge excess of savings over investment. Moreover, the surplus is exploding upward.

The sources of Chinese savings are also fascinating, because they are so different from what many believe them to be. Chinese households save enormously. But the core of the Chinese savings story over the past five or six years has been the rise in corporate savings (Figure 4.10). The Chinese government told state enterprises to become profitable, and they have done what they were told. The corporate sector has become profitable by disposing of surplus workers, yet the government has not taken some of the increased profits as dividends on the assets it owns, even to finance a safety net for displaced workers. Remarkably (and shockingly), the government has left the money with enterprise insiders. But the government itself is also a large saver. China has about 800 million poor people, yet the country now consumes less than half of GDP and exports capital to the rest of the world. This is highly peculiar. It is also why the country has such a huge current account surplus.

Now look at the oil exporters, who have become an increasingly important part of the picture. These countries have had a significant surge in income. So now they also have a large savings surplus, since they are unable to spend all the additional income, at least in the short run (Figure 4.11). One of the interesting characteristics of these countries is that they have been much more cautious about spending their excess income than in the 1970s. So while their savings rates have reached historically un-

Figure 4.8 Savings and Investment in East Asian Emerging Markets, Excluding China

Percent of GDP

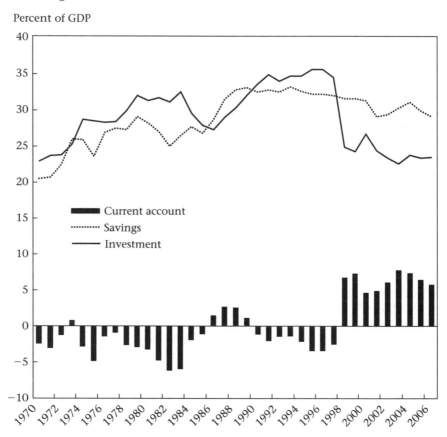

Source: International Monetary Fund, *World Economic Outlook,* April 2007.

Figure 4.9 Savings, Investment, and Current Account in China

Percent of GDP

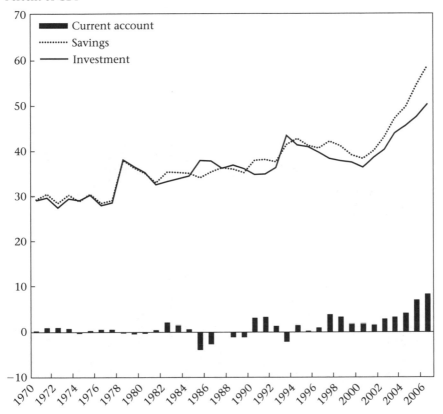

Source: International Monetary Fund, *World Economic Outlook,* April 2007.

Figure 4.10 Sectoral Breakdown of China's Savings

Percent of GDP

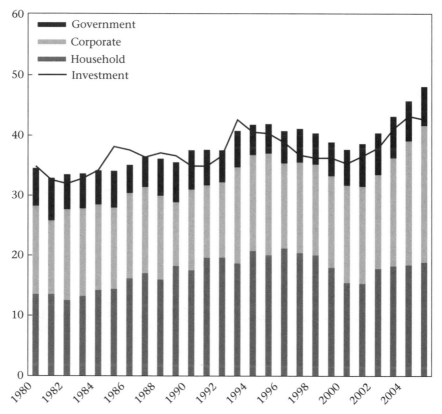

Source: UBS.

Figure 4.11 Savings, Investment, and Current Account of the
Oil Exporters

Percent of GDP

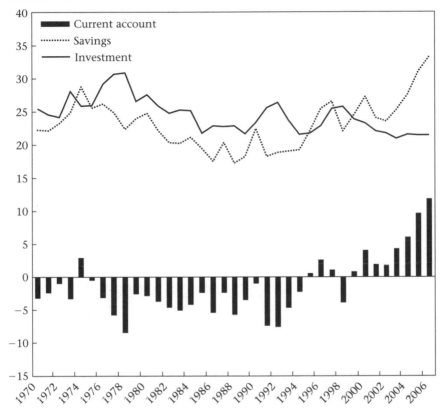

Source: International Monetary Fund, *World Economic Outlook,* April 2007.

precedented levels, investment rates have remained relatively low, and
their current account surplus reached 12 percent of GDP in 2006.

Finally, we have the other emerging market countries as a group. They
have been close to balance in recent years—a small surplus in 2002–4, followed by small deficits in 2005 and 2006 (Figure 4.12). They do not contribute to the savings glut. But they do nothing significant to eliminate it
either.

Now turn to the high-income countries. Japan has always been a relatively high-saving country. In 1970, the gross savings rate was 41 percent
of GDP. But this has since fallen steadily, to reach 28 percent of GDP in

Figure 4.12 Savings, Investment, and Current Account in Other Emerging Market Economies

Percent of GDP

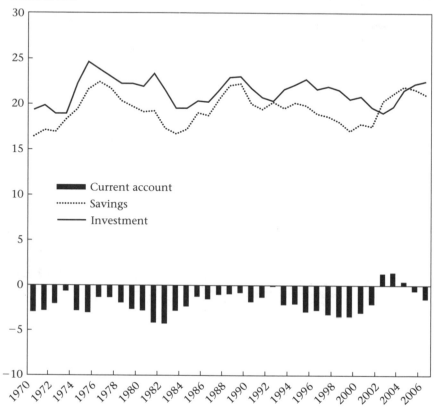

Source: International Monetary Fund, *World Economic Outlook,* April 2007.

2006. Yet investment has also fallen as economic growth has slowed. The country as a whole has had a chronic savings surplus that has shown up in a persistent current account surplus and export of capital. This is not new.

Since the bursting of the stock market bubble in 1990, the interesting part of the Japanese story has been sectoral.[9] Between 1990 and 2003, Japan's corporate savings (undistributed profits) soared from 14 percent to 21 percent of GDP. Meanwhile, household savings fell from 13 percent to 8 percent of GDP. But, given the sharp decline in investment, from 33 percent to 24 percent of GDP over the same period, the country had a growing surplus of private savings over domestic investment. Thus in 1990,

Japanese private savings were 6 percent of GDP less than overall investment (27 percent of GDP, against 33 percent of GDP). By 2003, however, private savings were 6 percent of GDP greater than total investment (30 percent of GDP against just 24 percent of GDP). In Japan's case, the principal offsetting adjustment was in public saving, which moved from 8 percent of GDP in 1990 to –3 percent. The massive deterioration in the public finances offset the combined impact of the modest rise in overall private savings with the sharp decline in investment, thereby preventing what would otherwise presumably have been either a huge recession or a big increase in the current account surplus or, more probably, a combination of the two.

Yet, as a result of the fiscal loosening, Japanese public debt has been on an upward path. Japan's rising public debt has allowed the corporate sector to improve its ravaged post-bubble financial position.[10] For the economy as a whole, though, debt has not been reduced, but rather shifted to future taxpayers. Meanwhile, there has been no large increase in overall Japanese excess savings for the rest of the world to absorb. But this situation may prove temporary. As the Japanese government cuts its fiscal deficit, the current account surplus may well rise.

The Eurozone has been in balance. There have been large deficits and surpluses: Germany, in particular, had a large surplus of savings over investment (5 percent of GDP in 2006), while Spain had a huge deficit (of around 9 percent of GDP in 2006). But overall the Eurozone has remained close to balance for most of the past fifteen years. This is why the Eurozone's monetary and fiscal authorities argue that it is not contributing to global imbalances. It is, however, certainly not contributing to their removal. Meanwhile, some European countries outside the Eurozone have large savings surpluses, notably Norway and Switzerland (both equal to 17 percent of GDP in 2006). In the aggregate, according to the IMF, western Europe (excluding the United Kingdom) had a savings surplus of $131 billion in 2006 (see Figure 4.14).

Having looked at the major players in the world economy—developing Asia, including China, and the oil exporters, Japan, and the Eurozone—nearly all of whom have moved into savings surpluses, just as Bernanke argued, let us examine the last big piece of the puzzle—the United States. The U.S. investment rate as a share of GDP has been reasonably constant. But the savings rate has fallen a long way. By the first quarter of 2007, it was running at 14 percent of GDP. Again, the components of U.S. savings are revealing (Figure 4.13). The business sector has increased its savings (which are its undistributed earnings), as a result of the surge in profits. If the business sector is saving so much, investment has been a reasonably constant share of GDP, and the flow of capital from abroad has been ex-

Figure 4.13 Sectoral Breakdown of U.S. Saving

Percent of GDP

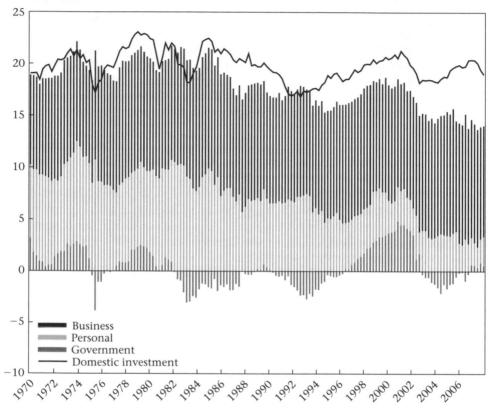

Source: U.S. national income and product accounts.

ploding, savings must have been falling sharply elsewhere. Indeed household savings were astonishingly low, at between 2 and 3 percent of GDP between the first quarter of 2005 and the first quarter of 2007. Meanwhile, the government moved sharply from a large surplus in 2000 back into a sizable deficit and then into a small surplus once again in 2007.

What then is the conclusion? A number of large and important regions have an excess of savings over investment. The United States has, in turn, been absorbing about 70 percent of the surplus savings in the rest of the world, with the difference accounted for not by increased investment but by higher consumption and a lower rate of savings.[11]

The Global Balance of Payments

The balance of payments is the vehicle through which capital flows across the world. Regions with capital surpluses run current account surpluses (and capital account deficits), while regions with capital deficits do the reverse. That is exactly what we now see as the savings surpluses and counterpart deficits build up.

There are two principal surplus regions: Asia and the oil exporters, with western Europe making a relatively modest contribution (Figure 4.14). The Asian developing countries have also played a significant role in the growth in world demand for oil, which has underpinned strong oil prices: between 2002 and 2005, almost half of global incremental demand for oil came from Asia. For the first time, developing countries—predominantly China and to some extent India and other Asian countries—have been more significant factors in the oil markets, at the margin, than the developed world. So what did we see in 2006? The total Asian surplus was $511 billion ($239 billion for China, $170 billion for Japan, and $102 billion for the rest of Asia). The surplus of the oil exporters was another $396 billion. The surplus of western Europe, without the United Kingdom, was $131 billion. The United Kingdom's deficit was $68 billion. But the U.S. deficit was $857 billion. The rest of the world, including the discrepancy in the global payments balance, ran a deficit of $112 billion.

This then was the picture for 2006. What trends can be foreseen? The IMF provides a useful analysis of global balances of payments as a share of global output (Figure 4.15). This study brings out clearly the extent to which the United States is the world's dominant borrower and Asia and the oil exporters the dominant sources of capital. It also highlights the steady rise of Asia as the dominant source of surplus capital in the world. What makes this trend even more extraordinary is that Asia is an important net importer of oil. For Asia to run such large current account surpluses at a time of high world oil prices is extraordinary.

If we look more closely at Asia, we find that the big story is the replacement of Japan by China as the biggest source of surplus capital. Japan has run a significant surplus for a long time. But China's is now far bigger (see Figure 4.14). China is, in fact, the dominant economy in the category of emerging Asia, shown in Figure 4.16. China's current account surplus was 9.1 percent of its GDP in 2006. The other giant, India, also in this group, was in an entirely different position: it ran a current account deficit of 2.2 percent of GDP in 2006. Japan has run a large surplus for a long time. But the share of GDP has remained fairly stable. It is also less than half of China's, at 3.9 percent of GDP in 2006. Japan's surplus has never come even close to 9 percent of its GDP. In fact, China is now play-

Figure 4.14 Global Current Accounts, 2006

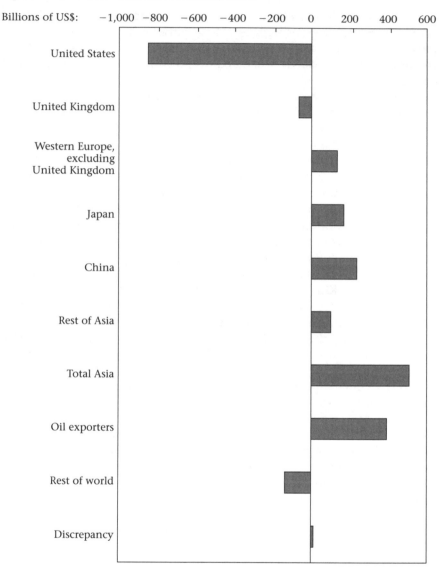

Source: International Monetary Fund, *World Economic Outlook,* April 2004 and April 2007, and World Economic Outlook Database.
Note: The "discrepancy" refers to the fact that the components enumerated in the figure do not add to zero owing to rounding.

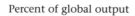

Figure 4.15 Global Current Account Balances

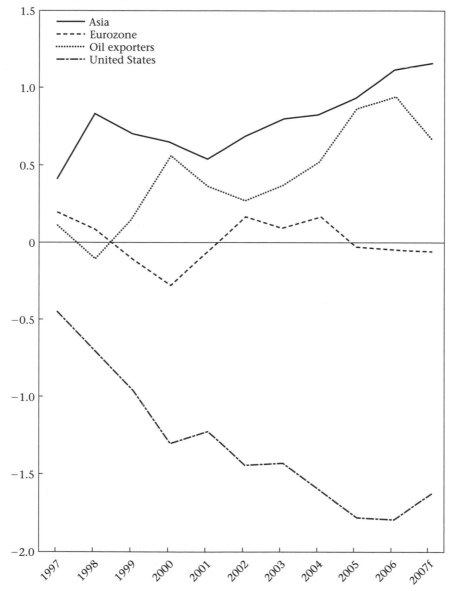

Percent of global output

Asia
Eurozone
Oil exporters
United States

Source: International Monetary Fund, *World Economic Outlook,* April 2007.
Note: f, Forecast.

Figure 4.16 Asian Current Account Balances

Percent of world GDP

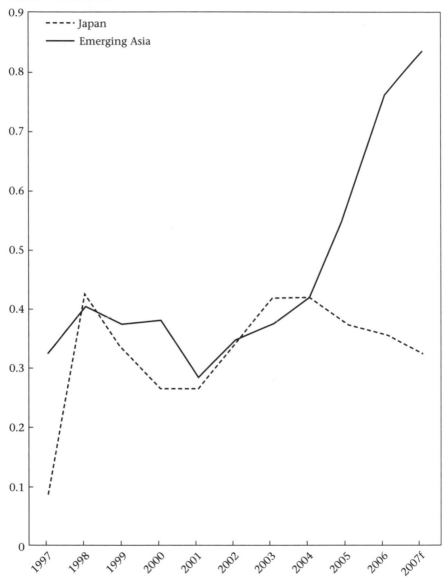

Source: International Monetary Fund, *World Economic Outlook,* April 2007.
Note: f, Forecast.

ing a unique dual role in the world economy: it is both the largest exporter of capital (as the United Kingdom was in the late nineteenth century) and the fastest-growing emerging giant (the role played by the United States at that time).

The global balance of payments ought to balance. (In fact, because of inevitable errors of measurement, it does not, but the discrepancy is not large.) What are the counterparts of the increased U.S. current account deficit? Between 1996 and 2006, the U.S. deficit increased by $740 billion.[12] Over that period the aggregate current account of the other established high-income countries (Australia, Canada, the United Kingdom, the rest of western Europe, and Japan) shifted by just $48 billion toward the black (with Japan alone shifting by $105 billion). China's shift was $232 billion, the rest of emerging Asia's (including the newly industrialized Asian countries, Hong Kong, Singapore, South Korea, and Taiwan) was $149 billion, the oil exporters' was $368 billion, and the rest of the world's was –$101 billion. Thus almost the entire counterpart of the United States' move into deficit was the move toward surplus by the emerging economies, including the oil-exporting developing countries.

Foreign-Currency Interventions of "Bretton Woods Two"

An appreciable shift into current account surplus must also mean a shift toward a surplus of savings over domestic investment. The policy question is why that shift happened. Was it the product of private behavior or was it the result of policy decisions, and, if so, whose? In fact the shift is, in large part, the result of policy decisions by governments. Their effect has been to support the move of a large number of emerging market countries toward a savings surplus. Yet this was not a change that simply happened.

Broadly speaking, the policy pursued by the Asian emerging countries is what my teacher Max Corden, a distinguished Australian international economist, called "exchange rate protectionism"—the attempt to promote production of tradable goods and services by deliberately engineering an undervalued real exchange rate.[13] The best evidence for exchange rate protectionism is the extent of official intervention in foreign-currency markets and the consequent accumulation of foreign-currency reserves. The motivations for exchange rate protectionism are complex: the aim is partly to influence industrial policy, via export promotion, and partly to insure against financial crises such as those discussed in Chapter 3.

The result has been the emergence of what some analysts call "Bretton Woods Two," in homage to the initial Bretton Woods agreement that codified the system of fixed, but adjustable, exchange rates, supposedly overseen by the IMF, that was in effect from the end of World War II to 1971.[14] The policy consequences include a need to generate the savings that are the counterpart of the current account surpluses. If that is not achieved, there will be excess spending, inflation, an erosion of competitiveness, and ultimately collapse of the policy.

Assume that a country tries to fix its real exchange rate below the market clearing level. Admittedly that market clearing level may itself be distorted by controls, most obviously controls on capital outflow, as in the case of China today. This may itself be one reason for government intervention to keep the exchange rate down. Two things will then tend to happen: current account surpluses will emerge, and, provided the capital account is sufficiently porous (as is likely to be the case for any economy sufficiently open to trade), speculative capital will flow in, because people with money will conclude that the currency has become a one-way bet.

The authorities must then buy the incoming foreign exchange from exporters (or their bankers) and put it into the foreign-currency reserves. But they must also ensure that the excess of income over spending implicit in the current account surplus is sustained. This can be done through a mixture of fiscal policy measures (higher taxes and lower spending) and monetary policy measures (aimed at "sterilizing" the consequences of the buildup of central bank money—predominantly deposits by the commercial banks at the central bank—needed to buy the surfeit of foreign currency coming onto the market).[15] These monetary measures will include some combination of reserve requirements imposed on the banks, direct controls on lending, and the sale of somewhat illiquid central bank or government liabilities to the broader public or the banks. The monetary measures are also likely to include higher domestic interest rates. These measures will have variable degrees of success: banks may find ways around reserve requirements; credit controls may be ignored; higher interest rates may attract even more capital into the country and also increase the fiscal cost of the operation (which arises as soon as domestic interest rates rise above those available on government holdings of foreign currency abroad).

Should the government be unsuccessful in controlling the impact of large-scale foreign-currency intervention aimed at keeping the nominal (and real) exchange rate down, the economy will overheat. The real exchange rate will then appreciate through higher inflation rather than through a rise in the nominal exchange rate.

So how has this new policy system evolved? Dramatically. The last year in which the emerging market economies as a whole ran a current account deficit was 1999. Since then they have moved into a massive current account surplus. The IMF believes it reached $544 billion in 2006 (Figure 4.17).[16] Recall that these countries have also been substantial and consis-

Figure 4.17 Balance of Payments of Emerging Market Economies

Billions of US$

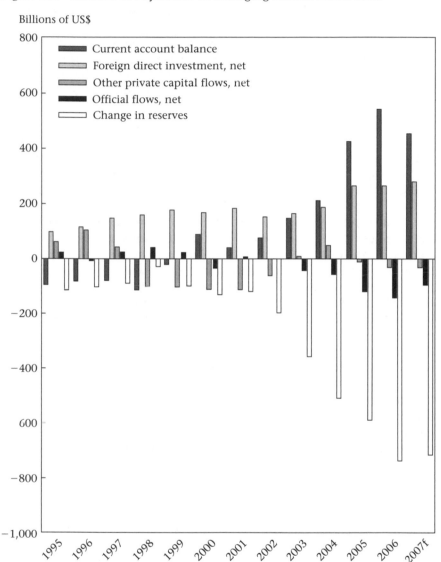

Source: International Monetary Fund, World Economic Outlook Database.
Note: Includes newly industrialized Asian economies and Israel. f, Forecast.

tent recipients of foreign direct investment (FDI), which reached $267 billion in 2006. "Other private capital flows" have been close to zero, on a net basis, during the 2000s, while official flows (other than reserves) have been substantially negative, on a net basis, mostly because of capital flows from oil exporters.

The dominant balancing item has been accumulations of foreign-currency reserves. These are the by-product of intervention in foreign-currency markets and represent an official capital outflow, which is why they are shown as negative. The increase in foreign-currency reserves of the emerging market economies between 2000 and 2006 inclusive was close to $2.65 trillion. The private sector wants to accumulate net claims on these countries, but governments are determined to prevent that from happening. In essence, governments have recycled the sums received from huge current account surpluses and from net inflows of direct investment as foreign-currency reserves. This is surely the biggest recycling operation in history.

What would have happened without the intervention? Presumably exchange rates would have soared, current account surpluses would have shrunk, and governments would have had to pursue more expansionary domestic policies to prevent their economies from falling into stagnation.

Now let us turn to the Asian developing countries, who are the biggest single piece of the story. The aggregate current account for this group has been in surplus since 1997, which was the time of the Asian financial crisis (Figure 4.18). But the surplus has exploded in recent years, entirely because of what is happening in China. In 2006 the current account surplus reached just over $250 billion. To that can be added a consistently strong inflow of FDI, which reached just over $100 billion in 2006. All this—and, it appears, even more—has poured into the accumulation of foreign-currency reserves, which rose by $1.93 trillion between 2000 and 2006 inclusive. Thus Asian developing countries accounted for almost three-quarters of the total increase in foreign-currency reserves of the emerging market economies.

China is the titan of reserve accumulation. Until 2004 it ran a modest current account surplus and a consistently positive net inflow of FDI. For some time there was a net outflow of other private capital. But two things have now changed: The current account surplus has exploded rapidly, from $69 billion in 2004 to $250 billion in 2006 (Figure 4.19). The IMF's most recent forecast was that this surplus would rise further, to $360 billion in 2007. Meanwhile, the principal balancing item is, again, the increase in official foreign-currency reserves, which grew by a little over $900 billion between 2000 and 2006 inclusive and jumped by $250 billion in 2006 alone. The rise in 2007 was much bigger still, at $462 billion.

Figure 4.18 Balance of Payments of Developing Asia

Billions of US$

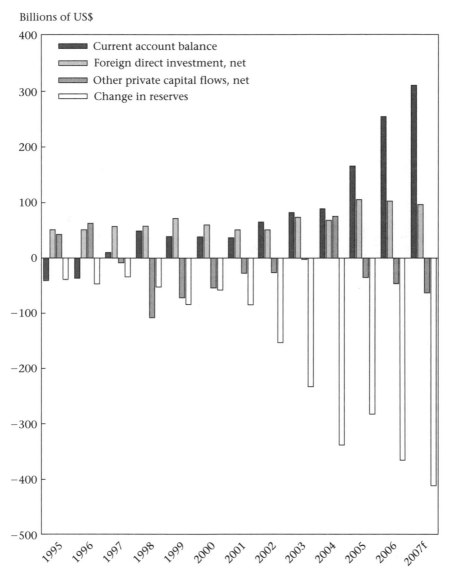

Source: International Monetary Fund, World Economic Outlook Database.
Note: Excludes newly industrialized Asian economies. f, Forecast.

Figure 4.19 Balance of Payments of China

Billions of US$

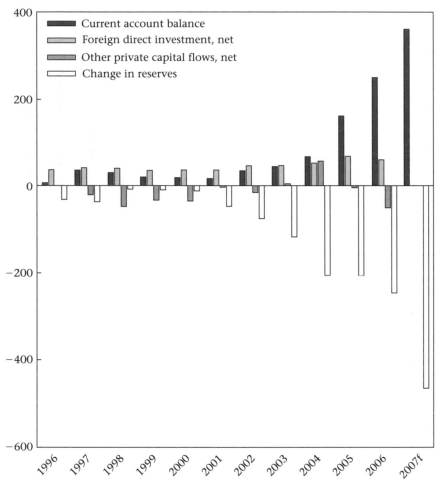

Source: International Monetary Fund, unpublished sources.
Note: f, Forecast.

After the Asian emerging markets, the next most important players are the oil exporters (Figure 4.20). The Middle East ran current account surpluses of close to $200 billion in 2005 and 2006, again balanced by official outflows and reserve accumulations. Meanwhile, the Commonwealth of Independent States (dominated by Russia) ran a current account surplus of $100 billion and accumulated $127 billion in reserves in 2006 (Figure 4.21). In the aggregate, the commonwealth accumulated $340 billion of reserves between 2000 and 2006 inclusive. In August 1998 Russia's government defaulted. As with the East Asians, the shock has endured. It has now made sure that it is very solvent indeed, by squirreling away both its oil and gas revenues and receipts of private capital in official reserves.

Even the Western Hemisphere ceased running current account deficits after 2002 and is accumulating foreign-currency reserves, although at a relatively modest aggregate rate of $140 billion between 2000 and 2006 inclusive. In fact, there is only one region of the emerging world still running large current account deficits today: central and eastern Europe (Figure 4.22). These countries—now almost all members of the European Union—have thrown caution to the winds. They ran an aggregate current account deficit of close to $100 billion in 2006, financed by capital inflow. While they too have been accumulating foreign-currency reserves, they have been doing so at a modest rate. In other words, in the 2000s central and eastern Europe became the only significant region of the emerging world to behave in the way that is familiar from the 1980s and 1990s.

Central and eastern Europe is, however, the exception. What we have been seeing across the emerging world are large current account surpluses, plus sizable inflows of private capital that are being recycled out via a government-managed capital outflow, predominantly in the form of foreign-currency reserves invested in dollars. The consequence of this policy—in fact, one of its motivations—is to keep the nominal exchange rate below what it would otherwise be. To the extent that governments are successful in curbing the potential inflationary effects of this policy, they are also able to keep the real exchange rate below what it would otherwise be, thereby making the sectors producing tradable goods (and, to a lesser extent, services) bigger and more dynamic than they would otherwise have been.

The overall consequence of these policies has been gigantic accumulations of foreign-currency reserves (Figure 4.23). By March 2007 the total global stock of foreign-currency reserves had reached $5.3 trillion. China alone had $1.2 trillion and Japan another $890 billion. Both Taiwan and South Korea held more reserves than the entire Eurozone. Asia held $3.3 trillion in all—just over three-fifths of the global total. Another big holder was Russia, with $330 billion. Oil-exporting developing countries held

Figure 4.20 Balance of Payments of the Middle East

Billions of US$

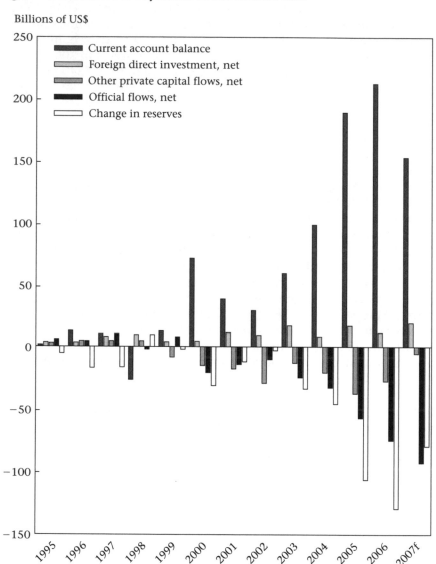

Source: International Monetary Fund, World Economic Outlook Database.
Note: f, Forecast.

Figure 4.21 Balance of Payments of the Commonwealth of
Independent States

Billions of US$

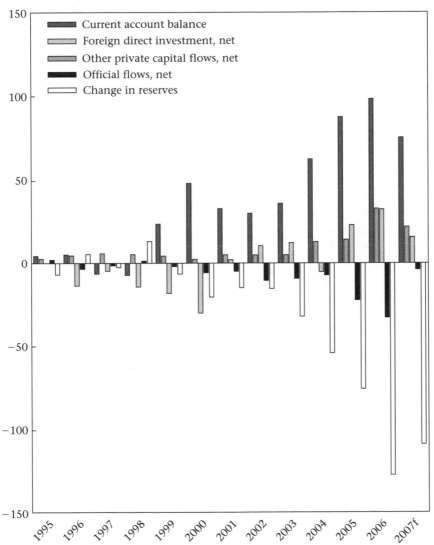

Source: International Monetary Fund, World Economic Outlook Database.
Note: f, Forecast.

Figure 4.22 Balance of Payments of Central and Eastern Europe

Billions of US$

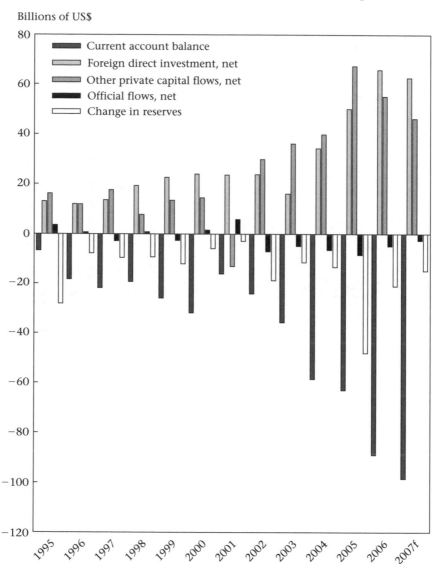

Source: International Monetary Fund, World Economic Outlook Database.
Note: f, Forecast.

Figure 4.23 Global Distribution of Foreign-Currency Reserves, March 2007

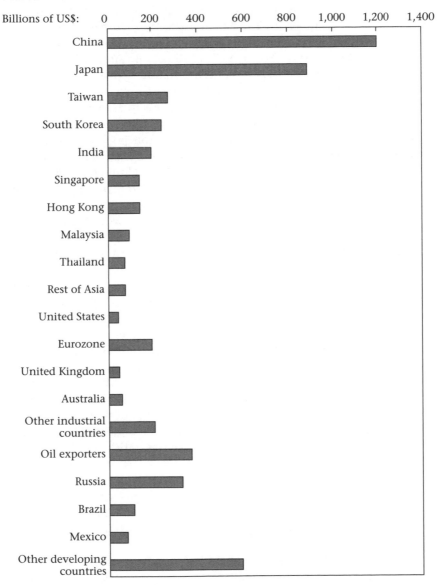

Source: International Monetary Fund, International Financial Statistics.

$370 billion in official reserves, although they held substantially more in investment funds.

More remarkably, two-thirds of all the foreign-currency reserves accumulated since the beginning were piled up within less than seven and a half years of the new millennium (Figure 4.24). The increase in China's reserves between December 1999 and March 2007 was close to $1.05 trillion, or roughly 40 percent of its 2006 GDP. Other large increases were those of Japan ($611 billion), South Korea ($170 billion), Taiwan ($161 billion), India ($160 billion), the oil exporters ($268 billion), Russia ($322 billion), and Brazil ($74 billion). The increase for Asia as a whole was $2.36 trillion—two-thirds of the global rise. The increase in foreign-currency reserves between December 1999 and March 2007 was the massive sum of $3.519 trillion. Foremost among these accumulators is China. Its currency reserves rose by just under $250 billion in 2006 and then at an annual rate of more than $500 billion in the first half of 2007. China has now far surpassed even Japan as an official creditor (Figure 4.25). In 2006 China invested about 10 percent of GDP in official holdings of foreign currency.

If these are freely floating exchange rates, what would managed exchange rates look like? We can safely conclude that we do not live in an era of floating exchange rates. Emerging market economies do not, for the most part, trust the merits of market-determined exchange rates, for perfectly understandable reasons, given the experience of "sudden stops" of capital during the 1980s and 1990s.[17] They are terrified of running large current account deficits. They trust in the age-old mechanism of export-led growth—particularly exports of manufactures. Freely floating rates are an idea only high-income countries endorse, and—as members of the Eurozone have shown by their decisions and the Japanese have frequently argued—by no means all of them endorse this idea either. This is, quite clearly, an era of heavily managed exchange rates, with huge efforts being made by the emerging market economies to keep rates down.

The conclusion many of these countries reached was not that it was a mistake to manage the currency. The mistake was, rather, to allow the exchange rate to appreciate, under the pressure of private capital inflows from abroad, to what subsequently proved to be an unsustainable, apparently "uncompetitive," level. They decided instead to aim for highly competitive exchange rates, at which the current account can be expected to remain strong and the trade surplus helps sustain high levels of domestic activity.

Knowledge of how reserves are invested is limited. Official sources provide no information at all on China's reserve holdings, which have become close to a quarter of the global total. For the rest, the U.S. dollar con-

Figure 4.24 Changes in Global Foreign-Currency Reserves,
December 1999–March 2007

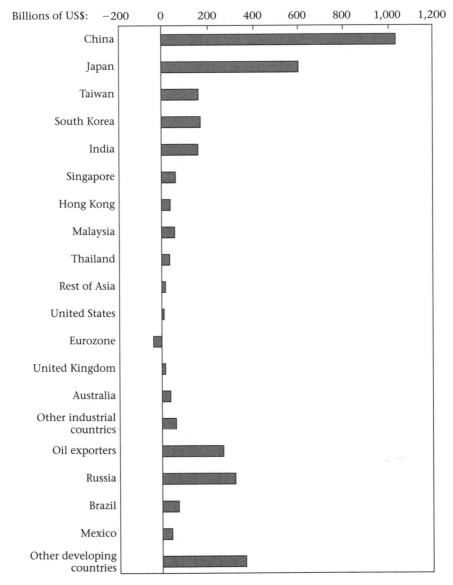

Source: International Monetary Fund, International Financial Statistics.

Figure 4.25 Foreign-Currency Reserves of China and Japan

Billions of US$

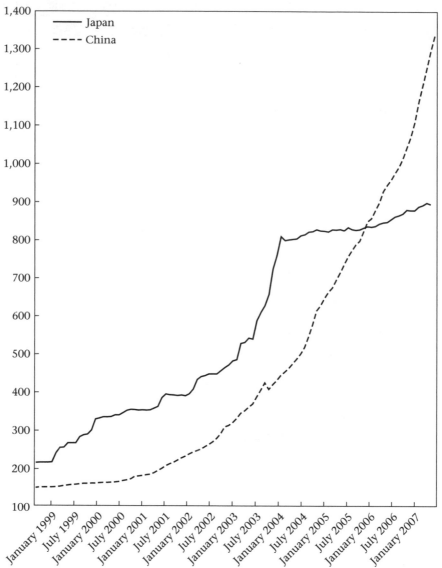

Source: International Monetary Fund, International Financial Statistics.

tinued to be the most important single currency denomination for official reserves. According to the Bank for International Settlements, two-thirds of reserves (excluding China's) were held in dollar-denominated instruments at the end of March 2006. This is not far short of the figure of 70 percent reported for 2001, despite the fall in the dollar against other reserve currencies (particularly the euro and sterling) in the intervening period. The proportion of incremental reserves invested in dollars also seems to be about two-thirds. It would not be surprising if the proportion of Chinese reserves held in dollars was substantially higher, given that the reserve accumulations are the by-product of an exchange rate target against the U.S. currency.[18]

An obvious question then is how far all this intervention has affected exchange rates themselves. The evidence strongly suggests that it has. The dollar fell a long way against most other currencies after the beginning of 2002 (Figure 4.26). It fell most against the currencies of those countries whose governments did not intervene on a very large scale. It is true that a few of these currencies—notably the South Korean won—did appreciate substantially in the end. It is also true that the Japanese yen barely appreciated over this period, even though official intervention ceased toward the end of 2004, because Japanese private investors started to move money out of the country, in a search for yield across the world. In general, however, East Asian currencies appreciated little. The Chinese yuan-renminbi is the most important example of the impact of intervention. Despite the huge current account surplus and private capital inflow and despite some freeing up of the currency in July 2005, it barely appreciated at all. It is, as the Chinese demonstrate, perfectly possible to buck the foreign-currency market, provided the pressure is for appreciation. It helps, however, if controls can be imposed on private capital inflow, as in the Chinese case.

Are these holdings of reserves excessive? One rule of thumb is that reserves should equal or exceed short-term debt—debt whose maturity is less than a year. Lawrence Summers used this measure in his March 2006 lecture, to show how disproportionate reserves had become.[19] By 2005 a number of important emerging market economies had reserves that were excessive by these standards (Figure 4.27). In some cases reserves exceeded not just short-term debt but all debt. The most remarkable example was China. At the end of 2005 its reserves exceeded short-term debt by $683 billion (30% of GDP)—and they exceeded total debt by the enormous amount of $549 billion. Even India's reserves exceeded its total debt, though by a more modest $15 billion.

At the heart of the story of the imbalances is official action to intervene in the foreign-currency market, to keep the currency down. A conse-

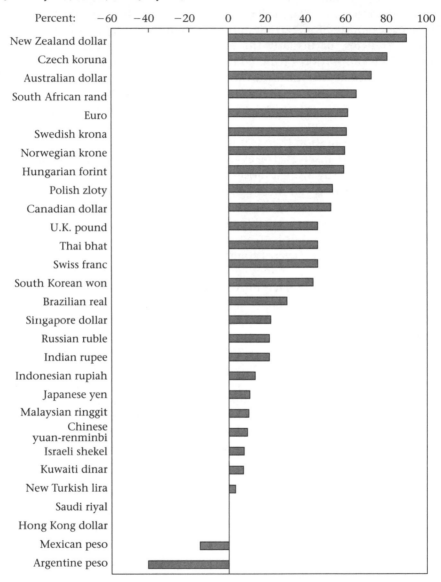

Figure 4.26 Change in Value against the U.S. Dollar between January 31, 2002, and July 18, 2007

Source: Thomson Datastream.

Figure 4.27 Excess Reserves, 2005

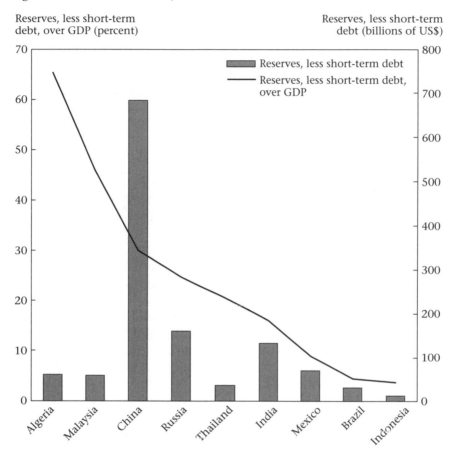

Reserves, less short-term
debt, over GDP (percent)

Reserves, less short-term
debt (billions of US$)

Source: World Bank, *World Development Indicators,* 2007.

quence of this policy has been gigantic accumulations of foreign-currency reserves, which are also, by definition, huge official capital outflows. Those outflows are the deliberate offsets to the foreign exchange receipts generated by current account surpluses and, in many cases, large inflows of private capital. The latter reflect the understandable desire to invest in the fastest-growing economies with the best prospects and, (as a result of their accumulation of reserves) high levels of solvency as well. It is an old story: the most attractive recipients of capital are always those who do not need it.

The United States as the Borrower
and Spender of Last Resort

What then is the role of the United States? If the rest of the world has in the aggregate a large surplus of savings over investment at home, it must invest this surplus elsewhere. And the place where it has sought to invest most of this money is the United States. For countries intervening to keep the dollar down against their own currencies, such a strategy is inevitable. If they did not invest in U.S. liabilities, the dollar would fall against their currencies. This group includes many of the most important surplus countries in East Asia and among the oil exporters. Some analysts describe this practice as "vendor financing": countries with surpluses of exports to sell finance their biggest market. For residents of countries not in this category, the United States provides attractive liabilities: property rights are secure, the economy seems dynamic in the long run, the dollar is the world's most important currency, and markets are liquid.

In this world, the tail wags the dog of U.S. macroeconomic policy. In the world of Bretton Woods, back in the 1950s and 1960s, analysts pointed out that, if every other country targeted the U.S. dollar, the United States itself could not have a currency policy. Its exchange rate is determined by the decisions of all the rest.[20] When President Richard Nixon and his treasury secretary, John Connally, decided to devalue the dollar in August 1971, they could not do this without forcing other countries to change their exchange rate policies. So, in addition to breaking the link between the dollar and gold, they decided to impose an import surcharge, to force other countries to appreciate their currencies against the dollar, rather than stick with it, as its value fell against gold.

Today the United States could have an exchange rate policy, if it wanted to, by targeting the exchange rate against currencies that float. But it cannot force its currency down by intervention against the currencies of countries that are prepared to invest in reserves without limit. And there is another sense in which U.S. policy makers are constrained: this time it is in the realm of macroeconomic policy.

Assume that U.S. policy makers are targeting what used to be called "full employment," "the natural rate of unemployment," "the nonaccelerating inflation rate of unemployment," or "internal balance." All these are different names for what economists would think of as essentially the same thing: the highest possible level of economic activity consistent with low and reasonably stable inflation. Assume that the rest of the world's desire to support the dollar, sterilize the monetary consequences, and hold U.S. liabilities generates a certain real exchange rate for the United States. Assume as well that, at this real exchange rate, the level of demand that generates internal balance also generates a very large U.S. excess demand for tradable goods and services—in other words, a large current account deficit. (It is not difficult to assume this: it is evidently the case.) Assume, finally, that policy makers in the United States—above all those at the Federal Reserve, whose job this is—target the achievement of internal balance.

Then the current account deficit that absorbs (or offsets) the desired excess savings of the rest of the world will emerge naturally. But to achieve this, the level of domestic demand within the United States must exceed the level of output consistent with internal balance by a large margin: in 2006 that excess of domestic demand over output (or GDP) was 6.5 percent of GDP. In essence, whatever the U.S. fiscal authorities do, the Federal Reserve must pursue a monetary policy sufficiently expansionary to generate this level of domestic demand, in order to secure the desired internal balance—that is, to avoid ever-falling inflation and ultimately deflation.

What would happen if the Federal Reserve failed to do so? The United States would experience a slowdown, possibly even a recession. If the United States entered a recession, so might the rest of the world. It is quite plausible that, if this were to happen, the rest of the world would alter its policies, to rely less on external demand and more on internal demand. In this sense, the American authorities are ultimately responsible—at least to an extent—for the persistence of the rest of the world's savings surplus: if the rest of the world could not rely on the United States to generate the domestic demand needed to offset their savings surpluses, then they could not safely pursue the policies they are demonstrably pursuing. But the path to such an alteration in the rest of the world's spending patterns would be an uphill one.

In the meantime, the United States would experience a significant slowdown for which the Federal Reserve would almost certainly be blamed. For the Federal Reserve to permit an unnecessary slowdown—one not required to eliminate excessive domestic inflation—would be politically intolerable, not to mention inconsistent with its "dual mandate." The Federal Reserve, unlike other modern central banks, is not governed by an inflation target alone, but by an explicit obligation to sustain real activity or, more precisely, full employment. In effect the Federal Reserve does indeed target internal balance, as I have argued, with the policies and behavior of the rest of the world as a given.

In considering U.S. policy, monetary policy is not all that matters. On the contrary, fiscal policy also strongly supported domestic demand in the period after the collapse of the stock market bubble in 2000 and the terrorist attacks of September 11, 2001. According to IMF calculations, the cyclically adjusted financial balance of the U.S. government shifted from a surplus of 1.6 percent of GDP in 2000 to a deficit of 4.6 percent in 2003, before improving to a deficit of 2.7 percent in 2006. This swing of 4.6 percent of GDP in the financial balance of the government was enormously expansionary—although, needless to say, the Bush administration did not present its policy in this way. It argued that the aim of the fiscal expansion was entirely to improve incentives. But the boost was effective in sustaining U.S. demand. There is no evidence that the private sector offset it by saving more. On the contrary, the savings rate of the U.S. household sector fell to record low levels (see Figure 4.13).

Without the huge fiscal boost, monetary policy would have had to be even more expansionary than it was. That might even have forced the Federal Reserve to lower the federal funds rate to zero, not 1 percent, which turned out to be the floor. It is possible that even zero would not have been enough. The Federal Reserve might have been forced to adopt some of the unconventional methods to counter disinflation discussed by Ben Bernanke when he was still a governor of the Federal Reserve.[21]

The bottom line is that the United States accommodates and offsets whatever the rest of the world throws at it because, as the issuer of the world's key currency, it suffers from no external constraint: it has been able, at least up to now, to borrow as much as it wishes in its own currency, at modest interest rates (both nominal and real). The market appears to have no fear of an inflationary collapse of the dollar—or, more precisely, it acts as if it believes (plausibly, in the light of experience) that foreign governments will step in to support the dollar whenever private financing proves inadequate. That indeed is what "Bretton Woods Two" implies. The result is that the Federal Reserve is free to pursue policies that balance the U.S. economy and, in doing so, also balance the world's, by absorbing the excess savings and so the surpluses of goods and services, at given real exchange rates, of the rest of the world.

One can explain what is going on, simply put, as follows: The rest of the world's capital outflow supports the dollar. At the resulting elevated real exchange rate for the United States, the output of the sectors in the U.S. economy that produce tradable goods and services shrinks, other things being equal. The Federal Reserve cuts interest rates to expand the economy, thereby preventing excessive unemployment. As it does so, a large excess demand for tradable goods and services emerges in the United States. This, finally, appears in the trade and current account deficits.

One consequence of all this is that U.S. domestic demand has had to grow faster than real GDP, to ensure that the latter grows in line with potential. The difference between the two is, of course, the increase in the current account deficit, in real terms. With trend growth in GDP between 3 and 3.5 percent a year, domestic demand has had to grow even faster. That is precisely what has happened. U.S. real demand (or "gross domestic purchases") grew faster than real GDP in 1993 and 1994 and then again in every year from 1996 to 2004 inclusive (Figure 4.28). Cumulatively, between 1993 and 2004 U.S. real GDP grew by 46 percent, while gross domestic purchases rose by 53 percent. That is how the current account deficit emerged. It is also how the United States absorbed the supply of excess capital from abroad.

The emergence of the U.S. current account deficit via the relatively rapid growth of demand in relation to output has also had important consequences for the structure of income and expenditure inside the U.S. economy. These in turn bear directly on the sustainability of the capital inflow, in the long run, and on the scale of the changes in incentives needed to combine external adjustment with the high levels of economic activity that Americans desire and indeed expect.

The most striking feature of the internal response to the external deficits is the role of personal expenditure: never before and for so long have U.S. households saved so little and borrowed so much. A simple way of showing this is in terms of sectoral financial balances—the difference between income and expenditure or savings and investment.[22] The relevant sectors are foreigners, the government as a whole, business, and personal. The latter two together make up the U.S. private sector. The essential point is that the sum of the balances of each of these four sectors has to be zero. If one sector spends more than its income, it must be selling financial claims or real assets to the other three. In this case, we know that foreigners are buyers of U.S. liabilities and real assets: that is what a current account deficit—or a capital account surplus—means. So it follows that the three U.S. sectors are, in the aggregate, sellers of such claims.

Figure 4.29 shows that the most significant seller of claims has been the U.S. private sector. There was a massive swing from financial surplus into deficit in the private sector during the bubble years of the 1990s. Until 1996 the sector was in balance. By the second quarter of 2000, however, its spending exceeded its income by 4.5 percent of GDP. The swing of the private sector from surplus into deficit between the first quarter of 1992 and the second quarter of 2000 was 9.3 percent of GDP. This is a powerful indication of how much faster spending grew than income in the private sector. Over the same period the government went into surplus. So, of course, did the foreign sector: it was a net supplier of capital to the United States or, in other words, was running a current account surplus with the United States.

After the bubble burst in 2000, the private sector's deficit shrank rapidly, though it never went into surplus. That itself was surprising. In previous recessions, the U.S. private sector had always cut back spending to well below its income. This time, however, the balance merely moved back

Figure 4.28 Growth of U.S. Gross Domestic Product and Gross Domestic Purchases

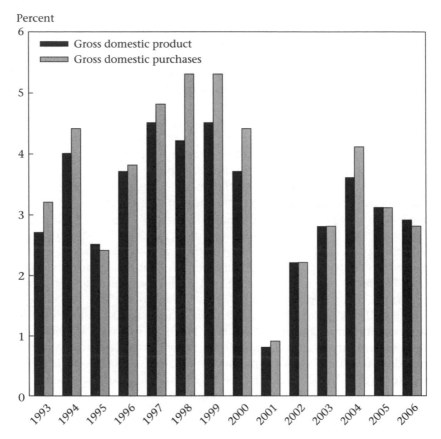

Source: U.S. national income and product accounts.

to zero. Since foreign lending—the global savings glut—continued to rise rapidly, however, the U.S. government went into a deficit that peaked at 5.4 percent of GDP in the third quarter of 2003. If that had not happened, the result would almost certainly have been a serious recession, since the U.S. private sector proved so cautious after the bursting of the bubble, even though the Federal Reserve reduced its rates to as low as 1 percent. Then, from the third quarter of 2003 onward, the private sector's deficit rose substantially once again, as the government's diminished. One indication that domestic spending is responding to foreign lending is the way that move-

Figure 4.29 Sectoral Financial Balances in the United States

Percent of GDP

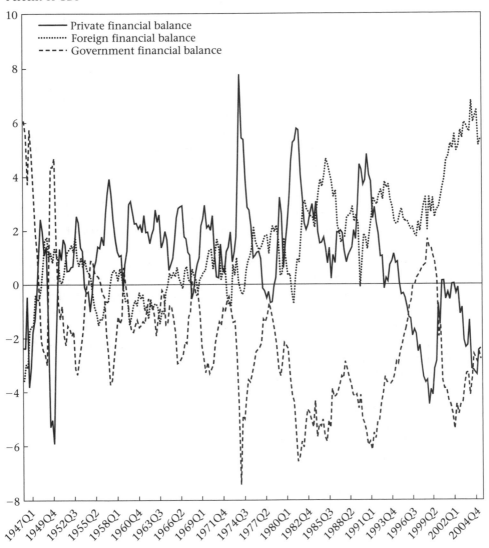

Source: U.S. national income and product accounts.

ments in the private sector and government financial balances are mirror images of one another. This pattern has seemed exceedingly clear since the early 1990s.

Now consider what has been happening within the private sector. Here there is a startling contrast between business and the household sector (Figure 4.30).[23] The business sector moved into a large deficit during the investment boom triggered by the bubble economy of the late 1990s and 2000. It then cut back sharply on investment and, after a short period of squeeze, built up profits again. More important, it also avoided any repeat of the investment surge of the 1990s. As a result, the business sector ran a financial surplus from the fourth quarter of 2001 to the first quarter of 2007. In all, there has been nothing exceptional about the behavior of the business sector, which is in line with historic norms.

The household sector is quite a different story. It has been running historically unprecedented financial deficits, consistently spending more than its income on consumption and residential investment. Between the third quarter of 1992 and the second quarter of 2005, the financial balance of the household sector moved from 3.7 percent of GDP to –3.6 percent of GDP—a swing of 7.3 percent of GDP. This was the consequence of both a collapse in gross personal savings, from 7.5 percent of GDP to 2.5 percent of GDP, and a surge in residential investment, from 3.7 percent of GDP to 6.1 percent of GDP.[24] What is important about the behavior of the household sector is that it moved ever deeper into deficit even after the bursting of the stock market bubble in 2000. It did so principally because of the boom in the residential property market, itself stimulated by the exceptionally low interest rates that the Federal Reserve introduced to sustain economic activity in the early 2000s.

It is therefore reasonable to conclude that the principal secular counterpart of the U.S. move into a massive current account deficit (or expanded capital inflow from abroad) has been the fall in household savings and, to a lesser extent, the boom in residential investment. Meanwhile the financial deficits of the government and business sectors have tended to oscillate quite violently, in opposite directions, rather than show a strong secular trend. The government's financial balance improved when the economy was very strong in the late 1990s and worsened sharply thereafter, while the business sector's financial balance moved in exactly the opposite direction. It follows from this picture that the principal counterpart of the external borrowing is household consumption and investment in housing, the latter being a paradigmatic example of a piece of fixed capital that produces a nontradable service—unless or until millions of prosperous Chinese decide to buy properties in the United States in which to live.

Figure 4.30 Composition of U.S. Private Sector Financial Balance

Percent

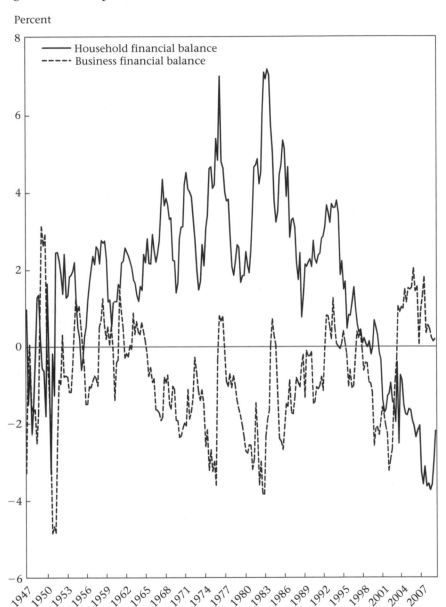

Source: U.S. national income and product accounts.

A necessary consequence of the persistent financial deficit of U.S. households has been a progressive increase in their indebtedness. Since the early 1990s the ratio of household debt to disposable incomes has doubled, to reach almost 140 percent (Figure 4.31). Furthermore, the growth of debt accelerated in the 2000s, as one would expect. The debt service burden has also risen to record levels. By the first quarter of 2007 it was 30 percent higher than it had been in the early 1990s. These developments will both seem supportable in a strong economy, where asset prices and so household wealth have been at record levels in relation to disposable incomes. In 2005 U.S. net household wealth was 5.7 times disposable income, well above the figure of 5.0 for 2002, though still below the value of 6.3 at the peak of the stock market bubble in 2000.[25] But higher prices of existing assets do not represent greater wealth for a society as a whole: the gains of current owners match the losses of would-be purchasers. There is at least a good chance that U.S. households will start to save significantly more and borrow less as their houses cease to provide the illusion of effortless increases in wealth.

In short the United States has indeed successfully absorbed much of the excess savings of the rest of the world. It has done so by promoting rapid growth of demand and, in particular, of consumption. The household sector has been principally responsible for the excess of spending over incomes. But in the early 2000s the government also played a significant part in offsetting the greater prudence of the business sector after the bursting of the stock market bubble in 2000. The big question, to be considered further in Chapter 5, is how long this pattern of spending can endure. If households went back into surplus, what would take the place of their spending? Or would there instead be a large recession?

Savings Glut versus Money Glut

What then is the explanation for why the "imbalances" emerged? What do they have to do with low real interest rates at a time of exceptionally rapid and sustained global economic growth? The argument advanced in this chapter has five elements:

1. As a result of the emerging market financial crises of the 1990s, the bursting of the Japanese economic bubble in 1990, the bursting of the U.S. and European stock market bubbles in 2000, the determination of China to pursue export-led growth and eliminate any risk of financial crisis, and, finally, the soaring oil prices of the 2000s (which represented a big shift in income toward high-saving countries), a significant surplus of desired savings over investment emerged in the early

Figure 4.31 U.S. Household Debt and Debt Service

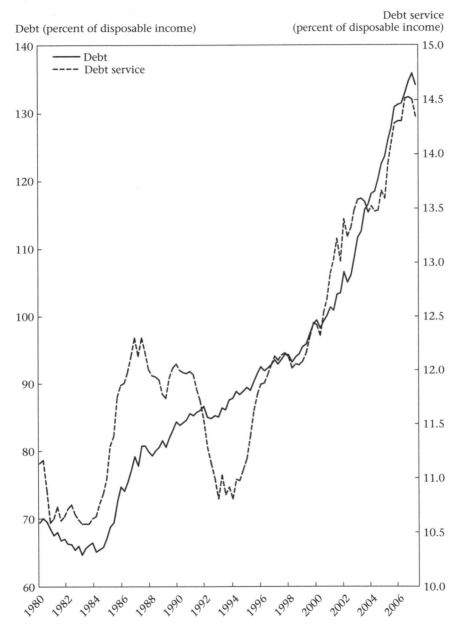

Debt (percent of disposable income)

Debt service
(percent of disposable income)

Source: Thomson Datastream.

2000s. In addition, several high-income countries, particularly Japan, have structural excess savings. One result of this situation has been the low long-term real interest rates that have become a feature of the world economy.

2. The distribution of these excess savings has been highly unequal across the globe. East Asia and the oil-exporting countries have become the regions with the surpluses. The latter are likely, in time, to spend the extra money they have earned. That seems less likely to be the case for East Asia in general and China in particular. Given current trends, a Chinese current account surplus of $400–500 billion a year within a few years no longer seems inconceivable. That could be no more than about 15 percent of GDP.

3. At the global level U.S. fiscal and monetary policy has acted to offset the excess savings elsewhere. This has not been the explicit intention of U.S. policy makers. Expansionary U.S. fiscal policy under George W. Bush's administration was justified by supply-side considerations. Similarly, the expansionary monetary policy of the early 2000s was designed to secure noninflationary growth in the United States. But, given the rest of the world's willingness to provide capital to the United States, these policies had the effect of offsetting excess savings elsewhere and so of generating higher levels of activity in the world as a whole.[26] In this view, easy monetary policy in the United States (and elsewhere) was a consequence of the global savings glut.

4. Governments in emerging economies have been directly responsible for much of the capital outflow. This is either because domestic residents are not allowed to hold foreign assets (as in China) or because most of the export revenue accrues to governments (as in the oil exporters). Moreover, the size of the savings glut is not just a given, but a consequence of the exchange rate targeting. That targeting has led, in the first instance, to large current account surpluses and reserve accumulations. The latter would, if unchecked, have led to rapid monetary growth, higher spending, and ultimately inflation. But the governments involved have tried hard to sterilize the monetary impact and control credit growth. The impact of such policies is to sustain savings at the required level.

5. Finally, the easy monetary conditions generated not just by the response to the savings glut but also by the gigantic reserve accumulations produced by exchange rate intervention produced what Brian Reading of London's Lombard Street Research calls a "liquidity tsunami."[27] Low nominal and real interest rates encouraged robust credit growth, a worldwide shift into risky assets, and compression of

risk spreads. Hedge funds and private equity funds boomed as investors sought high returns, though the buoyant asset prices and low real interest rates decreed the opposite.

In this time of the savings glut, the U.S. Federal Reserve has been the hero that has saved the world from the recession that excess savers would otherwise cause. But there are alternative views, which shed a different light on what is happening. What these have in common is the belief that U.S. profligacy is driving the global pattern of current account surpluses and deficits.

This view has both a simpler and a more complex version. The simple version suggests that Americans simply decided to spend "too much" and that this excess spending generated excess demand for the rest of the world's production and so the current account surpluses. This can be called the "U.S. profligacy" view. The argument against this view is that, if U.S. profligacy were indeed the driving force, one would expect real interest rates to be relatively high, not low. In essence, the argument is that U.S. dis-saving has been crowding out spending elsewhere. The mechanism through which this would happen is higher real interest rates. But that is not what we see. It is more plausible, given the relatively low real interest rates across the globe, to argue that excess savings in the rest of the world are "crowding in" U.S. spending—the savings glut hypothesis—than that excess U.S. spending is crowding out spending elsewhere—the "U.S. profligacy" view. This is not to suggest that there is nothing to the latter view. In particular, American policy makers had at least some influence on whether the counterpart of the capital inflow would be consumption or investment. While they could not compel companies to invest, they could have increased public investment. As it is, the counterpart has been consumption (see Figures 4.13 and 4.30).[28]

A more sophisticated version is what I call the "money glut" view. In this view as well the world's savers are passive victims, profligate Americans are agents of the imbalances, and the Federal Reserve is an antihero. In this world as well the U.S. central bank has been a serial bubble-blower, has distorted asset markets, and has inflicted excess monetary emissions on trading partners around the world, above all on those who seek monetary stability through pegged exchange rates.

The argument is that U.S. monetary excess causes low nominal and (given the subdued inflationary expectations) real interest rates. This causes rapid growth of credit to consumers and a collapse in household savings. The excess spending floods across the frontiers, generating a huge trade deficit and a corresponding outflow of dollars.

The outflow weakens the dollar. Floating currencies are forced up to uncompetitive levels. But pegged currencies are kept down by open-ended foreign-currency intervention. This leads to a massive accumulation of foreign-currency reserves. It also creates difficulties with sterilizing the impact on money supply and inflation.

In this view of the world economy, savings are not a driving force, as in the savings glut hypothesis, but a passive result of excess money creation by the system's hegemonic power. Profits (and so measured corporate savings) rise simply because of increased exports and output under economies of scale. Governments of countries that possess huge trade surpluses then follow the fiscal and monetary policies that sustain the excess savings needed to curb excessive demand and inflation.

It is no surprise that the Federal Reserve is a believer in the savings glut hypothesis. But many Asians blame their present predicament on "dollar hegemony," which is the core of the money glut hypothesis. The big questions, however, are which hypothesis is true—and whether it matters.

My answer to the first question is that the savings glut hypothesis is closer to the truth, for several reasons. First, monetary growth in the United States has not been unreasonably high. Second, inflationary expectations in the United States have remained contained. Third, it is hard to believe that the soaring savings in Asia and the oil exporters are passive responses to excess demand from outside, rather than deliberate choices. Finally, and most important of all, the pegged rates themselves are policy choices.

My answer to the second question is that indeed it does matter. If we live in the savings glut world, the U.S. current account deficit is protecting the world from recession. If we live in the money glut world, that very same deficit is threatening the world with a dollar collapse and ultimately a return of worldwide inflation.

The savings glut view is far more comforting. Excess savers will in the end learn to spend—sooner rather than later, if U.S. spending were to weaken dramatically. But if we live in the money glut world, the great gains in monetary stability of the past quarter century are at risk.

The plausible view is that both perspectives have merit. The Federal Reserve may have followed too loose a policy for too long in the early 2000s, thereby creating a money glut. But it surely did so in response to the global savings glut. The immediate question is how long these "imbalances" can—and should—last. That is the focus of the next chapter.

CHAPTER 5

Calm before a Storm

If you owe your bank a hundred pounds, you have a problem, but if you owe a million, it has.

JOHN MAYNARD KEYNES

If you owe your bank a billion pounds everybody has a problem.

THE ECONOMIST

AS I WRITE THESE WORDS in August 2007, there seems to be good reason to welcome the global imbalances discussed in Chapter 4: the world economy is growing strongly and in a more balanced way than in previous years, as demand picks up across the globe; the developing world is also performing well, particularly in Asia; and the world has not experienced a significant financial crisis in emerging markets since 2001, when Argentina defaulted. A world in which capital flows from poor countries to the world's richest seems to be more stable, more dynamic, and altogether more satisfactory than that of the 1980s and 1990s, with their repeated financial crises.

Why then should anybody complain? Is it not obvious that both sides gain greatly from these transactions? The United States, for its part, is able to consume considerably in excess of its income. Since the current account deficit has been bigger than its fiscal deficit, even at its largest—larger even than its spending on defense—the sole superpower has enjoyed both guns and butter. It has witnessed little more than a shadow of the burgeoning inflation that accompanied the Vietnam War and that was ultimately to prove so disastrous for both domestic and global monetary stability in the 1990s. One might argue that, willy-nilly, the oil exporters of the Middle East and the East Asians, particularly China and Japan, have once again paid for U.S. military "protection," just as many of these same countries did during the first Gulf War in 1991, but without any of the explicit and difficult political decisions of that time. This was a coalition of the sufficiently willing, even if financing U.S. wars is not what they had signed up to do.

Nor is this all. Those U.S. liabilities that are denominated in currency units (as opposed to being claims on real assets) are measured in the country's own currency. No difficulty, therefore, attends a reduction in the value of those obligations. If it wishes to improve its balance sheet position (and so its solvency), all the United States needs to do is allow the value of the dollar to fall against other currencies. The benefits of this strategy to the country are enormous. Not only does the United States, even more than other high-income countries, run no danger of the adverse currency mismatches that have proved so devastating to emerging market economies in the past, but any mismatches work in exactly the opposite direction: the country has assets denominated in foreign currency and liabilities denominated in domestic currency. The more unwilling the rest of the world is to hold the dollar, the more solvent the United States becomes.

Back in 1965, Valéry Giscard d'Estaing, then French finance minister, described the ability of the United States to borrow cheaply and apparently without limit in its own currency as an "exorbitant privilege."[1] The end of the Bretton Woods system of fixed exchange rates has made it no less exorbitant, as the extraordinary accumulations of foreign exchange reserves by emerging market economies and the cheapness of U.S. liabilities (about which more below) bear witness. A remarkable indication of these effects is what happened to U.S. net liabilities between 2001 and 2006.[2] The ratio of U.S. net liabilities to GDP fell by 3.4 percent of GDP over this period, despite current account deficits that ought, on their own, to have raised net liabilities by 28.2 percent of GDP.[3] The United States (as is true also of the United Kingdom) has been a vast and hitherto very profitable hedge fund.[4]

For the United States, this is not so much a free lunch as an apparently ongoing free banquet. Here is a country that is both so successful a speculator and so blessed with generous creditors that it can spend more than its income for years without increasing net liabilities faster than income.

The rest of the world is happy too. True, it is accumulating claims on the United States on which it is likely, in the end, to lose value, at least in relation to alternative investments. But its economies are growing, and they are doing so free of crisis. The oil exporters with small populations have to invest in foreign assets: they do not have sufficiently safe and high-yielding opportunities at home. The countries hit by significant financial crises in the past—such as the East Asian nations, Russia, and Brazil—want a more-than-comfortable cushion of foreign-currency reserves as insurance against future mishaps. China, the single country dedicated to outward-oriented growth and reliant on inward FDI for the technology and managerial know-how it needs, is able to sustain export-led growth at 10 percent a year or more. The rich countries with surplus savings—notably Japan—are able to accumulate the assets they will want to live on as their populations become increasingly elderly.

At the most fundamental level, the possibility of large flows of capital, both net and gross, is the most obvious justification for liberalizing capital markets. They allow "intertemporal trade" in goods and services: people can decide *when* they want to consume their incomes, not just *what* to consume. Why, as Max Corden asks, should that be any more problematic than trade in goods and services at any moment in time?[5] Moreover, as he also notes, "it is not at all surprising that globalization—above all increased capital mobility—has increased this type of trade." What else, after all, was the point? Few may have imagined that the result would be huge flows of capital from poor countries to the world's richest countries. But since this represents the free choice of the peoples and governments concerned, why should that be deemed problematic?

Is this a desirable and sustainable solution to the challenge of managing a globalizing world economy? Is it natural and normal that the world's biggest, richest economy, with the most sophisticated, deepest, and most liquid financial markets, should also be its borrower and spender of last resort? Is this the best way—as it proved to be in the early 2000s—to ensure strong recovery after the end of the stock market bubble followed by rapid economic growth, successful absorption of the world's surplus savings, "recycling" of the (probably temporary) surpluses of the oil exporters, and opportunities for export-led growth in the developing world?

Indeed, in a world with many distinct currencies that move erratically against one another and in which countries can borrow safely only in their own currencies, who else but the issuer of the world's most important currency is able to borrow almost without limit? But, if this is true, is it of any great use to promote a more liberal global financial system when it generates a huge surge of capital that flows "uphill"—not from the world's most advanced economy, as happened in the nineteenth century under British hegemony, but toward it?

These are important and, I would now accept, far more open questions than I thought in the early 2000s. Let us consider them a little more deeply, examining both the desirability and the sustainability of these trends, because a solution to our present challenges that is feasible and even desirable today may not work forever. That being the case, it may be useful to consider what is to replace it when this extraordinary—and extraordinarily fascinating—episode in the history of global finance comes to an end.

In order to assess the desirability and sustainability of current developments, let us start by looking at the arguments of those who consider present patterns unsustainable, before turning to the arguments of those who take the opposing view.

A Case for Unsustainability—The View from the United States

The case that recent U.S. current account deficits are unsustainable comes down to the following simple propositions: An economy that runs a current account deficit of 7 percent of GDP and whose nominal GDP grows at about 5 percent a year (3 percent real, plus 2 percent inflation) will end up, in the long run, with a ratio of net external liabilities to GDP of 140 percent. Moreover, to keep the current account deficit to even 7 percent of GDP, the trade deficit must improve substantially, since the balance on net investment income is sure to deteriorate massively. If, for example, the average (nominal) cost of funds were to be as low as 4 percent, the trade deficit would have to decline from 7 percent to 2 percent of GDP to keep the current account deficit at 7 percent of GDP.

Moreover, as Barry Eichengreen of the University of California, Berkeley, notes, the share of the capital stock owned—directly or indirectly—by foreigners would be even higher, to the extent that Americans own assets abroad.[6] At the end of 2006 Americans owned wealth abroad worth 116 percent of U.S. GDP (with FDI valued at market prices). Assume these gross assets rose to 160 percent of U.S. GDP. Assume net liabilities were to reach 140 percent of GDP. Then the gross U.S. liabilities must reach 300 percent of U.S. GDP. As it happens, 300 percent of GDP is the value of the entire U.S. capital stock. So foreigners could own it all. Of course, they might own financial claims on income (e.g., bonds or bank accounts) rather than real assets (e.g., equities). But they would probably then demand a substantial risk premium to guard themselves against the risks of inflation and dollar depreciation. For they would be aware that the very feature that makes borrowing large sums relatively safe for Americans—that they are borrowing in a currency the United States can create at will—also makes borrowing riskier for their creditors.

It seems difficult to imagine that net debt of this scale would be feasible. It would be extraordinarily high by global standards, even for relatively small economies and, therefore, ones whose liabilities would make up a relatively small proportion of creditors' portfolios. Figure 5.1 gives some of the relevant comparisons, though it also shows how low U.S. net liabilities still are (for reasons to be discussed further below). Not surprisingly, a host of international macroeconomists have argued that these

Figure 5.1 Net Foreign Debt

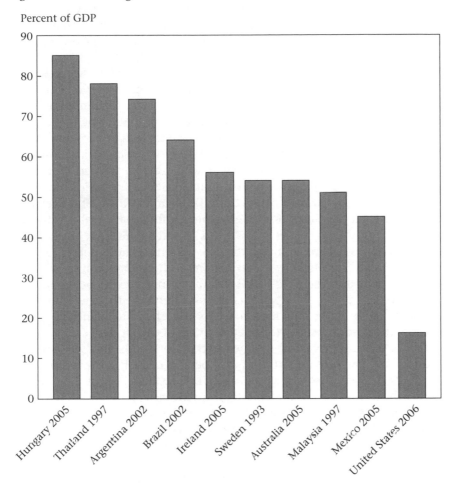

Percent of GDP

Source: McKinsey Global Institute, *The U.S. Imbalancing Act.*

deficits cannot continue unchecked.[7] In March 2007 a group of economists associated with the Brussels think tank Bruegel, the Peterson Institute for International Economics in Washington, D.C., and the Korea
Institute for International Economic Policy (KIEP) emphasized the conventional view among international macroeconomists that the trends
were unsustainable and undesirable.[8]

The continuation of these trends also presents significant political
risks. How likely is it, for example, that Congress would allow foreigners—

particularly foreign governments—to buy up as large a proportion of the U.S capital stock as trends suggest might be necessary? Not very, one would think. Just look at the fierce complaints over Chinese attempts to purchase the oil company Unocal or over the efforts of Dubai Ports World to buy the right to manage six U.S. ports. Consider, too, the growing protectionist concern over the yawning trade deficit and the backlash against rising Chinese bilateral and overall trade surpluses. Perhaps it would be rational for Americans simply to lie back and enjoy their ability to spend more than their incomes at what seems to be modest cost. But that is not, in fact, how many Americans see the situation. Many see it instead as a foreign plot to buy up America, destroy good jobs, and lay waste to American industry.

Many economists also argue that it would take a substantial real depreciation to make the needed adjustments.[9] The survey carried out by the economists associated with Bruegel, the Peterson Institute, and KIEP concludes, for example, that "the models generally find that a real effective depreciation of the dollar of between 10 and 20 percent from the current level [March 2007] is needed to shrink the U.S. current account deficit to 3 percent of GDP over the next few years."[10] The United States is after all a large economy and must achieve very substantial increases in penetration of world markets if it is to expand its exports significantly; the volume increases must be bigger than mere inspection of the initial deficits suggests, because the terms of trade—the relative prices of exports and imports—will deteriorate as exports expand. Since exports of goods and services have been so low relative to imports (just 11.6 percent of GDP in the second quarter of 2007, even after a period of recovery, against 16.8 percent for imports), the former must grow far faster than the latter if the deficit is to close significantly. All these facts suggest that large changes in both external competitiveness and domestic relative prices would be needed.

If this logic is correct, the dollar, already a long way down from recent peaks, has considerably farther to fall (Figure 5.2). By March 2007 the decline in the real exchange rate, on the JP Morgan trade-weighted index, had already reached 22 percent from its peak in February 2002 (by June 2007 it was down 25 percent). If the real exchange rate needed to fall by a further 20 percent, the cumulative decline would reach 40 percent (comparable to what happened in the late 1980s), and the real exchange rate would reach record lows.[11] Moreover, because of incomplete pass-through of changes in the nominal exchange rate to prices, the depreciation of the trade-weighted nominal exchange rate would need to be substantially greater than that of the real exchange rate.[12] The risk of a "run" from the dollar in these circumstances cannot be small.

The longer the trends continue and the larger U.S. net liabilities become, the bigger the correction in the trade balance will have to be and

Figure 5.2 Real Effective Exchange Rate for the United States

Source: JPMorgan.
Note: Values are trade-weighted.

the larger will be the associated fall in the real exchange rate. Moreover, should foreign investors become better aware of the risks they are running with their growing unhedged dollar exposure, they might suddenly impose higher risk premiums on their dollar assets in the form of higher interest rates. The combination of higher long-term real interest rates with a falling dollar could severely constrain the Federal Reserve's room for maneuver, triggering a deep recession in the U.S. and world economies. This would be a "hard landing" indeed.[13]

Nor are the external trends the only subject for concern. As already noted in Chapter 4, the domestic counterpart of the rise in external indebtedness has been a large increase in the indebtedness of U.S. households. While it is difficult to argue convincingly that any particular level of such indebtedness is "too much," one may still wonder how long the trends can or should continue. Furthermore, as experience has shown, such an expansion in credit has inevitably been associated with risky lending, evident in so-called subprime lending and securitization of mortgages. In any case, with the weakening of the housing market and falling home prices, household spending is likely to decline as a share of disposable income, as saving returns to more normal levels. It would take a very aggressive change in monetary policy to reverse that shift. Such a change in the Federal Reserve's policies might in turn threaten the dollar's external stability, raise the specter of inflation, or both. The alternative means of sustaining demand in the presence of a continued inflow of capital from abroad would be another big increase in the fiscal deficit. That too would be undesirable, possibly politically difficult, and once again frightening to foreign creditors, creating a sudden and costly turnaround. For these reasons as well, an earlier decline in the inflow of capital (and so of the current account deficit) would seem highly desirable.

Moreover, in an international political crisis some official creditors might choose to dump their claims on the United States. Of course they would stand to lose a great deal from such a policy, and this outcome should prevent them even from considering it. But suppose the alternative, from their point of view, would be sequestration of their assets by the United States. Such a decision could even seem attractive for the United States, since it would amount to a cheap default. Suppose foreigners feared precisely that choice by angry U.S. legislators. They might then dump their assets out of fear of this alternative. Then, because of either sequestration or large-scale dumping of claims, the United States' credit would be damaged, perhaps severely. The fact that the Chinese government is the biggest single creditor of the United States is an indication of the rising superpower's commitment to maintaining a good relationship with the incumbent one. But should the relationship go badly wrong, U.S. credit itself might be damaged more widely, with incalculable longer-term consequences.

A Case for Sustainability—The View from the United States

The view that the path on which the United States is set is unsustainable, while held by many economists, is challenged by others. The longer the United States has pursued its present course and the larger the deficits have grown, the greater the opposition to the conventional wisdom has become. In a survey of the issues, Eichengreen groups the skeptics into three intellectual camps: proponents of the "new economy," "dark matter," and "savvy investor" schools of thought.[14] But there are more: our old friend the "global savings glut" is one; others are the "optimizing United States," "sophisticated U.S. finance," and "safe haven" perspectives.

Harvard University's Richard Cooper has a characteristically broad perspective.[15] He makes five points:

1. The proposition that the United States saves too little is mistaken and is based on a misunderstanding of the relevant forms of saving in the contemporary advanced economy.
2. The excess savings in the rest of the world are large and permanent, particularly in other high-income countries with low birth rates, such as Germany and Japan.
3. Since the United States generates a quarter to a third of world output (depending on movements in exchange rates) and has well-developed financial markets that account for half of the world's marketable securities, it is perfectly reasonable for the rest of the world to invest up to 10 or even 15 percent of its gross savings in that country, which it is doing precisely because both the private and the official foreign sectors believe that U.S. assets are both safe and rewarding.
4. Should the deficit continue at a nominal level of $600 billion indefinitely, while the U.S. economy grows at 5 percent a year (again in nominal terms), the ratio of net foreign claims to U.S. GDP would peak at 50 percent in fifteen years, and the current account deficit would fall to 2.5 percent of GDP by 2019.
5. Nevertheless, the deficit cannot continue to grow indefinitely as a share of GDP—but this is very different from saying it cannot stay at a historically unprecedented level for a long time.

Let us elaborate and assess these arguments in turn, since they represent a balanced, broad, and authoritative assessment. Let us also note that they incorporate the "savings glut" perspective and as such seem very similar to the position of Ben Bernanke, chairman of the Federal Reserve.

First, it is true that properly measured savings in the United States are substantially higher than shown in the national accounts, where gross savings for 2006 were 14.1 percent of GDP and net savings a negligible 1.9 percent. Cooper argues that an appropriate concept of savings today would include investment in consumer durables, in education, and in research and development. These three categories alone have amounted to about

19 percent of GDP in recent years (9 percent for consumer durables, 7 percent for education, and 3 percent for research and development). Given these levels of saving, the consistent fall in the price of investment goods, and, most obviously, the sustained rise in national income per capita, the product of both investment and sustained rises in total factor productivity (or overall technical progress), Americans as a nation have little reason to believe that they are saving too little. Moreover, the development of the financial markets has made it far easier than ever before for individuals to turn illiquid assets—such as homes—into spending. This then might be called the "optimizing United States" perspective.

Yet it is not necessarily easy to turn much of this capital—lawyers, for example, or shopping malls—into the capacity to earn or save foreign exchange and so service or repay the country's liabilities. That may require large changes in the composition of the capital stock, which, in turn, could take a long time and require significant changes in relative prices.

Second, argues Cooper, the excess savings of much of the rest of the world are structural—the "savings glut" view. He points particularly to Germany and Japan and a few other rich countries (e.g., the Netherlands, Norway, Singapore, and Switzerland, which have very large current account surpluses, despite being so small).[16] Aging, rich societies with modest growth prospects are likely to have high savings and relatively low demand for new investment. This argument is convincing. Figure 5.3, from the McKinsey Global Institute and the Organisation for Economic Cooperation and Development, which shows the sum of the surpluses of all surplus countries, would appear to support Cooper's view of the role of western Europe in particular.[17]

It should be noted, however, that western Europe's surpluses are offset by the deficits within Europe: the Eurozone ran a current account deficit of $29 billion in 2006 (with France, Greece, Italy, and Spain, in particular, offsetting Germany's surplus); the United Kingdom a deficit of $68 billion; and central and eastern Europe a deficit of $89 billion. This more than absorbed the excess savings of Denmark, Norway, Sweden, and Switzerland (a total of $159.9 billion in 2006). Moreover, Japan is currently generating only a third of East Asia's surpluses. Thus, on a global level, much depends on the future surpluses of the oil exporters and of East Asian countries other than Japan. It is likely that the former's surpluses will fall, even if oil prices remain at high levels, as they spend more of their additional income. The future of China's surpluses, now the world's biggest, are an enigma, about which more below. Yet a plausible future is one in which the sum of the surpluses shrinks. A desirable future, one would have thought, is one in which some of these surpluses flow to developing countries, rather than to the United States. Nonetheless, Cooper's view that the United States will

Figure 5.3 Surplus Savers and United States as Borrower of Last Resort

Current account balance (billions of US$)

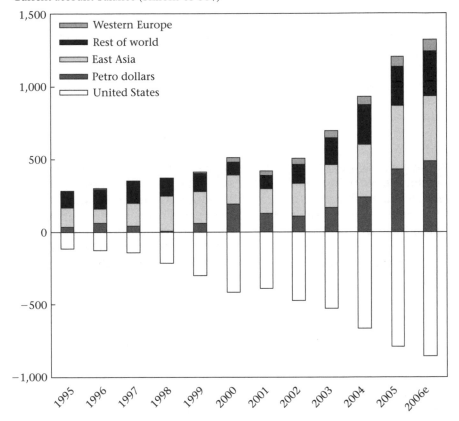

Source: McKinsey Global Institute and Organisation for Economic Co-operation and Development.
Note: e, Estimated.

be able to run significant deficits (though smaller than in recent years) for a very long time is indeed convincing.

Third, Cooper maintains, the United States offers a good home for investment—a broad version of the "new economy" and "safe haven" perspectives. Another economist who suggests that the United States is an attractive home for investment is Richard Clarida of Columbia University. He argues that "the U.S. current account deficit is a general equilibrium phenomenon and is, in part, a reflection of a global excess of savings, relative to profitable investment opportunities in the post-bubble world."[18]

He also suggests that it was a natural consequence of the relatively rapid growth of the U.S. economy, compared to the economies of other high-income countries.

Ricardo Caballero, Emmanuel Farhi, and Pierre-Olivier Gourinchas, the first two at the Massachusetts Institute of Technology and the last at the University of California, Berkeley, have advanced a variant of this argument, which I call the "sophisticated U.S. finance" view.[19] They note that U.S. assets now amount to over 17 percent of the rest of the world's financial wealth, which is equivalent to 43 percent of their annual output. In essence, they suggest, the world has three regions: relatively dynamic advanced economies that produce first-rate financial instruments (the United States, the United Kingdom, Australia); relatively less dynamic regions that also produce good instruments (Japan and the Eurozone); and dynamic developing countries that save a great deal but suffer from inadequate financial markets and so offer a poor home for their liquid savings. This model explains the pattern of net capital flows to the relatively dynamic rich, the relatively high real exchange rates for those countries, and the low real interest rates, which result from the high demand from the rest of the world's savers for the first-rate assets offered by the United States and its smaller English-speaking peers.

Beyond doubt, these broad lines of argument—all of which stress some favorable feature of the United States as a home for capital—have some plausibility. But they also face some important difficulties.

The argument that the U.S. current account deficit necessarily reflected faster U.S. economic growth is incorrect. A rising deficit must mean that domestic demand grows faster than output (see Figure 4.28 for the U.S. experience), not that output itself grows particularly rapidly. If one doubts this, one need only look at the recent performance of China, both the world's fastest-growing country and the country with the largest current account surplus. Thus the fact that the U.S. economy grew faster than the economies of Japan or western Europe in the early 2000s does not itself explain the explosive rise in its deficits

The fact that the United States is the "world's banker"—the central country of the global financial system, as the United Kingdom was in the nineteenth century—does not mean that it has to run large current account deficits. The United Kingdom did not at that time. Similarly, the United States ran current account surpluses after World War II, when it was far more central than it is today. The fact that the United States offers attractive assets for foreigners to hold, as Caballero and associates argue, does not necessarily lead to current account deficits, provided the United States saved enough to finance its investment and exported the capital it was receiving.

Figure 5.4 Financing of the U.S. Current Account

Trillions of US$ (without statistical discrepancy)

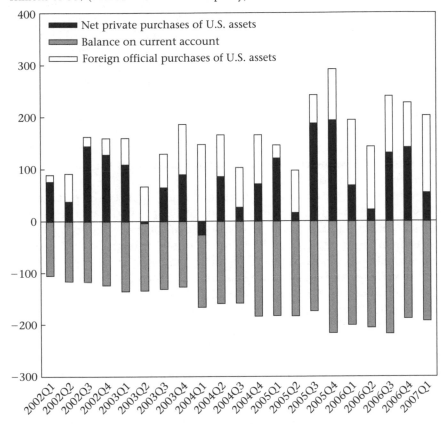

Source: U.S. Bureau of Economic Analysis.

Yet another difficulty with the notion of the invincible attractions of the United States is that it was foreign governments, not profit-seeking private investors, that provided such a high proportion of the financing of the U.S. current account deficit in the 2000s (Figure 5.4). From the beginning of 2002 to the second quarter of 2007, inclusive, foreign governments invested $1.64 trillion in the United States (81 percent of which went into U.S. government securities). On a net basis, foreign governments financed 48 percent of the U.S. current account deficit. Even on a gross basis, they provided 24 percent of the external finance.

Another and more important difficulty is that foreign investments in the United States did not offer the supposedly wonderful returns of a dynamic "new economy"; the returns were actually quite poor. Gourinchas and Hélène Rey show that the returns on U.S. assets were 3.26 percentage points higher than the cost of its liabilities between 1973 and 2004 (Figure 5.5).[20] Of this differential, 2.39 percentage points were due to higher returns on similar assets, while 0.88 percentage points were attributable to the fact that U.S. assets were skewed, relative to its liabilities, toward higher-return and presumably riskier classes, such as FDI and other equities. Overall, foreigners who invested in the United States over this period obtained real returns of 9.4 percent on equities and 9.3 percent on FDI, as one might expect, since this was a period of buoyant equity markets—but a miserable real return of 0.32 percent on debt and 1.2 percent on the "other assets" (bank loans and trade credits).

What makes this so important is that a huge part of the foreign purchases of U.S. liabilities takes the form of debt instruments (including bank accounts), and that is particularly true of the investments by foreign governments. At the end of 2006, for example, foreign-owned assets in the United States (with direct investment valued at market prices) were worth $17.418 trillion, according to the U.S. Bureau of Economic Analysis.[21] Of this total, 6.8 percent was in financial derivatives and the remaining 93.2 percent in conventional assets. Of the latter, 17.1 percent (the huge total of $2.77 trillion) were assets held by foreign governments in the form of Treasury liabilities, bank deposits, and so forth. Another 47.5 percent were privately held debt claims, 19.8 percent was in foreign direct investment, and 15.6 percent was in portfolio holdings of corporate equity. In all, almost two-thirds of the foreign holdings of U.S. assets (other than financial derivatives) took the form of debt. Thus the signal—and, for the United States, very favorable—characteristic of foreign ownership is that a high proportion of foreign capital is invested in assets with low returns, denominated—even better for the United States—in depreciable dollars.

Between the end of 1989 and the end of 2006, the country's cumulative net financial inflow, to cover its current account deficits, was $5.308 trillion. Yet over the same period the U.S. net external position deteriorated by a mere $2.151 trillion. Thus the United States enjoyed offsetting gains of $3.157 trillion, or almost a quarter of 2006 GDP. The explanation for this massive differential was partly favorable exchange rate movements, which gave a positive shift worth $200 billion. But it was mainly due to favorable relative price movements on U.S. assets relative to liabilities (that is, better price performance of assets owned by Americans abroad than of U.S. assets owned by foreigners), worth $1.488 trillion, and so-

Figure 5.5 Determinants of Superior U.S. Returns on Assets against Liabilities, 1973–2004

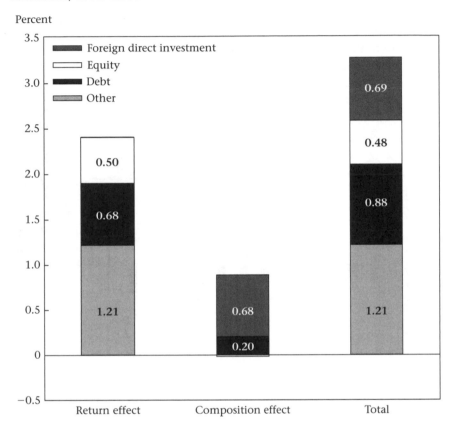

Percent

Source: Gourinchas and Rey (2005b).

called other changes, worth $1.469 trillion.[22] The picture is even more dramatic since the end of 2001, when the dollar began its steady slide. Over that period U.S. net liabilities actually fell by $199 billion, despite cumulative financial flows of $3.209 trillion. This time the explanation was $892 billion in favorable exchange rate movements, $1.694 trillion in favorable price changes (because of the relatively poor performance of U.S. equities), and $1.469 trillion in those other changes.

Figure 5.6 shows the total financial flow to the United States to cover its current account deficit in each year between 1989 and 2006. But it also shows the change in each year's overall net liabilities (the sum of the net flow and all changes in valuation). The difference is caused by changes in

Figure 5.6 Financial Flows and Change in U.S. Net Liabilities

Trillions of US$

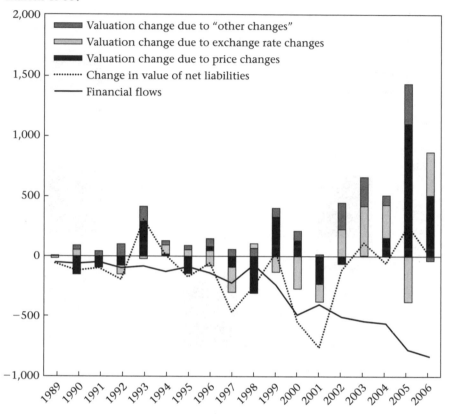

Source: U.S. Bureau of Economic Analysis.

valuation. These can dwarf any given year's net inflows of capital. Valuation effects were particularly dramatic in 2005: a net gain of $1.033 trillion, which turned a net financial inflow of $777 billion into a change in net liabilities of *–$256 billion* (that is, a gain to the United States).

The overall impact of these changes is shown in Figure 5.7. If one simply adds the cumulative current account deficits to the net liability position in 1976, the United States would have had net liabilities equal to 44 percent of GDP by the end of 2006. As it was, according to the Bureau of Economic Analysis, the net liability position was only 16 percent of GDP, down from 23 percent at the end of 2002. Thus at the very time when its current account deficits were particularly large, valuation effects were par-

Figure 5.7 U.S. Net International Investment Position as a Share of GDP

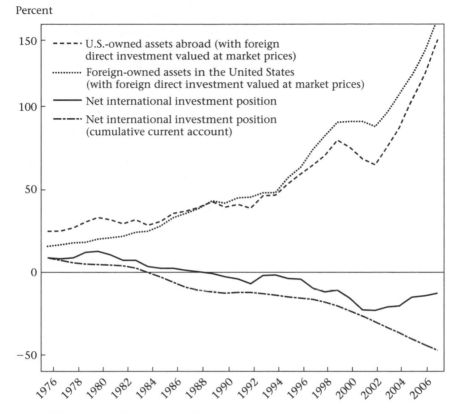

Source: U.S. Bureau of Economic Analysis.

ticularly favorable to the United States. This is the result of both the high ratio of assets and liabilities to GDP (116 and 132 percent of GDP, respectively, by the end of 2006) and the far better price performance of assets than of liabilities in recent years: between 2002 and 2006 the dollar value of U.S. foreign assets jumped by 124 percent, while the dollar value of U.S. liabilities rose by just 88 percent.

In short, the proposition that it makes sense for foreigners to invest in the United States because of high returns looks like nonsense. It is because just the opposite has been the case that the United States has been able to run huge current account deficits, while its net liability position has actually been improving in the 2000s. Nor is this a new phenomenon.

What Gourinchas and Rey call the "valuation channel," including changes brought about by falls in the value of the dollar, has "contributed about 30 percent of the process of international adjustment."[23] To put the point bluntly, reductions in the external value of a currency are an elegant, painless, and entirely legal way for the United States to default.

The United States is enjoying its free banquet, because it has been a relatively poor place for foreigners to put much of their money. It might seem to have been particularly foolish to buy U.S. dollar debt instruments. Yet foreign investors—and particularly those buying low-yielding debt instruments exposed to the decline of the dollar—may not have been foolish to make these investments. They may indeed have offered better prospects than the alternatives. But the evidence does at least raise questions about the propositions advanced by Cooper, Clarida, Caballero, and co-authors that the inflow reflects the attractiveness and quality of investments in the United States. Indeed, as I point out below, it is obviously hard to argue at the same time that the U.S. can obtain almost infinite quantities of credit cheaply and at minimal risk to itself—namely, that it is enjoying an "exorbitant privilege"—and that putting money into the United States has been a good investment.

Yet, at the least, proponents of this position can argue, investments in the United States are safe from expropriation or other forms of criminal malfeasance—the "safe haven" view. Up to a point, that is indeed the case. During the twentieth century the United States won a reputation for protecting the rights of outside investors that it certainly did not possess in the nineteenth. More broadly, foreigners are able to avail themselves of the same protections as citizens. Yet it is important to offer three qualifications even to this argument:

1. As the United States demonstrated in the course of the 1970s, it is possible for the country to choose to inflate away its dollar-denominated debt.
2. As was made clear once again after 2002, the dollar is indeed a floating currency, with a capacity to lose much value against other currencies (see Figure 4.26). It is therefore far from a reliable store of value—as proponents of the monetary role of gold frequently remind us.
3. The U.S. government is more inclined to sequester or freeze assets owned by foreigners—and particularly by foreign governments that the U.S. government deems hostile—than any other in the advanced world. Indeed, as we will see further below, one group of analysts makes this demonstrated vulnerability of foreign assets to seizure an argument for the official inflows.[24]

Thus the argument that investments by, say, the Chinese government or by the governments of Middle Eastern oil exporters in the United States are particularly secure is false.

This point also bears on another related argument, again from Corden. He argues that the Chinese current account surplus may be a way to "park" a proportion of funds abroad until efficiency in domestic investment allocation improves.[25] This is perfectly possible. But a rational investor trying to put funds away for a rainy day (or, in this case, a sunnier day at home) would wish to preserve the purchasing power of those funds. Investing primarily in U.S. government securities would be risky. It would make more sense to own a diversified portfolio. Indeed there is already some evidence of this behavior. At the end of December 2006 the total world stock of official foreign-currency reserves was $5.037 trillion. According to U.S. statistics, however, foreign official holdings in the United States itself were only $2.77 trillion. The difference presumably consisted of holdings in other currencies and in foreign jurisdictions. Neither would necessarily finance the United States.

Now let us turn to Cooper's fourth argument: that a deficit of $600 billion a year (in nominal terms) is indefinitely sustainable. While certainty is impossible, this seems entirely plausible, since it would imply a steady decline in the ratio of the current account deficit to GDP and would cap the net liability position at no more than 50 percent of GDP. As the thorough study of the prospects for the U.S. current account by the McKinsey Global Institute shows, this would be well below the ratios for many other countries that have fallen into difficulties with external liabilities over the past two decades. Of course, because it is so big, exposure for the United States would be far larger than in those other cases. But the United States is also far less likely to get into difficulties (as discussed further below), because it is borrowing entirely in its own currency and also has a sufficiently closed economy to be able to depreciate significantly without risking much inflation. Moreover, even if the ratio of the current account to GDP were to stabilize at, say, 5 percent of GDP, U.S. net liabilities would never exceed 100 percent of GDP, even if one ignored the likelihood of favorable valuation effects (see below), as adjustment began.

This brings the discussion to Cooper's final point: that the current account deficit cannot continue to rise indefinitely relative to GDP. Until the fourth quarter of 2005 this had been exactly what was happening (see Figure 4.3). The growth of the deficit relative to GDP had continued for a long time, as the growth of imports greatly exceeded that of exports. Then came signs of a turnaround, shown in Figure 5.8. The big question (discussed further below) is whether that turnaround is durable, reflecting both fun-

Figure 5.8 Real U.S. Exports and Imports

Billions of US$

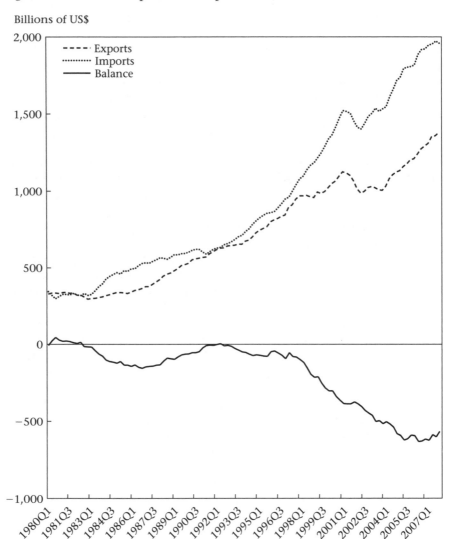

Source: U.S. Bureau of Economic Analysis.
Note: Values are at 2000 prices.

damental improvements in competitiveness (including the steep fall in the real exchange rate of the dollar) and changes in relative growth of demand across the globe, or temporary, reflecting the slowdown in demand in the United States after the bursting of its housing bubble. From the second quarter of 2005, real year-on-year growth of exports exceeded that of imports, at least until the second quarter of 2007. Over that period, moreover, the average real growth of exports was 7.5 percent, against just 4.8 percent for imports. As a result the deficit fell slightly in real terms over this period. If that trend were to last, the path of the deficit would no longer be explosive, and sustainability would be correspondingly closer.

These are not the only arguments that the present pattern of inflows into the United States is sustainable or at least easily manageable. A particularly intriguing one comes from Ricardo Hausmann and Federico Sturzenegger of the Kennedy School of Government of Harvard University. Essentially they argue that the United States is not running a current account deficit, never has run a current account deficit, and is unlikely ever to run a current account deficit. Thus the U.S. and global balance of payments and GDP accounts are false, because they exclude huge U.S. exports (and so imports to the rest of the world) of what they call "dark matter." (Here they borrow the name given by physicists to the unobserved stuff that is supposed to explain the difference between the observed and indirectly measured mass of the universe.)[26]

The argument is, in essence, very simple. Despite becoming a net debtor on an ever-larger scale, the United States, argues Hausmann and Sturzenegger, continues to earn a modest surplus on investment income. Over the four quarters to the first quarter of 2007, for example, the United States ran an overall surplus of $43.1 billion, with a surplus of $183.5 billion on FDI, a deficit of just $1.8 billion on other private income, and one of $138.6 billion on government income (because of the very large foreign holdings of U.S. government liabilities). But, they argue, "the income generated by a country's financial position is a good measure of the true value of its assets. Once assets are valued accordingly, the United States appears to be a net creditor, not a net debtor, and its net foreign asset position appears to have been fairly stable over the last 20 years."[27] The authors argue that the explanation lies in invisible U.S. exports of services that have created a permanent stock of dark matter investments.

What are these exports? They fall into three categories: global liquidity services, which explain the willingness of foreigners to "pay" in return for holding dollar liabilities; insurance services, which show up in the difference between the yield on U.S. Treasury bonds and that on comparable bonds issued by other governments; and knowledge services, which are bundled together with U.S. FDI and reappear in the subsequent flows of income. True U.S. foreign assets are then measured by applying a universal price-earnings ratio of 20 or yield of 5 percent to net income. This generates a "true" net asset position. The difference between that and the measured net asset position consists of the stock of dark matter. The change in each year is equal to the flow of dark matter exports. In this way—presto!—the United States becomes a permanent net creditor. How large is the cumulative value of these invisible exports or stock of dark matter? The answer is the far from small sum of $3 trillion, as of the end of 2006, according to my calculations.[28]

Is this a legitimate procedure? In a word, no. First and most importantly, it assumes without any justification that the figures for U.S. net income are right, while the figures for U.S. trade and investment are wrong. But, as both Willem Buiter of the London School of Economics and Goldman Sachs and Daniel Gros of the Centre for European Policy Studies in Brussels show, this is an entirely illegitimate assumption.[29]

As Gros points out, when one looks carefully at recent U.S. accounts, there is only one asset class for which returns on the assets Americans own abroad are significantly and consistently higher than the returns on the assets owned by foreigners in the United States: direct investment. He demonstrates, for example, that between 2000 and 2005, the difference in rates of return on portfolio equity and debt investments was zero, while for "other investments" the difference was just 1 percentage point in favor of the United States. But the difference for direct investment was 4 percentage points: the United States earned 7 percent abroad, while foreigners who invested in the United States earned 3 percent—less than they would have received on investments in U.S. bonds. Furthermore these returns, unlike those on portfolio equity, refer to total profits, not just dividends. They should therefore give a relatively accurate picture of the profitability of investment by foreigners in the United States against that of Americans abroad (on the assumption that capital gains would be similar). The conclusion one might reach—very much contrary to the view that foreign companies should invest in the United States because it is so profitable—is that they should not do so because it is so unprofitable.

If one adds in more recent U.S. data, one finds that, between 2000 and 2006, the average difference between the ratio of payments to the stock of U.S. outward FDI and the ratio of payments to the stock of FDI in the United States was 5.0 percentage points, with FDI valued at current cost, and 3.9 percentage points, with equity valued at market prices. In 2006 the differentials were 4.4 percentage points and 2.9 percentage points, respectively (Figure 5.9). Above all, the absolute figures are large: in 2006 reported U.S. receipts were $310 billion on a stock of outward FDI valued at $4.378 trillion (at market prices), while payments to foreigners were only $133.8

Figure 5.9 U.S. Return Advantage on Direct Investment

Percent

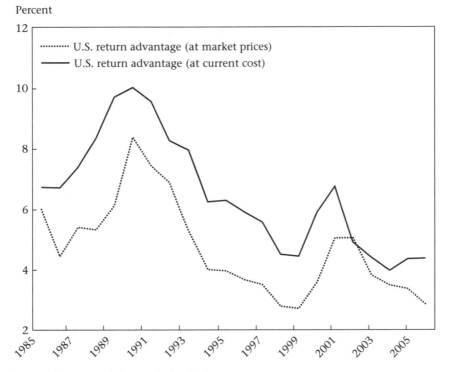

Source: U.S. Bureau of Economic Analysis.
Note: Values are difference between U.S. returns on foreign assets and foreign returns on U.S. assets.

billion on a stock valued at $3.222 trillion. If foreigners earned the same returns as those reported by U.S. investors abroad, U.S. outward payments would have been $229 billion, or almost $100 billion greater. That would have created a sizable change in even the massive current account deficit of the United States.

Is it plausible that foreigners should continue to invest in the United States when they are earning such miserable returns? The answer must be no. No doubt foreigners are foolish and perhaps even generous, but can they be *that* foolish? Remember that these are overwhelmingly sophisticated corporate investors from other high-income countries. Gros notes, moreover, that the difference is entirely explained by reinvested earnings (i.e., reported earnings minus repatriated dividends). He notes too that, between 1999 and 2004, average annual reinvested earnings were $103.4 billion on U.S. investment abroad and $6.9 billion (effectively zero) on foreign investment in the United States. But, as Gros notes, reinvested earnings are an accounting item: they affect reported payments and returns, but no money changes hands. To compute them, moreover, one must rely on corporate accounts. But the reporting of profits in a particular jurisdiction depends on tax considerations. If, for example, it makes sense for both foreign and U.S. multinational companies to shift their reported profits outside the U.S. (to minimize U.S. tax liabilities, since the U.S. corporation tax is relatively high), the result will be an artificial increase in U.S. companies' reported reinvested profits abroad and an equally artificial reduction in foreign companies' reported reinvested profits in the United States. One reason for believing that such tax considerations matter is, as Gros notes, that reported payments on U.S. investments abroad account for a half of U.S. corporate profits, but only a fourth of value added and a fifth of employment.

Gros adds further reasons to doubt the massive reported differences in the payments on FDI. First, there is no difference in returns on portfolio equity. This suggests that foreign companies get a market rate of return, until their investment goes above the threshold that defines it as FDI. Second, why should foreign companies be willing to earn miserable returns in the United States if returns available at home to their U.S. peers are much higher? Third, there are no powerful reasons why investors from other high-income countries should particularly value U.S. political stability or access to U.S. know-how (and so accept very low returns), as is sometimes argued. Is the U.S. more stable than the United Kingdom or Japan? Does Toyota need U.S. know-how?

In all, concludes Gros, the data on payments on FDI are highly suspect and, in all probability, the reported net income position is correspondingly dubious.[30] In any case, what is relevant are overall returns, including capital gains. As I have already noted (see Figure 5.5), Gourinchas and Rey show that, between 1973 and 2004, U.S. investors earned higher overall returns on all equity classes except FDI. What drives this result and how much of it is explained by earlier years in this dataset are unclear.

Apart from very good reasons to question the income data, as laid out above, there are also good a priori reasons for questioning the rationale for dark matter. Buiter provides the clearest analysis. He agrees that the United States provides liquidity services to foreigners. These are measured by the stock of U.S. dollars held abroad. But in 2006 this was only $364 billion—a mere 2.1 percent of total U.S. liabilities—according to the official statistics on the U.S. net investment position (though, it must be admitted, it is not a liability at all, since it costs nothing whatsoever to create).

The second category, insurance services, supposedly exists when the United States can issue public debt at lower risk-adjusted rates than the debt issued by emerging market economies. But, as Buiter notes, if the bonds issued by emerging market governments gave consistently higher returns than those issued by the U.S. government (or other high-quality issuers, such as the governments of Germany or Japan), even after the risk of defaults, there would exist a money-making machine. All the U.S. government would need to do is issue dollar debt to buy up the world's emerging market debt, saving its taxpayers vast amounts of money in the process.

But Hausmann and Sturzenegger offer no evidence that the risk-adjusted dollar return on emerging market debt is higher than that on safe U.S. government debt. Just consider the defaults that have occurred over the past decade and a half in Pakistan (1998), Russia (1998), Ukraine (1998 and 2000), Venezuela (1998), Ecuador (1999), Peru (2000), and Argentina (2001). Moreover, the fact that Americans appear to be earning consistently positive returns from buying risky bonds and selling safe U.S. Treasuries proves nothing, since any offsetting write-offs would not appear in the income accounts. This is yet another reason why income accounts, on their own, provide little information. Moreover, even if the write-offs have not happened yet, they could still occur. The outcome could be particularly costly when, as has recently been the case, spreads on risky debt have been very small and so the cushion against loss has been correspondingly modest.

The third category, knowledge services, shows itself above all in direct investment. But, as I have already noted, there are good reasons to question the gap between the apparent returns on U.S. direct investment abroad and FDI in the United States. If there is no such gap, the dark matter automatically disappears. The big question, as Buiter notes, is why one would suppose that the knowledge services bundled up in U.S. direct investment abroad are fundamentally different from those offered by foreign investors in the United States. For what it is worth (not much, given the extreme difficulty in making calculations of market value), the ratio of estimates of market value to current cost of U.S. direct investment abroad and FDI in the U.S. in 2006 were exactly the same, at between 153 and 154 percent. This suggests that the impacts of know-how, managerial skills, and all the other things that make the market value of companies higher than the cost of acquiring the capital they employ are much the same.[31] No dark matter unique to U.S. direct investment appears here.

A final line of argument—close to that underlying dark matter, but without its heroic conclusion on missing accumulations of valuable assets —is that of the "savvy investor." This contention argues that the United

States has the capacity to earn higher returns on its assets than it pays on its liabilities indefinitely, because its citizens are just better at investing. What Gourinchas and Rey have described for the past is, it is argued, a structural feature applicable to the present and the future as well. John Kitchen of the Office of Management and Budget has advanced this argument particularly clearly. He shows that, with the continuation of past differentials in returns on direct investment, past valuation effects, and significant falls in the dollar (of 14% over ten years), U.S. net liabilities will reach only 39 percent of GDP by 2015. Under more pessimistic assumptions, they can be double that level.[32]

If one looks carefully, one finds that the United States' "exorbitant privilege" results from four features of U.S. capital flows and valuation of assets and liabilities. The first is the very different composition of U.S. assets and liabilities. If one ignores financial derivatives, 61 percent of U.S. assets at the end of 2006 consisted of direct investment and corporate equity, while they made up only 36 percent of its liabilities. This has created overall return differentials, in favor of the United States, because of capital gains.[33] The second feature is the superior reported payment returns on U.S. outward FDI, compared to inward FDI. For reasons discussed above, there are reasons to question the reality of this differential. And even if it is real, it seems to be declining (see Figure 5.9). Finally, if it is real, it suggests such poor investment skills on the part of foreign businesses that it is hard to imagine the flows can be sustained indefinitely. Between the beginning of 2001 and the first quarter of 2007, inclusive, only 10 percent of the gross inflow into the United States took the form of direct investment. The third feature is huge unexplained valuation adjustments. Essentially, the United States appears to be a black hole for foreign capital. The sums involved are gigantic: a $1.469 trillion adjustment in value between 1989 and 2006 and an $822 billion adjustment between 2001 and 2006. Gros suggests that this is because the Bureau of Economic Analysis relies on data from U.S. custodians, which will, he suggests, omit a substantial proportion of foreign holdings of U.S. assets.[34] Finally there is simply the adjustment of the currency itself, as a painless way of lowering liabilities relative to assets.

How plausible are these arguments for the sustainability of the pattern of capital flows from the world at large to the world's richest country? The "new economy" view is implausible, in its pure forms, though related elements make some sense—the "optimizing United States," "safe haven," and "sophisticated U.S. finance" views. But the investments being made by foreigners are not those most likely to benefit from superior U.S. returns. The striking feature of foreign investments in the United States is how low returns have been. Moreover, greater productivity growth in the

United States does not guarantee higher returns to foreign investors and does not eliminate the unpleasant arithmetic of long-term debt accumulation. The "dark matter" hypothesis is simply implausible, since it places total faith in figures on net income and rejects data on investment. Moreover, it is simply another way of restating the puzzle: why are U.S. returns so much higher than those of foreigners investing in the United States? What looks most plausible is the "savvy investor" hypothesis. That is just another term for "exorbitant privilege."

As Eichengreen notes, these arguments are also mutually incompatible.[35] If Americans earn far higher returns on foreign investments than foreigners earn in the United States, the argument that the latter are rationally deploying their capital in a lucrative market collapses. One cannot simultaneously argue that the United States can go on running huge current account deficits because foreigners are enticed by high prospective returns and stress the United States' ability to earn far higher returns on its assets than it pays on its liabilities. In the end, the best argument for the view that high current account deficits are indefinitely sustainable is that Americans are "savvy investors," fleecing the naïve. That is not a view wise Americans should trumpet too often. In any case, it seems dangerous to assume it will continue forever. In the long run, the deficit must surely fall as a share of GDP. The question is when and how.

A Case for Unsustainability—The View from the Creditors

Why should the process of funding the United States be unsustainable from the point of view of the creditors? The short answer is that it cannot be. Provided they wish to transfer some part of their production to the benefit of U.S. spenders, they can if they wish continue forever. Many of those who expected them to cease long before now did not allow for the scale of government financing that would be offered when private financing dried up.

Nevertheless, credit lines are never infinite, even if those to residents of the United States are far greater than those to residents of any other country. For foreign investors an important consideration must be the risk-reward ratio. As the proportion of their portfolios invested in the United States rises, they are likely to seek higher returns, to compensate for their growing exposure. Given how poor their returns have apparently been and their role as buyers of U.S. assets, such a shift in attitudes could trigger substantial changes in pricing. This obviously applies to private investors. But even official investors cannot be indifferent to returns. China's foreign-currency reserves, for example, are now close to half of GDP. As the assets grow, returns will become increasingly important. That is obviously even more true of oil exporters, whose sovereign wealth funds will make up much of the assets of the nation over the long term. This then is a matter of diversifying assets and ensuring adequate returns to compensate for risk. So far foreigners seem to have been doing a poor job in both respects—though they may be doing even worse with investments elsewhere.

The second consideration for the creditors is monetary. This is particularly important for countries with pegged exchange rates or similar arrangements, which make necessary heavy intervention in exchange markets to keep the currency down. The normal consequences of intervention include the expansion of the monetary base and declining interest rates, either as a direct consequence of the desire to slow the inflow of speculative capital or as a result of attempts to sterilize the monetary expansion. Such sterilization works by selling nonmonetary assets to the nonbank private sector (in China's case, simply the nonbank sector) or, if necessary, to commercial banks. (In China the dominant instrument is the sale of so-called sterilization bonds.)

This policy of sterilization seems to be achieving the objective of curbing the growth of the monetary base, which consists predominantly of deposits of the commercial banks at the People's Bank of China (Figure 5.10). Proponents suggest that low domestic interest rates (enforced by controls on capital outflows) ensure that the fiscal cost of sterilization is also low. Against this, Morris Goldstein and Nicholas Lardy of the Peterson Institute argue that the policy of sterilizing foreign-currency intervention creates a host of difficulties. Among these are the need to impose direct credit controls on banks, which undermines the policy of financial reform; the damage done to the commercial banks by forcing them to hold low-interest sterilization bonds; the danger of shifting an increasing proportion of lending into curb markets, outside the purview of official regulation; the impossibility of raising interest rates, given the risk of accelerating the capital inflow; the need to impose direct controls on investment, which is inconsistent with liberalization of the economy; and the risk of another round of excessive lending and nonperforming loans.[36]

Furthermore, they argue, the interest rate on sterilization bonds is artificially low and so understates the opportunity cost of funds. Finally, allowance must be made for the ultimate losses when—as seems almost certain to happen—the currencies move upward. An appreciation of 30 percent, for example, would impose a domestic-currency loss of $450 billion on Chinese reserves of $1.5 trillion—$350 for every man, woman, and child in a country that still had an income per capita of only $2,000 in 2006. If the reserves reach $3 trillion—as seems quite plausible and not in the too

Figure 5.10 Sterilization of Foreign-Currency Intervention

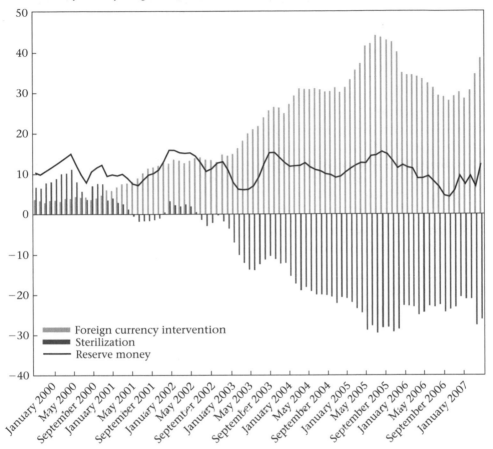

Growth rate, year-on-year (percent)

Source: UBS.

distant future—the losses would be double that. It is inconceivable that any even moderately democratic polity could pursue so wasteful a policy.

Some observers—notably the financial analyst Richard Duncan—argue that the inability to sterilize massive reserve accumulations inherent in foreign-currency intervention has lain behind a long series of financial bubbles over the past two decades, notably in Japan and the developing countries of East Asia.[37] Thus, such observers would argue, any apparent success in sterilizing reserves must be temporary. Ultimately the policy of open-ended intervention by central banks is doomed to generate excessive growth of credit and domestic money, asset-price bubbles, excess investment, and financial collapse. Even where these disastrous outcomes do not occur, the stimulus to demand should generate higher prices and so ultimately a loss of the external competitiveness that the policy of currency intervention is designed to preserve.

The creditors face one other danger: protectionist backlash. Policies of open-ended currency intervention, to preserve export competitiveness, or of large accumulation of foreign-currency assets in the hands of governments, to shift consumption into the future (as in the oil-exporting countries) risk creating opposition in countries whose assets are being bought. This may be irrational, but it is a reality. For a country as big as China, the sustainability of a policy of export-led growth must be in question, at least if its current account surpluses continue to rise as rapidly as they have in recent years (see Figure 4.19).

A Case for Sustainability—The View from the Creditors

The view that the accumulation of current account surpluses and reserve assets cannot continue also has important challengers. One view is the "nationalization of capital outflow," proposed by Cooper. The broadest perspective may be described as "Sino-American co-dependency." In addition, there is "Bretton Woods Two" and the international monetarist perspective of Ronald McKinnon of Stanford University.

Cooper argues that "if the Chinese were permitted to invest abroad, there is little doubt that many of them would do so, particularly after the institutional developments required to make such investment easy, such as the formation of mutual funds of foreign securities and brokerage houses to sell them." But there are good reasons, given the weak state of the domestic financial system, not to lift controls on private outflows. So "one way of interpreting the People's Bank of China's behavior is that it is undertaking the foreign investments that residents are not allowed to undertake, in anticipation of the day when controls on capital outflows will be removed and the Chinese will invest extensively abroad."[38] Since the gross foreign assets of the United States now exceed its GDP, it is not unreasonable for China to own foreign-currency assets worth close to half of its GDP by 2007. This is almost certainly not the motivation for the reserves. But it is still a reason for having them. If Cooper is correct, the Chinese authorities will be in a position to prevent the depreciation of the currency that would otherwise follow the decision to liberalize controls on capital outflow.

The co-dependency argument is in essence that Asian countries are risk averse, are running their economies under conditions of constrained domestic demand, are accumulating reserves for precautionary reasons, and are reliant on net exports as a source of demand. In other words, they have a policy of generating savings gluts, precisely as I argued in Chapter 4. Their surpluses require offsetting deficits in a country to which they—and the rest of the world—wish to lend. That country, as I have also argued, is the United States. The argument is a valid one. But the process cannot continue indefinitely in its present form, as Catherine Mann of Brandeis University and the Peterson Institute has noted.[39]

An extreme version of the co-dependency thesis comes from Michael P. Dooley of the University of California, Santa Cruz, and David Folkerts-Landau and Peter M. Garber of Deutsche Bank.[40] The argument is brilliant and, to me, entirely unconvincing, in equal measure.

The Bretton Woods Two thesis has two elements: "rapid industrialization requires a large inflow of direct and portfolio equity investment; and, in turn, a large current account surplus is required for the periphery to provide the collateral." On the first of these elements, "the key assumption in our framework is that much of the savings intermediated by domestic financial markets in poor countries is not transformed into productive capital. . . . Gross international capital flows replace domestic financial markets with an efficient alternative."[41] Productive capital, these authors add, is invested in globally competitive production, particularly manufacturing. A particularly important objective is to transfer workers into urban employment. Moreover, they argue, those flows will not be forthcoming without protection against expropriation. The accumulation of official foreign-currency reserves provides collateral against such an eventuality.[42] Moreover, because the collateral has to exceed the value of the equity (to cover the returns on the latter), the FDI-importing country must run a current account surplus and so become a net creditor.

My answer to these fascinating propositions is that what is true is not new, what is new is not true, and neither what is true nor what is new explains what is happening in the world economy. Moreover, even if this were a good policy for emerging market economies to follow, it is not a policy they are following.[43] Finally, the theory is not necessary to explain what is happening.

Consider first what is true, but not new.

It is true that many emerging market economies, particularly in East Asia, believe that the development of export-oriented manufacturing is an indispensable basis for economic growth. Their experience with the financial crises of 1997 and 1998 will have strengthened that belief. It is also true that the Chinese government thinks along similar lines.

It is true as well that the Chinese government believes that inward FDI is an important tool for generating an internationally competitive industrial sector. But China has not limited inward FDI to the industrial sector or to production for world markets. Some of the FDI it has attracted is to support production for the home market behind protectionist barriers. It is unlikely that this FDI is creating an internationally competitive industrial sector. Much of it is not generating significant employment either. Yet what is true for China is not true for other East Asian countries, notably Japan and South Korea. These countries were, and to a substantial extent still are, resistant to affording any such role to FDI.

Now consider what is new, but not true, on exchange rate policy:

1. It is not true that the only export market that matters to the emerging market economies in general, and China in particular, is the United States. More than half of China's exports go to other markets. Thus it is not a rational competitiveness strategy to target the dollar exchange rate alone. A more sensible policy, from this point of view, would have been to target the real effective exchange rate, which has in fact been quite volatile (Figure 5.11). True, the dollar target worked out well, from China's point of view, between 2001 and 2005, when the dollar was losing value. Yet before that the peg severely undermined Chinese external competitiveness, notably so when China stuck to it throughout the Asian crises of 1997 and 1998.

2. FDI financed under 5 percent of China's fixed investment over the past few years. This is far too small an amount to determine the efficiency of the overall capital stock, which can be raised only by an efficient domestic financial system. The same argument undermines the view that the "round-tripping" of Chinese funds via U.S. capital markets can transform the efficiency of capital in the Chinese economy. The tail is not big enough to wag this dragon.

3. The export sector created by an undervalued real exchange rate does not necessarily—or even plausibly—embody an efficient capital stock. On the contrary, given the prospective rises in the real cost of labor and in the real exchange rate, much of it will have to be scrapped. Indeed over the next decade or two China is likely to find that it is no longer the world's most competitive supplier of labor-intensive manufactures.

4. China does not conform to the hypothesis that currency undervaluation will bias domestic investment in favor of tradable goods, thus adding to the supposedly superior foreign-financed capital stock. Goods that are exported from China and so meet what the Deutsche

Figure 5.11 China's Real Effective Trade-Weighted Exchange Rate

Source: JPMorgan.

Bank authors call "the acid test of efficiency" use a mere 6 percent of the stock of fixed assets, according to Goldstein and Lardy.[44]

5. Much of the foreign investment in China is not oriented to world markets, but to the Chinese market, and a third of it is in nontradables (retail and so forth). About half of the foreign capital stock in the tradable goods sector is used to produce goods for the domestic market, some of it uncompetitively: motor vehicles seem an important example. U.S. investment seems to be heavily biased toward the domestic market.

6. Consider the argument that supernormal profits generated by companies exporting from China persuade U.S. investors to lobby Congress to keep markets open; this line of reasoning founders on the twin facts that they do not appear to make supernormal profits and do not export much from China.

Now consider what is new, but not true, with the idea of accumulating foreign-currency reserves as collateral against seizure of part or all of the inward stock of FDI:

1. There is no reason for China to imagine that the U.S. government would default on Treasury bonds China owned if it were to seize assets owned by European, Japanese, South Korean, or Taiwanese companies. Indeed it can be pretty skeptical over the chances that the United States would do so even if China seized American assets. China need only look at the example of Russia, which has seized assets belonging to—or defaulted on contracts with—BP and Shell, both influential companies, with no such response by the U.S. Treasury.

2. The large outright emerging market defaults have been on bonds or bank debt, not on equity investments. In the latter case, there are many options for a national government, local government, or investment partner short of outright seizure, including changes in the tax regime, removal of favorable treatment of various kinds, discrimination in government purchases, regulatory hassling, and simple theft. Any of these could be ruinous for the investor. None is likely to lead to default by the United States on the debt it owes to its most important single creditor. As Eichengreen puts it, "the way that foreign investments in China have been expropriated historically is through the surreptitious stripping of assets by Chinese managers and joint-venture partners, not through overt nationalization. It is hard to imagine that the U.S. government would risk tarnishing its public credit in response to more such instances."[45]

3. The true constraint on large-scale seizures of stocks of FDI is the knowledge that new investment would cease. That matters to any country trying to become a leading player in the world economy, particularly one envisaging a future as an owner of capital abroad.

4. The accumulation of massive reserves by China is recent (see Figure 4.25) and coincides with a decline, not an increase, in its dependence on inward FDI, which has fallen from financing 12 percent of Chinese fixed investment in the mid-1990s to financing only 4 percent in the mid-2000s.

5. The accumulation of reserves is obviously a by-product of the pegged exchange rate. The Chinese government did not plan the swing in flows of capital (other than FDI) that drove the reserve accumulations in the early 2000s nor the explosion in the current account surplus that drove them after 2004.

6. Official reserve accumulations in favor of the hegemonic financial power are a new phenomenon. They were entirely absent in the late

nineteenth century, when the net flow of capital was from the United Kingdom. Yet U.K. investors also confronted the possibility of defaults, at least outside the empire.

7. Empirical work by Eichengreen shows that, once a wide array of determinants of FDI inflows are included, those inflows no longer explain accumulation of reserves.[46]

Moreover, neither what is true nor what is new explains what is happening in the world economy as a whole. For the argument is essentially China-specific:

1. China itself generates only a fifth of the world's current account surpluses (while the United States generated 70 percent of the deficits), and even this high share is very recent. China's behavior cannot explain the U.S. deficits on its own.
2. Other East Asian countries with current account surpluses, such as Japan, South Korea, or Taiwan, are not encouraging inward FDI to develop their backward economies or secure the emergence of internationally competitive manufacturing. If they were, these countries would not need foreign-currency reserves to prove to the United States that they are not about to seize American assets—or, for that matter, each other's. Can one imagine circumstances under which the United States would seize South Korean holdings of U.S. Treasury bonds if the South Korean government seized the assets of a Japanese investor in South Korea?
3. The second group of countries with large current account surpluses, the oil exporters, are also not trying to attract large inward FDI to create a globally competitive manufacturing sector. Moreover the evidence strongly suggests that many are avoiding putting their money into U.S. government liabilities precisely because they fear that the United States might seize their assets, though for political reasons.
4. Even if China did want to own more U.S. Treasury bonds than it receives in FDI, this need not create a huge U.S. current account deficit. This policy would be perfectly consistent with, say, a modest current account surplus for China and the United States, with current account deficits elsewhere.

Now let us consider the penultimate point: even if this were a good policy for emerging market economies to follow, it is not a policy they are following. The Deutsche Bank authors, following Milton Friedman, argue that it is a mistake to measure the usefulness of a theory by the realism of its assumptions. I strongly disagree. In a science incapable of reliable testing of theory, the reality of the assumptions is essential to judging the likely robustness of the results. Certainly where the assumptions concern motives, as they do here, we benefit from the fact that we are dealing with chatty human beings, not mice. If the Chinese authorities were accumulating foreign-currency reserves in order to convince inward investors that they would not seize their assets, one might expect them to say so. After all, it is useful information. If the Chinese did not say so, one might expect some of the investors to have pointed this fact out to their shareholders. I am unaware of any statements to either effect.

Finally, the theory is unnecessary. All one need suppose is that the Chinese authorities have two predominant objectives: monetary stability and satisfactory levels of economic growth. For a country with a primitive financial system and an economy increasingly oriented to the outside world, the exchange rate peg is a simple way of providing the former. It has also proved consistent with the latter. In recent years, the peg has led to the rapid accumulation of foreign-currency reserves. Initially this was almost certainly welcome as a form of insurance. Subsequently it has been something of a problem, not least because of the challenge of sterilization (not insurmountable, but tricky) and the friction with the United States. But that difficulty has not yet been enough to warrant changing the policy radically, since there is a significant risk that doing so would imperil China's two primary objectives.

What I have just outlined is, more or less, the position of McKinnon. He is, together with the Nobel laureate Robert Mundell, one of the principal proponents of the "international monetarist" position, that all currencies should be fixed. In essence he desires a return to a version of the gold standard that ruled the global economy between 1870 and 1914. His view is clearly expressed in the following quotation: "If we jettison the still well-entrenched theory that the real exchange rate is a useful device for balancing international payments on current account and with it jettison the idea that a 'free float' is possible or desirable in the presence of a huge overhang of dollar assets, how can one best theorize about 'optimal' exchange rate policy? The alternative view is that a controlled nominal exchange rate is part and parcel of the national monetary policy for targeting the national price level."[47] In other words, China's best monetary policy is to become a region of the United States—a federal reserve district without a Federal Reserve Bank.

In arguing for this position, McKinnon makes essentially the following argument:

- Current account surpluses and deficits are expressions of the difference between a country's savings and investments—of savings glut and savings dearth.

- Movements in real exchange rates cannot affect these savings and investments balances in any significant, predictable, or durable way.
- For a country with a structural savings surplus, such as China or Japan, a floating exchange rate threatens the needed smooth outflow of excess capital, because of periodic bouts of anxiety among domestic savers over the likely appreciation of the exchange rate.
- Such anxiety is greatly increased by the perception of pressure for appreciation from abroad—particularly from the United States—because of the persistence of trade surpluses.
- The only reason that the Chinese and Japanese governments have had to intervene so heavily in the foreign-currency markets is the expectation of an appreciation, which creates a "one-way bet" for speculators.
- If these governments do not then intervene in the foreign exchange market, to purchase the foreign exchange generated by the structural trade surpluses, the currency will soar.
- That will then generate outright deflation, as nominal prices of tradable goods and services are pushed down.
- The prospect of steady appreciation of the currency will also drive down interest rates below levels in the United States, perhaps to zero, as happened to Japan.
- At that point the country will be in a "liquidity trap," threatened by a long period of deflation. That has been the fate of Japan.
- It is one that China must avoid at all costs, not least because it would impose savage adjustment pressure on the internationally open sectors of the economy, particularly agriculture.

The answer, suggests McKinnon, is a credibly fixed nominal exchange rate. Furthermore, should China and Japan both fix their exchange rates against the U.S. dollar, they will also automatically fix them against each other. Smaller East Asian countries can do the same, thereby creating a de facto area of monetary stability without any need for a formal agreement.

This is an important argument, with which I have some sympathy. But on several points I disagree. First, for reasons discussed at length in Chapter 4, it is difficult to believe that China's savings surplus is simply the result of private decisions and is independent of exchange rate policy. In the case of Japan, that is more plausible. But since almost all the savings are now being generated even there by the corporate sector, it is hard to believe that retentions of corporate profits (which are astonishingly high in Japan) are not subject to fiscal influence or to legislation that would increase the power of shareholders over companies.

Second, it is equally hard to believe that substantial changes in current account balances can be achieved without sizeable shifts in real exchange rates, if the aim is also to avoid severe recessions in countries being forced to reduce deficits and equally severe overheating in countries in the process of reducing surpluses.[48] Should a significant correction of the United States' external deficit be required, a sizable depreciation of the overall real exchange rate will likewise be necessary. The alternative—adjustment solely via demand and recession—will not be tolerated. It is true that a sufficiently prolonged recession would bring about a sufficiently sustained period of low—or even negative—inflation for the needed real depreciation to occur without a nominal decline in the value of the dollar. That is more or less what Germany achieved within the Eurozone in the first half of the 2000s, through "competitive disinflation." What would be required of the United States would probably be even deeper and more prolonged. It is simply not going to happen. If the United States would demand the ability to depreciate under these circumstances, China would probably have to find a way to adapt to appreciation, unless all the adjustment could be shifted elsewhere.

Third, the liquidity trap argument is oversold for China. The principal difficulty created by deflation is that it puts a lower bound on real interest rates: if, for example, the relevant price level is falling at 3 percent a year, the real interest rate cannot be lower than 3 percent (with nominal interest rates at zero). For a low-growth economy with high savings, like Japan, this is a big difficulty. For China, however, it should be much less difficult. A very-high-growth economy should be able to pay positive real interest rates and grow quite easily. The only reason why that might not be the case for China is its staggering overall national savings rate—estimated at just under 60 percent for 2006.

Last, China is not living by the standard rules of a fixed nominal exchange rate regime, since it is trying to have both an exchange rate target and an inflation—or domestic monetary—target. This is possible because the country has exchange controls, which give it substantial monetary freedom, even under a pegged exchange rate. Moreover, sterilization seems feasible in a country with China's characteristics, not least the rapid growth in the demand for money. The result seems to be an ability to avoid the real appreciation that a country growing so fast would be expected to show. China is, as a result, steadily increasing its competitiveness, generating larger trade surpluses, and having to accumulate more reserves and generate the needed savings through a range of public policy decisions. That seems to be consistent with the soaring current account surpluses and savings rates, which apparently came close to the incredible figure of 59 percent of GDP in 2006.

On the Sustainability and Desirability of the "Imbalances"

Are the trends in external "imbalances" sustainable? If they are sustainable, will they be sustained? If they are sustained, are they desirable?

The answer to the first of these questions is yes. This is so for a simple reason. If creditors wish to provide the finance, they can do so, without limit. Moreover, as the discussion has shown, the creditors do have reasons for continuing to finance the United States. Some (e.g., Germany, Japan, Singapore, and Switzerland) are rich countries with structural savings surpluses. Others (e.g., the East Asian emerging economies) rely heavily on export-led growth. Yet others (e.g., Brazil or Malaysia) fear the consequences of another round of current account deficits and external borrowing. Some (the oil exporters) have enjoyed large recent windfalls which they wish to squirrel away for a rainy day. And one—China—seems to be a mixture of all four: it has a huge structural savings surplus, despite being poor; it relies quite heavily on export-led growth; it certainly fears financial instability; and its rapid growth itself generates what seems to its people to be something of a windfall. While the challenge of managing huge surpluses is not small, many of these countries do seem able to do so, if not forever then certainly for a long time. I do not accept some of the explanations for the behavior of the creditors—the Bretton Woods Two hypothesis, for example—but they all have some truth.

Now turn to the second question: will the imbalances be sustained? Here both creditors and the big debtor will be heavily involved. As the external deficits piled up, the dollar fell. This is fairly predictable. The significant point is that an explosive path for the deficit was never going to be sustained—and has not been. Investors will insist on more favorable prices: higher yields or lower exchange rates, with correspondingly smaller currency risk. The decline in the real exchange rate then facilitates the adjustment in trade flows and reduces the real value of U.S. liabilities. The outcome seems benign, but it is also dangerous. It is one of several reasons why returns to creditors have been so poor. But there are others: the disappearance of no less than $1.5 trillion in net liabilities accumulated between 1989 and 2006 and $820 billion between 2001 and 2006 is staggering, and so is the consistently miserable return on inward foreign direct investment.

One comes to the conclusion that the U.S. borrowing spree looks affordable because creditors have enjoyed such miserable returns. It is little surprise that foreign governments have had to provide almost half of the net financing of current account deficits between 2002 and the first half of 2007, inclusive. The private sector has not provided the funds required.

If governments are willing to do this, the finance must be sustainable. But why should it be sustained? What if they start to cut and run? It would be a brutal landing, as interest rates jump in the United States and the exchange rate tumbles.

What might the debtors' attitude be? It is of course mixed. There is pleasure in what the finance affords, worry over what would happen if the credit were swiftly cut off, and a host of specific interests on all sides, but most vociferously on the protectionist side. There is a limit to the amount of borrowing households are likely to do, even if it is initially on very favorable terms. The economy has become adapted to the deficits. The proposition that sizable current account deficits—even if not as large as those seen in recent years—will be observed for many years to come is not that difficult to accept.

Finally, is all this desirable? The answer is yes, because it is far better than the repeated financial crises that preceded it. It is also no, because the opening of global financial markets, in order to generate an open-ended line of credit from the poor to the world's richest consumers, looks—how does one put it?—peculiar. Surely we can do a little bit better than that. In fact, we will probably have to do a little bit better than that, as the explosive rise of the U.S. deficit tails off and, in all probability, reverses. This is the challenge to be addressed in the following chapters.

CHAPTER 6

Toward Adjustment and Domestic Reform

Asia has become the source of finance, the source of savings. It now has the human capital to manage that well. Why doesn't it take the advantage of that opportunity to try and create financial markets that work better for the people of Asia?

JOSEPH STIGLITZ, NOBEL LAUREATE IN ECONOMICS

SO WHAT IS TO BE DONE? The U.S. current account deficit is shrinking. But if the rest of the world is to move rapidly forward without the engine of U.S. demand, these countries must themselves achieve more balanced growth. At the very least, their aggregate demand must grow as fast as potential output. Ideally it should grow faster, thereby allowing the U.S. current account deficit to shrink comfortably.

How is this to happen? The argument in this chapter is that it can happen only if the increasingly significant emerging market economies play their part. Indeed that follows almost automatically from the picture of capital flows presented in Chapter 4. Yet such flows will be impossible if these countries consider it too risky to run current account deficits. Such a shift in the direction of capital flows seems self-evidently desirable. It does, ultimately, make more sense for capital to flow from rich and aging societies to poorer countries with good investment opportunities than to the consumers of the world's richest country (as well as a few other high-income countries in a similar position, such as Australia and the United Kingdom).

What then should we seek?

1. We should seek an international financial system that is liberal and market based. But it should also be far less prone to the shattering fi-

nancial crises of the 1980s and 1990s, with the enormous costs they imposed in terms of both fiscal solvency and lost output and incomes.

2. We should seek a global economy that is not as reliant for its overall macroeconomic balance on the United States as borrower and spender of last resort, as it has been over the past decade or so.

3. We should seek a set of domestic and international reforms that lets emerging market economies feel they can be net importers of capital—that is, run current account deficits—without fearing exchange rate collapses, sovereign default, mass insolvency of domestic businesses, and the resulting humiliation and economic and political crises.

4. We should seek an international monetary system that supports these goals and a set of international institutions—of which the IMF is the most important—that helps make them achievable.

In short, as Stanley Fischer, erstwhile first deputy managing director of the IMF and subsequently governor of the Bank of Israel, put it: "The vision that underlies most proposals for reform of the international financial system is that the international capital markets should operate as well as the better domestic capital markets."[1] For reasons explained in Chapter 2, that is impossible, since one cannot wish away the reality of multiple jurisdictions. But one should be able to come closer to this ideal than we have so far.

Yet let us start by considering how urgent such changes are. How long is the present pattern of global capital flows likely to last? Could it end without any significant change in the behavior of emerging economies?

Adjustment of Global Imbalances: When, How, How Much?

Some idea of what will happen to the stock of global net assets and liabilities if trends merely continue is shown in Figure 6.1, where it is assumed that there will be no further change in real exchange rates and no further huge valuation shifts in favor of the United States similar to those shown in Figures 5.6 and 5.7. Without some adjustment, the stocks of net assets and liabilities will grow substantially faster than world output. The United States can cope with this, because of the structure of its liabilities and their denomination in its own currency. The question is whether the creditors will be happy with their growing exposure and what price they will demand to compensate them for their growing risks. And emerging Asia is set to become the largest net creditor, with China playing by far the dominant role.

Figure 6.1 Net Foreign Assets and Liabilities

Percent of global output

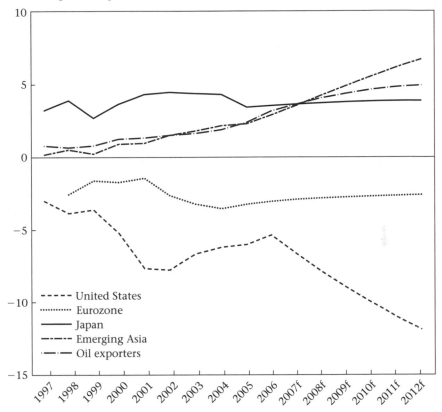

Source: International Monetary Fund, *World Economic Outlook,* April 2007.
Note: f, Forecast.

Could such a continuing increase in the U.S. net liability position continue? In its study of the underlying trends, the McKinsey Global Institute suggests that it could.[2] Given the trends it analyzed, the U.S. current account deficit would have reached almost $1.6 trillion by 2012 or 9 percent of GDP. The U.S. would then have a trade deficit in goods and mineral fuels of $1.46 trillion, a surplus of $140 billion in services, negative net transfers of $145 billion, and negative net foreign income of $120 billion. Net foreign income would still be less than 1 percent of GDP, on the assumption that the remarkable U.S. return advantage would endure. Net foreign liabilities would reach $8.1 trillion (if one assumed no exchange rate changes and a continuation of the rate of appreciation of assets and liabilities seen over the past 15 years). But net debt would still be only 46 percent of GDP, below levels reached in other, smaller countries (see Figure 5.1).

Since U.S. liabilities are denominated in dollars, these would be safer for the United States and riskier for the creditors than in many other cases. Creditors might demand higher risk premiums, with adverse effects on the net income position of the United States. Indeed there is already some evidence of this.[3] It is also important to ask what the domestic counterparts of these huge external deficits would be. Would investment in the corporate sector take off, corporate profitability collapse, households go even deeper into financial deficit, or the fiscal deficit explode? Some combination of these scenarios must happen if the current account deficit is to rise by a further 2–3 percent of U.S. GDP (see Figure 4.29). This domestic side of the external capital flows must not be neglected.

To fund these huge inflows, surpluses must grow elsewhere. That, says the McKinsey Global Institute, is feasible. The gross capital inflow into the United States as a share of the rest of the world's gross savings would rise slightly, from just under 20 percent to 23 percent. But, given present trends, the Institute argues that the aggregate of global current account surpluses could reach almost $2.1 trillion by 2012: $800 billion in East Asia, $620 billion in western Europe, $390 billion in the oil-exporting countries, and $270 billion in the rest of the world. The U.S. share of these surpluses would rise to 77 percent, up from close to 70 percent between 2001 and 2006.

Would the rest of the world allow the U.S. share of the capital flow to rise still further? That depends on how much concentrated risk foreign investors would be willing to run. A guess—but it can only be a guess—is that market forces (a combination of higher risk premiums on the supply of funds to the United States and a declining dollar) would prevent this from happening even if no overt policy decisions were made. As a result of a weakening currency and weak growth, the year-on-year growth of U.S. real exports of goods and services was faster than that of imports after the first quarter of 2005. In the three years from the second quarter of 2004 to the second quarter of 2007, real GDP rose by 8.2 percent, real imports by 14.2 percent, and real exports by 22.9 percent. But exports have to grow faster than imports for a long time to make a meaningful dent in the deficit, because imports start off much bigger: in the second quarter of 2007 imports were 16.8 percent and exports still only 11.6 percent of GDP (Figure 6.2).[4]

So what might adjustment look like? Three points emerge from any close analysis:

1. Higher foreign growth alone would not begin to close the U.S. deficit. The McKinsey Global Institute concludes, for example, that even if U.S. exports of manufactures were to grow at 7.5 percent a year—well

Figure 6.2 U.S. Exports and Imports over GDP

Percent (nominal and at constant 2000 prices)

Source: U.S. national income and product accounts.

above the 4.2 percent consistent with current trends—the current account deficit would still be 6.3 percent of GDP in 2012. Moreover,
achieving even this growth would require either a huge increase in foreign growth rates—by 5 percentage points a year, which is absurd—or
a sharp and (in the absence of a big boost to competitiveness) highly
implausible reversal of the long-term decline in the share of U.S. exports in world trade.
2. There must therefore be shifts around the world in real exchange rates
as well as changes in absorption—or expenditures—relative to GDP.

3. These changes in real exchange rates are too big to be brought about without movement in nominal exchange rates as well, since that would mean either outright deflation in the depreciating countries (such as the United States), a surge in inflation in the appreciating countries, or both.

What sort of shifts might market forces alone generate? One possibility —the European nightmare—would be a continuation of Asian exchange rate targeting against the dollar and large surpluses in oil-exporting countries, with a still bigger decline in the dollar against the euro (and other floating exchange rates). This would be the market's attempt to shift the capital flows from the United States to the Eurozone and other high-income countries (probably including Australia, Canada, Denmark, Sweden, Switzerland, and the United Kingdom).

Under admittedly restrictive assumptions, Maurice Obstfeld and Kenneth Rogoff have argued that, if the Asians were to stick to their exchange rate pegs and the U.S. current account deficit were to be eliminated, "the real value of the European currencies would have to rise by almost 50 percent relative to the baseline."[5] Moreover, the appreciation of the nominal exchange rates would be substantially greater, because of incomplete pass-through of changes in exchange rates to domestic prices. This large real appreciation is needed partly because the Asian currencies would be falling together with the dollar. There would then be an increase in the Asian current account surplus (of 70 percent, according to their model). Thus Europe would have to adjust to both shrinkage of the U.S. deficit and a rise in the Asian surplus. This is a recipe for a trade war: Europe would protect itself against imports, thereby trying to negate the impact of the appreciation.

An important point in evaluating a market-led adjustment, in the absence of a change in policy by emerging market economies, is that high-income countries were, in the aggregate, running a huge current account deficit in 2006 (Figure 6.3). If we think about the possibility of adjustment among the high-income countries alone, we notice that some countries, such as Australia and the United Kingdom, already had sizable current account deficits of $41 billion and $80 billion, respectively, in 2006. How much bigger these could become must be open to question. Moreover, Japan seems to have a structural savings surplus, as Richard Cooper of Harvard University has argued.[6]

Meanwhile, as is shown in Figure 6.4, the European economy already contains huge internal divergences. A large external adjustment, triggered by a big appreciation of the euro, would put substantial pressure on relationships within the European economy and particularly inside the Euro-

Figure 6.3 Current Account Balances of High-Income Countries, 2006

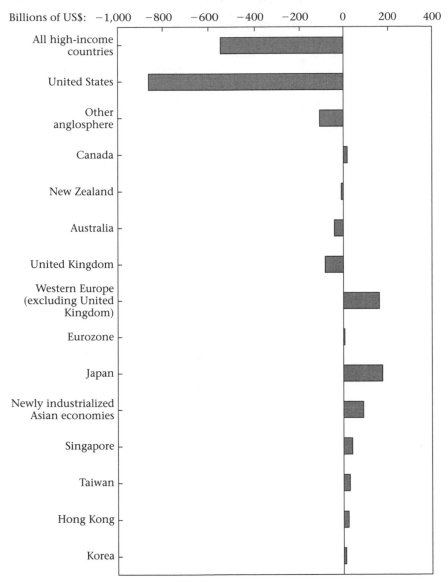

Source: International Monetary Fund, *World Economic Outlook,* April 2007, and Organisation for Economic Co-operation and Development, *Economic Outlook,* June 2007.

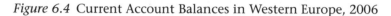

Figure 6.4 Current Account Balances in Western Europe, 2006

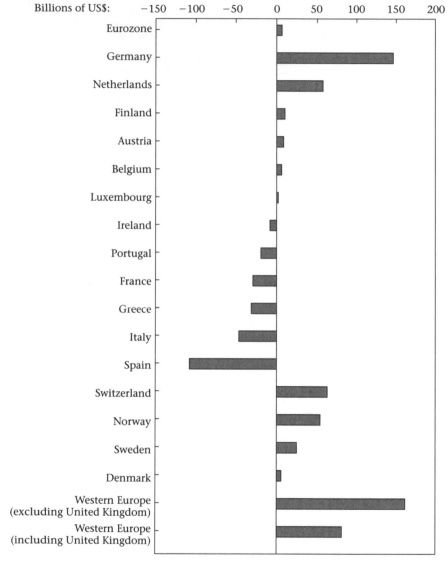

Source: Organisation for Economic Co-operation and Development, *Economic Outlook,* June 2007.

zone. It is hard to imagine a further increase in the current account deficit of Spain, which was already 9 percent of GDP in 2006. Big countries like France and Italy could run bigger deficits. But any large increase in the current account deficit of the Eurozone as a whole would presumably require a significant shift in Germany's current account surplus.

This would not happen easily. If the mechanism were to be a big appreciation of the euro combined with an offsetting relaxation of European Central Bank monetary policy, it is more likely that Germany would go into recession than that demand would strengthen and the current account surplus diminish. Germany's household spending seems to be highly interest inelastic (that is, unaffected by interest rates), while investment is strongly affected by the performance of exports. Meanwhile, its fiscal policy tends to be conservative. There is little likelihood that, under normal circumstances, strong German demand would deliver a big fall in its current account surplus in the context of a large loss of external competitiveness.

Thus any manageable global adjustment—one that retained an open world economy—would have to include shifts in the external positions of emerging market economies, particularly the oil exporters and the East Asians. As Figure 6.5 shows, this is where the big current account surpluses are. That has indeed been the premise of the IMF's "multilateral consultation on global imbalances," which has included China, the Eurozone, Japan, Saudi Arabia, and the United States. (Yet neither China nor Saudi Arabia is able to speak for other emerging countries.)[7]

Examination of the "dollar bloc" as a whole underlines the role of emerging economies in global adjustment. Figure 6.6 shows the current accounts and reserve holdings of the significant economies whose currencies are either pegged to the dollar or more or less actively managed against it (a group that includes Japan). The bloc as a whole is close to current account balance, with huge surpluses elsewhere offsetting the huge U.S. deficit. The bloc owned almost $4 trillion in reserves by the end of 2006— $3.786 trillion, to be precise, or three-quarters of the global total. Most of this vast total was accumulated in the 2000s, to keep currencies down against the dollar.

The figure has three important implications. First, internal "recycling" of current account surpluses within the dollar bloc can be perfect. The area is not dependent on any outside funding. Second, if anybody tries to take money out of the United States and put it into the economies of other members of the bloc, the latter will send much of it back to the United States as official reserves. Provided the members of the bloc are prepared to do this, the bloc can survive, and the peripheral members can hold the dollar up against their currencies. (Because they are not prepared to do so without limit, some of the member currencies have in fact moved upward

Figure 6.5 Current Account Balances in the Emerging Economies, 2006

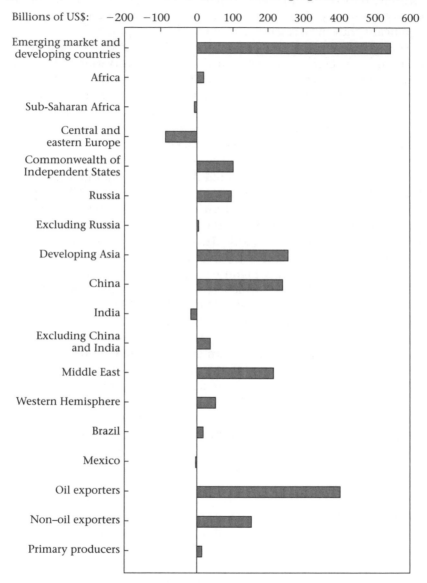

Source: International Monetary Fund, *World Economic Outlook,* April 2007.

Figure 6.6 Current Accounts and Reserves of the "Dollar Bloc"

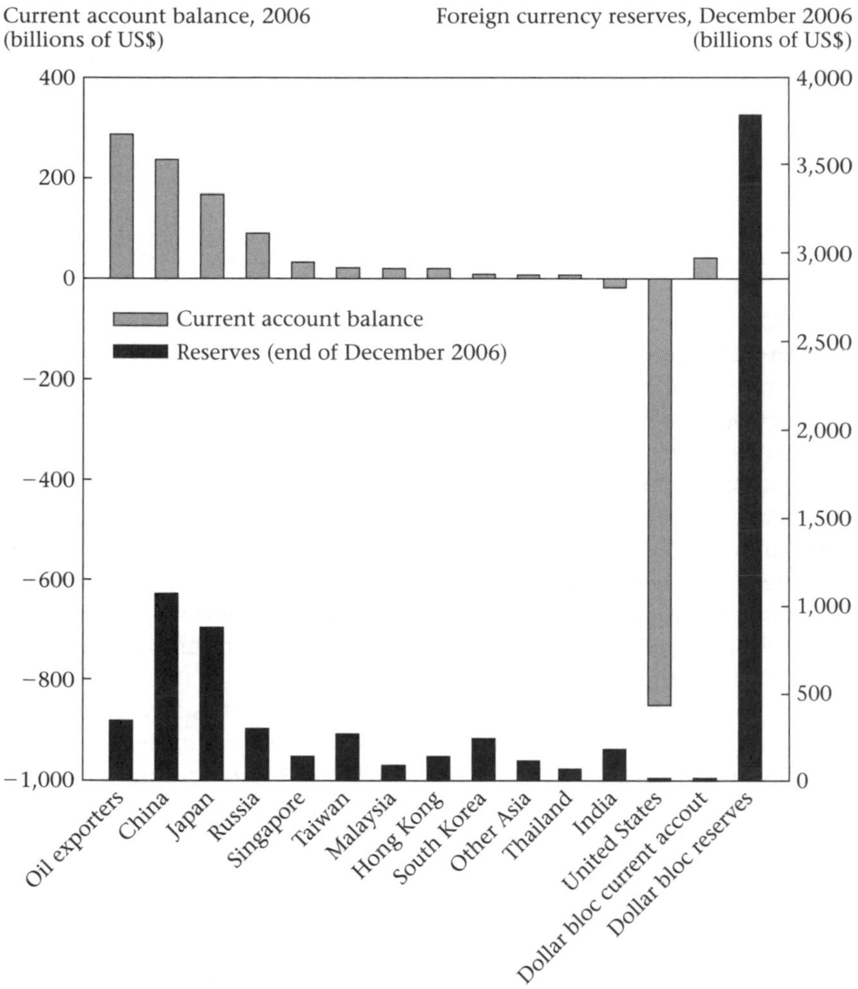

Current account balance, 2006
(billions of US$)

Foreign currency reserves, December 2006
(billions of US$)

Source: International Monetary Fund.

somewhat; see Figure 4.26.) Finally, because of this intrabloc recycling, the dollar moves down against the floating currencies only when people want to shift money out of the United States into these currencies. But then not only the dollar but all the dollar bloc currencies will fall against the floating currencies, with painful and unpopular consequences in the latter.

Of the two most significant groups, the oil exporters are most likely to see their surpluses fall, unless oil prices jump upward again. If oil prices stay where they are, pressures for additional spending are likely to prove overwhelming, particularly in relatively populous oil exporters, a category that would include Saudi Arabia. If oil prices fall, their surpluses will dwindle automatically. In any case, since oil exporters are losing a nonrenewable resource, it makes good sense for them to save a considerable proportion of the revenue they gain, thereby switching one asset for another. What matters for them is gaining the best possible blend of risk and return on these assets.

In Asia the dominant player is China, which is running the world's largest and most rapidly rising current account surplus. A large reduction in this surplus certainly does not guarantee an equal reduction in the U.S. deficit. On the contrary, it is likely to be spread across the world. If the Chinese surplus were to shrink by $200 billion and the U.S. deficit were to shrink in proportion to its share in the rest of the world's economy, the reduction would be about $60 billion. But it is also hard to imagine any plausible global rebalancing that does not include a substantial reduction in the Chinese surplus.

Now suppose China did begin to act in this way. Suppose that other Asian countries followed its exchange rate lead. Suppose as well that the Japanese yen's weakness at least halted as the risks of investing abroad became more obvious to the Japanese people. Suppose too that the savings surpluses of the oil exporters began to dwindle. What might this mean for the global adjustment process?

One would have to imagine a rise in real interest rates as surplus savings started to be absorbed at home. This would automatically tend to cut spending in the United States, particularly by the increasingly exposed household sector. It would be natural for the Federal Reserve to cut short-term interest rates as well. This might further weaken the dollar, allowing needed switching of expenditures. In such a context, with everybody contributing, one could envisage a gradual reduction of the U.S. current account deficit as a share of GDP, not to zero but perhaps to 3–4 percent of GDP, at which level it would comfortably offset the structural savings surpluses of some of the other high-income countries. Tighter fiscal policy in the United States would increase the room for adjustment. This is certainly not a plan for a globally coordinated response. That would be insane. But this is at least an imaginable path. It is one that would happen more or less automatically, without serious risk of a significant global slowdown, provided action began with more spending in the surplus countries, to which the United States was forced to respond, rather than the other way around.

If we consider any such adjustment process, three important points emerge. The first aspect of any such scenario for depreciation is that a huge part of the adjustment would result from changes in the country's net assets and net income from investment. Thus, "even with a balanced current account the U.S. would continue to run an overall trade deficit in 2012 under all scenarios. This would be composed of a $720 billion deficit in merchandise and $430 billion surplus in services." So how could the United States have a current account balance? The answer would be a huge improvement in net income from capital, resulting from a transformation of the country's net foreign asset position. This would come about because of a revaluation of U.S. liabilities, denominated in dollars, relative to assets, denominated in foreign currencies or in real terms (such as equities). This in turn would trigger a corresponding revaluation of income receipts relative to payments. According to the McKinsey Global Institute, "the U.S. net foreign debt position would swing from a projected negative $8.1 trillion in 2012 to a positive $4.9 trillion at the same point. Instead of being a large net debtor to the tune of 46 percent of GDP, the U.S. would instead be a significant net creditor equal to 28 percent of GDP. In addition we assume that the positive spread between the interest that the U.S. earned on its foreign assets versus liabilities in 2006—which is lower than the 15-year average—will continue. As a result U.S. net foreign income would turn positive, growing to some $435 billion per year by 2012."[8]

The gains of the United States would be the losses of its creditors, in terms of their home currencies. Since the shift in the U.S. asset position would be $13 trillion, this would in effect be the biggest default in the history of the world—equal to perhaps a quarter of the rest of the world's GDP at that time. This is taking the notion of "exorbitant privilege" to heights previously undreamed of. The risk is that such an outcome would destroy confidence in the dollar and generate a huge shift from dollar-denominated assets to assets denominated in other convertible currencies, particularly the euro. Dollar interest rates might also soar, creating a major challenge for U.S. monetary policy. Indeed the Federal Reserve would have to act to sustain foreign confidence in the U.S. dollar if it wanted to prevent a run. This could lead to a head-on clash with lawmakers in Washington, and the Federal Reserve might find its freedom of maneuver limited. Such severe dollar weakness combined with the enormous U.S. liability position could result in a rerun of the 1970s. Thus, as noted previously, the very thing that makes a huge net liability position relatively safe for the United States makes it relatively unsafe for its creditors. This has the potential to inject significant instability into the world economy.

The second aspect of adjustment is that it would indeed have to be broadly shared, as the analysis by Obstfeld and Rogoff suggests. If there were to be a large nominal depreciation of the U.S. dollar, it would, suggests the McKinsey Global Institute, indeed help bring about a big reduction in the current account deficit. The McKinsey study finds that "the dollar would need to depreciate on a trade-weighted basis by 30 percent from its level in January 2007 if the U.S. current account deficit were to close by 2012. . . . Although very large, the magnitude of this change is in line with the findings of other economists."[9] If the deficit were to shrink to 3 percent of GDP, the dollar would need to fall by 23 percent, adds the study. But since the dollar was already 5 percent below its post-1970 average, such declines would bring it to an all-time low. This would be highly disruptive for other economies. The needed fall against the floating currencies would be particularly large if the Asians did not participate: to eliminate the U.S. current account deficit, for example, the dollar's depreciation against the euro would be 40 percent, which would raise the value of a euro to well over $2.00—a level at which the Eurozone would certainly be in a state of panic! That merely underlines the need for a broadly shared adjustment.[10]

The third point is that any adjustment process in trade itself (as opposed to changes in valuation) requires the rest of the world to generate more rapid growth of purchases, or demand, than of output. If the world economy is to grow satisfactorily, demand needs to grow faster than potential output. Some countries now in surplus would find themselves moving into deficit. The natural countries to run such deficits are fast-growing ones with vast opportunities and huge inflows of FDI, because FDI is a fairly risk-free way of financing a current account deficit. In other words, they are big and successful emerging market countries, such as China. Moreover, now that these countries possess enormous cushions of foreign-currency reserves, they could run current account deficits safely, particularly if these were financed by FDI. But this raises the big policy issue: is it possible to persuade emerging market economies that they might become net borrowers again, without risking a relapse into crises? The preconditions for such a shift are the focus of the rest of this chapter, starting with reform in the emerging market economies themselves.

Reform in Emerging Market Economies

What reforms would be needed in emerging market economies if some of the larger ones were willing and able to become substantial net borrowers once again? The scope of this question is huge. This discussion will focus on just three reforms: a simple recognition of the limits of export-led growth, reform of the financial sector (a discussion that will bring us back to the themes of Chapter 2), and reforms in macroeconomic policies, including exchange rate regimes, monetary arrangements, and fiscal policy.

Limits of Export-Led Growth: The Case of China

China's development path, though unique in some respects, is also similar to that of other Asian economies with abundant supplies of labor, such as Japan. But, for its size, the country is remarkably open to trade: the ratio of trade to GDP (measured at market prices) is not much below that of South Korea—a country with 4 percent of China's population. China is also running extraordinarily large current account surpluses as a share of GDP. Interestingly the Chinese leadership itself has come to recognize the limits of this approach to development.

As far back as December 2004, at the annual Central Economic Work Conference, China's leadership agreed to rebalance its growth strategy away from investment and exports and toward domestic consumption.[11] In July 2005 the exchange rate regime was altered in the direction of greater flexibility. But the simple truth is that since then very little has happened, in either direction. Figure 6.7 charts the exchange rate.

As Nicholas Lardy of the Peterson Institute for International Economics puts it, "at least through early 2007 China's policy initiatives have been relatively modest, with only a slight change in China's underlying growth dynamic."[12] He is being generous in his assessment. The truth is that developments have been strongly in the opposite direction. The current account surplus is exploding upward: in the *World Economic Outlook* of April 2007, it was forecast by the IMF to reach 10 percent of GDP in 2007, bringing the basic balance (the sum of the current account and net long-term capital inflow) to at least 12 percent of GDP. In 2006 the increase in net exports generated between a fifth and a quarter of China's growth, which is greater than ever before. China's national savings rate reached close to 60 percent of GDP in 2006, while its investment rate reached 50 percent of GDP. These are the highest rates ever achieved, let alone by such a big economy. Correspondingly, household consumption is less than 40 percent of GDP and is declining as a share of GDP. Together with the rise in net exports, the increase in investment generated most of the rise in demand.

The case for the shift in strategy was strong. There is substantial evidence that the high-investment, high-growth, high-export strategy is creating huge domestic and international problems. At home this capital-intensive pattern of growth is leading to more inefficient use of resources, which is demonstrated by the rising incremental capital output ratio. I myself have noted that the surprising thing about China's growth is how slow it is, given the incredible rate of investment.[13] Excess capacity is a pandemic: by 2005, to take just one egregious example, excess capacity in China's steel production was 120 million tons a year—greater than the en-

Figure 6.7 China's Modestly Flexible Peg

Renminbi to the dollar

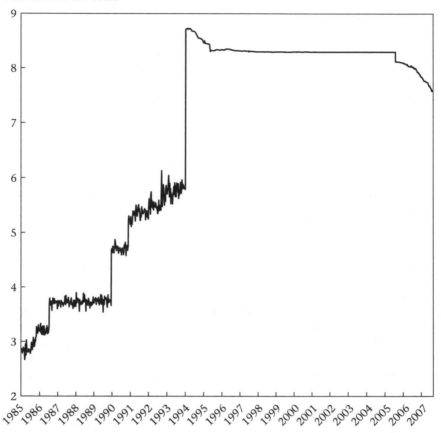

Source: Thomson Datastream.

tire output of Japan, the world's second largest producer. Employment growth is slowing: between 1993 and 2004, it was only 1 percent a year. Pollution has become a huge, even life-threatening, problem. The energy intensity of the economy has also been rising, not falling, despite increased energy efficiency within individual sectors, because of the economy's shift in a more capital-intensive direction. China is already the world's second largest emitter of greenhouse gases and could soon become the largest, because of its heavy reliance on coal. Inequality is also rising rapidly, partly because economic growth is so heavily concentrated on the coast and employment growth is so low. Furthermore, the huge growth in investment is threatening another round of nonperforming loans in the banking system.[14]

Difficulties are also arising in China's international relations. The exploding current account and bilateral surpluses with the United States, combined with the very modest movement in the exchange rate, act like a red flag to the U.S. Congress's bull (Figure 6.8). The probability that an unprecedentedly protectionist U.S. administration will emerge after 2008 is strong. Should the United States go in this direction, the Europeans will, alas, be only too happy to follow. The risk of a breakdown in the open global trading system is substantial, since the willingness of the incumbent powers to keep their economies open to the disruptive exports of the rising power must be in question. In the end, however beneficent "Bretton Woods Two" may be for China, the country is simply too large to follow the development path of a South Korea or even a Japan.

Assume, for example, that China's economy continued to grow at 10 percent a year; its investment rate fell modestly, to, say, 45 percent of GDP; and its savings rate remained at 60 percent of GDP. Then China's current account surplus in 2012 could be close to $700 billion in today's dollars, 15 percent of GDP at that time. If one also assumes that the current account surplus were to rise smoothly from 2007's 10 percent of GDP to 15 percent in 2012 (as the gap between savings and investment rises), the net inflow of FDI remained $60 billion a year (a conservative assumption), and there were no speculative net capital inflow (despite the likelihood of a massive appreciation of the renminbi), then by 2012 China's foreign exchange reserves would be well over $4 trillion (in 2007 dollars), close to that year's GDP (Figure 6.9). Even if the current account surplus were to remain at 10 percent of GDP, it would be quite close to $500 billion by 2012, and reserves would have reached $3.7 trillion. Anything is possible. But it is hard to imagine any of this happening without a global explosion.

It is also in China's own interests to prevent this from happening.[15] It is hard to imagine that what is still a poor country—with a GDP per capita, at purchasing power parity, of $6,600 in 2005 (about a sixth of U.S. levels), significant levels of internal inequality, and a huge number of impoverished people—should be postponing so much of its consumption to what is expected to be a far richer future. Lardy notes, for example, that, while China's GDP per capita was two and a half times that of India in 2004, its consumption per capita was only two-thirds higher. It is still harder to believe that it makes sense for this country to lend so much money abroad at what are low nominal returns, in dollars, and will ultimately prove to be negative real returns, once one allows for the virtually certain appreciation of the real exchange rate. Indeed it is something of a surprise that such an appreciation has not yet happened, through either a nominal

Figure 6.8 U.S. Bilateral Trade with China

Trillions of US$

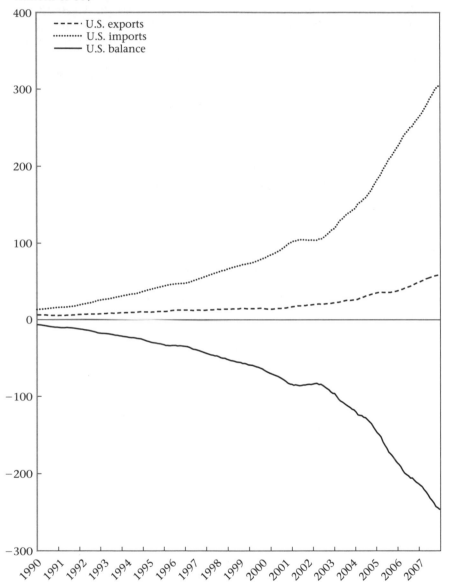

Source: U.S. Bureau of Economic Analysis.
Note: Values are for previous twelve months.

Figure 6.9 A Possible Path for China's Current Account and
Foreign-Currency Reserves

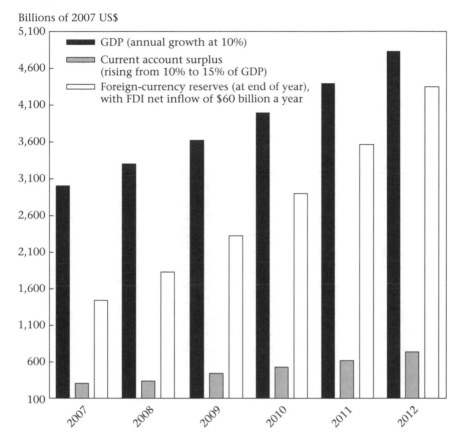

Billions of 2007 US$

Source: Author's calculations.

appreciation or higher inflation. It is equally hard to imagine that it makes
sense to pursue a domestically costly strategy that risks creating huge ten-
sions abroad. For all these reasons a shift in strategy is indeed justified,
as the Chinese leadership recognizes. Unfortunately nothing effective is
happening.

What should be done? The key is expanding demand, relative to supply, with a focus on public and private consumption. The exchange rate
should be allowed to rise to the extent needed to curb inflation. If this were
done, Ronald McKinnon's fears about deflation would automatically disappear. This policy would recommend the fundamental truth that changes

in external balance depend, in the first place, on shifts in demand relative to supply, with changes in real exchange rates eliminating excess demand (or excess supply, in the case of a country with an initial current account deficit).

Obvious modifications in public policy would include increased spending on health, education, and rural infrastructure and the creation of a reliable and credible safety net, particularly for the elderly. These would involve direct spending by government and increase the incentive for households to lower their precautionary savings (currently about a quarter of disposable income). The government could also tax enterprises more heavily, thereby forcing them to go to the financial markets and so increasing their exposure to market discipline. This should also lower corporate savings. The proceeds should then be fully spent by the government or used to lower other taxes. The exchange rate should be made somewhat more flexible. The move to greater flexibility should be accompanied by gradual liberalization of capital outflow and accelerated liberalization of imports. These changes would reduce substantially the needed currency appreciation. These requirements are all well known. What is needed is more action.[16]

It is not hard to understand why the Chinese government has been more prepared to talk about what it needs to do than to do it. It is obviously hard to put at risk a policy that, albeit imperfect in many respects, is at least generating rapid growth and reasonable macroeconomic stability. But the leadership should also be aware of the risks it is running, both domestically and internationally, and avoid waiting until it may be too late for a shift in policy. In particular the explosive increases in investment and net exports in the mid-2000s must be worrying to China's leaders, since these take the country's economy into uncharted waters.

Financial Reform

Let us start by imagining that the significant emerging economies, including China, agree that their foreign-currency reserves provide adequate insurance. So they are prepared to consider running current account deficits. How should they do so?

The starting point has to be liberalization of those inflows that create relatively small risks of instability or even crisis. The least risky, from this point of view, is FDI. Once a foreign investor has made its investment, it is more or less captured. The investment is illiquid in any case. Even if it could be liquidated in a crisis, it would probably be liquidated at a much reduced price and in domestic currency. Thus, at the very least, the foreign investor would share the losses inflicted on the recipient country in such a crisis.

The second least risky form of finance is portfolio equity. While such investments are generally far more liquid than FDI, they share the latter's other characteristics: in a crisis the investor automatically shares the losses, as both the equity market and (normally) the exchange rate tumble.

The third least risky form of finance, from the point of view of the recipient country, is domestic-currency bonds with relatively long maturities. While most bonds have fixed nominal coupons, the value of the bonds is fixed in domestic, rather than foreign, currency. The great advantage of such bonds is that they eliminate the dire consequences of currency mismatches when the currency is forced to devalue. Indeed the big difference between currency crises in high-income economies and those in most emerging economies is the absence of currency mismatches in the former. If a country with large gross foreign-currency liabilities devalues, the debt burden will jump at once. If many private nonfinancial companies or banks have such liabilities, they are also likely to suffer mass bankruptcy, as happened during the Asian financial crisis.[17] This danger is limited only if the country or companies are able to match their foreign-currency liabilities with foreign-currency assets, or at least if they have very large foreign-currency earnings.

In contrast to the historic position of most emerging economies, the debt liabilities of the United States are denominated in its own currency. When the dollar falls, there are no adverse balance sheet effects. On the contrary, balance sheet effects are strongly positive in this case, as has already been noted, because Americans own large quantities of foreign-currency-denominated assets, including foreign real assets. The same is true for the other high-income countries, to a greater or lesser extent.

Thus if a country is to finance itself abroad, it should do so via either equity or bonds denominated in the domestic currency. Foreign-currency debt is dangerous, and short-term foreign-currency debt, given the risks of "sudden stops" (or more precisely a sudden bout of market illiquidity), most dangerous of all. The only circumstance under which foreign-currency debt makes sense is if the currency is credibly pegged to another one. In practice that situation seems hard to achieve. Hong Kong has sustained its currency board with the dollar since 1982. But that is an exception. Actual adoption of the other currency as one's own seems to be necessary to make such a link work. Even Argentina's one-to-one link between the peso and the dollar failed.

As long as we live in a multicurrency world, each country does best to borrow in its own currency, thereby eliminating the risk of significant currency mismatches. This fundamental distinction between the so-called "first globalization" of the industrial era, the period between 1870 and 1914, and the past three decades was essentially missed. For a long time policy makers took a relatively relaxed view of the widespread practice of issuing dollar-denominated debt, despite the crises that followed. That was a grave error. Arguably the biggest single policy difference between the two eras—one that is also a political difference—is that the first globalization was the epoch of the gold standard, while the second was the epoch of adjustable exchange rates. Under adjustable exchange rates, the only safe way to borrow is in one's own currency. If that is impossible, borrowing must be limited.

Fortunately emerging market economies have made substantial progress in developing local-currency bond markets, based on an important study published by the Bank for International Settlements in 2007.[18] The evidence is that a country must first establish a market that the local citizenry trusts; then foreigners will join in. The logic here seems obvious. Domestic residents are normally better informed about their own country than outsiders. If the former are unwilling to lend to their own government in the currency it issues, they are sending an important signal. Conversely, if a large domestic debt market develops, residents are indicating a reasonable level of confidence.

At the end of 2005 the total value of outstanding emerging country bonds issued domestically and overwhelmingly denominated in domestic currencies was $3.515 trillion (Figure 6.10).[19] This was a big increase from the total value of $1.681 trillion in 2000. But the total value of bonds issued internationally by emerging countries was only $618 billion in 2005, up from $498 billion in 2000. Thus the outstanding stock of domestic bonds not only was much larger but also grew far faster than that of international bonds. Three-quarters of the domestic bonds outstanding in 2000 were public. Asian economies were the largest issuers, with $1.69 trillion outstanding at the end of 2005, followed by Latin America, with $872 billion. The largest individual issuers were South Korea ($499 billion of public bonds and $289 billion of private bonds), Brazil ($390 billion and $36 billion), China ($361 billion and $266 billion), India ($216 billion public), Mexico ($122 billion and $86 billion), and Turkey ($185 billion public).

There is also substantial international issuance of emerging country bonds in local currencies. According to the study by the Bank for International Settlements, the total outstanding reached $69 billion at the end of 2005 and $102 billion at the end of 2006. The biggest issuer was South Africa, with $23 billion outstanding in rand. Also significant were the Czech Republic with $12 billion in domestic-currency bonds outstanding, Brazil with $10.7 billion, Mexico with $9.9 billion, and Turkey with $9.5 billion.

The development of healthy domestic-currency bond markets, both public and private, is a necessary—and significant—step toward a health-

Figure 6.10 Emerging Market Bonds Outstanding

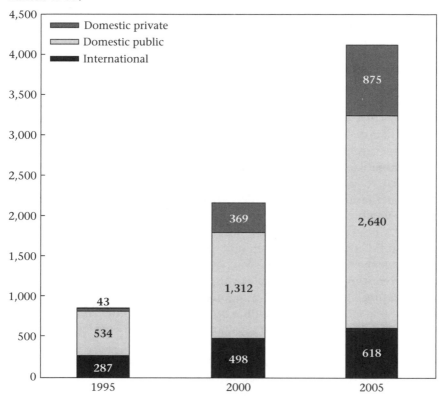

Billions of US$

Source: Bank for International Settlements (2007).

ier global financial system. The next step is to increase access by foreign investors to these markets. It is evident that there is substantial interest on the part of investors, because of the relatively high interest rates offered and because these markets provide diversification for bond portfolios. The underlying logic here seems evident: Wall Street can readily create baskets with bonds denominated in every currency in the world. It can diversify its risks. Debtors cannot diversify their risks in the same way because, if they borrow overwhelmingly in dollars, the dollar exchange rate becomes a source of systemic risk for the entire economy. Hedging may be too expensive or even impossible in their currencies. But investors are readily able to hedge against such risks through the simple process of diversification, without relying on complex derivative products. Thus a world in which countries borrow in their own currencies and investors hold diversified portfolios of bonds is likely to be far more stable than one in which countries borrow heavily in a foreign currency that their central banks are unable to issue and in which, as a result, their governments cannot operate as effective lenders of last resort.

Some economists have argued that this development is impossible. They have instead advanced the "original sin" hypothesis.[20] This is a good Catholic doctrine. The assumption underlying this hypothesis is that there is nothing emerging countries can do to create internationally credible domestic-currency bond markets. For this reason, the economists argue, an international solution is needed to persuade foreigners to invest in the domestic currencies of emerging economies.

Fortunately this hypothesis is at the least exaggerated, if not altogether unpersuasive. International action may accelerate the development of an active international market in emerging country domestic-currency bonds (a point to which I turn in the next chapter). But it is unnecessary for that purpose. Countries can do a great deal for themselves. If this development were indeed impossible, the present high-income countries would not have made the breakthrough. As Michael Bordo of Rutgers University notes in an interesting analysis of historical parallels to the present situation of the emerging countries, "what is required is the development of a domestic bond market, in turn based on a broad-based and efficient tax regime, combined with a sound banking system. These are the key elements to the creation of financial stability, which is crucial to reliable access to the world capital market."[21] This, he argues, is the foundation of country trust. In addition, "currency trust is based on the ability to adhere to a credible nominal anchor."

The hypothesis of original sin also suggests that international markets will never be interested in more than a small handful of emerging market currencies, since diversification would be achieved adequately without including the bonds of most emerging countries. This may be true, though financial markets happily cope with thousands of different equities, many of which are quite similar to those of other companies. But, for the purposes of the argument in this book, that restriction hardly matters. If the domestic-currency bonds of the larger emerging market countries were readily acceptable abroad, it would be possible for the world economy to be substantially better balanced than it has been. Nor does this seem intrinsically unlikely, since the larger emerging economies are sizable: China, India, Mexico, Brazil, Russia, Turkey, Indonesia, South Africa, Argentina, and Thailand are all surely large enough to attract substantial investor interest.

Yet evidently they have to be made reasonably attractive. Fortunately what makes them attractive to domestic investors is also likely to make them attractive to foreigners. The idea that resistance to holding the domestic-currency bonds of emerging countries is the product of an unbreakable intellectual prejudice is simply wrong. On the contrary, potential investors have had good reasons not to hold the liabilities of governments that they could not trust to keep their promises—or rather that they could trust not to keep their promises. The pressure to issue foreign-currency or index-linked debt was a direct consequence of this rational skepticism. This was not an irrational prejudice—as suggested by the hypothesis of an original sin from which external redemption is required—but an entirely rational "postjudice."

In 2005 46 percent of outstanding Latin American domestic bonds had floating interest rates, 23 percent were inflation-indexed, and 5 percent were foreign-currency-denominated, leaving just 23 percent for straight fixed-rate bonds.[22] But 91 percent of the bonds issued by the emerging Asian countries were straight fixed-rate domestic-currency bonds. This is exactly what the respective histories of inflation would lead one to expect. This is not a case of original sin, but of the wages of sin. This is not to suggest that the legacy of past mistakes is not an enduring one. But that is a long way from concluding that there is nothing countries can do to develop deep, liquid, and reasonably safe domestic financial markets, with substantial domestic-currency bond offerings, in which foreigners can invest with some feeling of safety.

So what must these relatively advanced and sophisticated emerging countries do to establish the markets they need and so ultimately the reputations they hope to deserve? They need to create an environment of credible macroeconomic stability. That is the subject of the next section. But they also need to create a healthy financial sector, while recognizing, as recent experience in the U.S. demonstrates and the arguments in Chapter 2 explain, that they will never succeed in eliminating crises. The fragility of finance is ineradicable.

What is involved in creating a healthy, domestic-currency-based financial sector, apart from sound macroeconomic policies?

The necessary policies will have positive and negative elements. The positive elements include encouraging the emergence of long-term domestic investors, such as pension funds and insurance companies. This does not mean that these institutions should be forced to hold domestic-currency debt, since that is likely to weaken pressure for sound policies by the borrowers. It means that a group of investors will emerge that have a need for long-term domestic assets to match their long-term liabilities.[23] As they emerge and demand better transparency from borrowers (which should be supported by improvements in the regulatory regime), foreigners will become increasingly interested in the domestic markets, some of which—notably in China and India—seem bound to become of enormous size.

The negative elements include:

- direct regulation of currency mismatches, particularly in the banking system, for which the state always has some responsibility;
- insistence that financial institutions hold foreign-currency assets that match foreign-currency liabilities, in terms of currency composition, maturity, and liquidity (since in a foreign exchange crisis the domestic central bank will be unable to act as lender of last resort against a run on foreign-currency liabilities);
- insistence that banks regulate—or compensate in their own lending for—the foreign-currency position of their nonfinancial borrowers (this turned out to be an important source of weakness during the Asian financial crisis of 1997–98);
- assessment of the overall national balance sheet in terms of foreign-currency assets and liabilities (including derivatives) and consequent adjustment of holdings of official currency reserves in the light of changes in that balance sheet;
- maintenance of foreign-currency reserves at a level suitable at least to meet relatively short-term official liabilities; and
- encouragement, through regulation or taxes, of relatively long-term foreign-currency borrowing.[24]

An important step is defining precisely the assistance a government will give to an institution that falls into difficulty. If banks and other businesses confidently expect to be rescued from the consequences of their mistakes, they will have less of an incentive to act prudently. Of course, in the euphoria of the moment some may forget prudence because they are overwhelmed by greed. But others may be influenced by the perception of the risks they are running. Since governments will want to reward the latter for their good sense, it is even more important for them not to rescue the imprudent—and to make clear in advance that they have no intention of doing so.

An important issue is the role of direct controls on foreign-currency transactions. Since the vulnerability is created by borrowing rather than lending, it is there that such controls should be concentrated. Persistent controls on capital inflow do not create the disruptions to property rights that emergency controls on outflows in a crisis are sure to do. For this reason it makes sense to impose such controls while the financial system itself remains fragile and poorly managed: prevention is far better than an emergency cure. But emerging countries must also recognize that, as their econ-

Figure 6.11 Proportion of Developing Countries with Exchange Controls

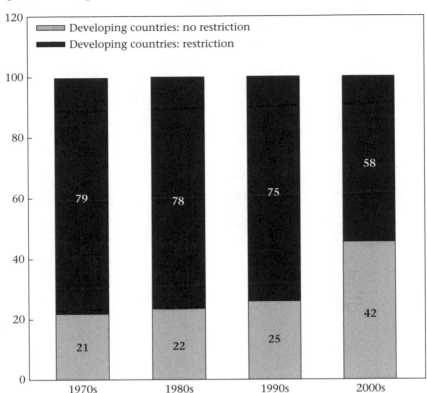

Source: International Monetary Fund, *World Economic Outlook,* April 2005.

omies become more open to trade and other forms of capital inflow (FDI and others), the effectiveness of controls on capital inflows is bound to decline. Capital controls are problematic, because they make intensive use of what most emerging markets lack: effective and honest government. They are also inevitably somewhat distorting. Taxation or special deposit requirements are probably the most effective and least damaging policy choice.

As Figure 6.11 shows, the proportion of developing countries with exchange controls is falling. India, for example, is now discussing getting rid of them. Here the developing countries are following the industrial countries, with a lag of about twenty-five years (Figure 6.12). So we are in a world that is moving away from exchange controls.

Needless to say, the effectiveness of specific regulatory interventions aimed at encouraging the development of a domestic-currency-based fi-

Figure 6.12 Proportion of Industrial Countries with Exchange Controls

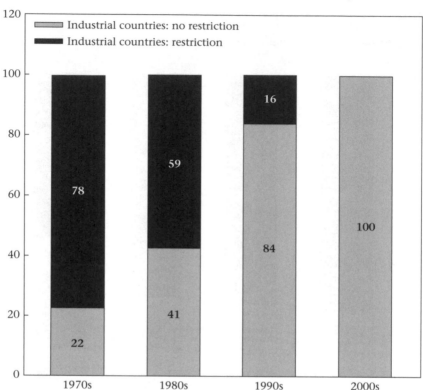

Source: International Monetary Fund, *World Economic Outlook*, April 2007.

nancial system depends on the creation of a sound financial system in the first place. The list of necessary features is well known: credible property rights; an effective bankruptcy regime; adequate capitalization; deposit guarantees sufficiently credible to reduce the risk of bank runs, but with precise limits, to contain the extent of moral hazard; transparent accounts, since no financial market can operate if people do not know the financial condition of companies; the entry of effective foreign competitors; and strong and independent regulation.

The political and technical difficulties of achieving all this are evident. But at least the more advanced emerging countries are now in a reasonable position to try—even if China cannot, under its present political dispensation, create regulators independent of the Communist Party. In all, much has been achieved since the crises of the late 1990s. Whether it is enough will not be known before the next test of the financial system. One will come, no doubt. The only question is when.

Macroeconomic Reform

A necessary condition for a sound financial system is macroeconomic stability. In particular, high and variable inflation, usually caused by fiscal profligacy, not only undermines the financial system but is the principal cause of reliance on lending in foreign currencies. Thus fiscal and monetary policy must be viewed together. This is particularly true in emerging countries, where, in the absence of deep bond markets and good external credit ratings, large fiscal deficits are likely to be monetized sooner rather than later: in the last (and sometimes even the first) resort, profligate governments borrow from the central bank.

The requirements of a sound fiscal policy are so simple in principle yet so difficult in practice. A government has to ensure solvency in the long run and flexibility in the short run. This means that there must be discipline over the fiscal positions of all layers of government at any one time and over all fiscal promises, actual and contingent, over time. Yet achieving these objectives is hard for all governments, since fiscal dishonesty can play so well at the polls or, in their absence, with a disenfranchised populace whose acquiescence needs to be bought.

It would be wrong to believe that high-income countries are necessarily superior to emerging countries in these respects. But their credit is better. Emerging countries also suffer from a number of handicaps: their economies tend to be more volatile and shock-prone, particularly if they are heavily reliant on a small number of commodity exports; they are likely to have particularly large contingent liabilities toward the financial system, as the evidence presented in Chapter 3 showed; and, it goes without saying, their ability to borrow abroad in a crisis is relatively limited. For all these reasons, emerging market governments need to be particularly cautious in what they regard as "normal" levels of indebtedness and deficits.

Emerging countries tend to borrow too much—that is, they run excessively large fiscal deficits, given the low confidence everyone (but particularly their own citizens) has in their determination to service their debts consistently, let alone repay them. Lengthy histories of borrowing too much in response to populist pressures in countries with weak institutions, and so of defaulting too often (usually via domestic inflation), drive governments into bouts of external borrowing (when markets are open), domestic borrowing denominated in foreign currencies, index-linked borrowing, short-term borrowing, and outright dollarization.[25]

All these developments constrain the governments' freedom in crises and so increase the likelihood of further defaults. This can easily become a vicious circle. Governments spend years trying to rebuild their credit only to have it destroyed again, almost overnight.

What can governments do to tie their hands? They can try to make their fiscal position as transparent as possible. They can also introduce a fiscal policy framework that sets down the rules they intend to follow. Such frameworks have become increasingly popular in recent years, as governments have become persuaded of the dangers, in terms of loss of credibility and predictability, of maintaining the maximum amount of discretion. But rules are only convincing if they are followed. Nor do rules help to increase credibility if sticking to them becomes itself incredible. Ultimately rules cannot dictate to politics unless they are themselves internalized within the body politic.

The monetary requirement for a stable domestic financial system is credibly low inflation. One of the most remarkable phenomena of the past decade and a half has been the emergence of low inflation throughout the developing world. This is part of a global—and as yet not fully understood—move to low inflation.

The first condition for maintaining such low and stable inflation is fiscal discipline. In the absence of such discipline, the temptation to debauch the currency is great. While it is possible to adopt a monetary constitution with a view to eliminating the risk of debauching the currency—notably by adopting another country's currency as one's own—the country then risks fiscal default and financial collapse. Under such circumstances the likelihood of reintroducing some sort of domestic money is high. Nevertheless, a small, open country that not only does a great deal of trade with a far bigger one, but also has weak domestic institutions, may consider adoption of the latter's currency as its own, despite the costs of forgone seignorage (namely the ability to supply domestic cash at zero cost) and the risks of severe fiscal crises.

At present a worldwide move toward abandonment of national currencies seems a remote possibility, other than in the exceptional situation of the European monetary union, which is as much a political as an economic project. Relatively sophisticated and large countries should consider adopting an inflation target with an independent central bank. This structure has become increasingly common in the developing world in recent years. It implies a fully floating currency, however, and thus abandonment of attempts at targeting nominal or real exchange rates.

While developing countries have in general moved toward more flexible exchange rates over the past decade and a half, relatively few have given up intervention altogether. This "fear of floating" is driven by the combination of foreign-currency liabilities, fear of reliance on sizable capital inflows, desire to preserve export competitiveness, and desire to accumulate foreign-currency reserves for prudential reasons.[26]

The predominant regime is managed floating. Such a regime is manageable, though it prevents assignment of monetary policy to an independent inflation-targeting central bank. It is possible to target the real exchange rate at a highly "competitive" level, provided it proves feasible to sterilize the monetary impact. This policy does create distortions, but it reduces some risks. Now that many countries have accumulated substantial foreign-currency reserves, less management and more floating would generally make sense. A policy of heavily subsidized export-led growth (subsidized via accumulation of overpriced foreign currency) is decreasingly reasonable for the emerging countries, particularly for very large ones. Such a shift toward more flexible exchange rates would make even more sense if borrowing in domestic currencies were feasible. Fortunately a floating exchange rate encourages domestic businesses and banks to borrow in the domestic currency, as a simple way of reducing foreign-currency risk.

So most countries are likely to move toward greater flexibility, with a few experimenting with outright abandonment of the domestic currency instead. Currency boards are also effective, in those cases in which a country can generate a credible commitment. Possession of a highly flexible economy, like that of Hong Kong, or an economy heavily intertwined with another much bigger one, like that of Estonia, makes a currency board workable. But it is important to recognize a fundamental fact about a hard peg or outright dollarization or euroization: it does not mean that the currency ceases to float. In a world in which the big currencies continue to float anyway, fixing to another currency merely determines *how* one's own currency is going to float.

Significant risks arise if one chooses the wrong anchor. Argentina, for example, had a relatively closed economy with low trade ratios, and within that its exposure to trade with the United States was modest. It also had a relatively inflexible labor market and chronic fiscal indiscipline. The combination made the convertibility law of the 1990s immensely vulnerable to untoward movement in the dollar's exchange rate against other currencies. As it was, Argentina's peg might have worked if it could have held on for another few years, as the dollar depreciated. But it could not hold on—and so the peg did not work.

An alternative is regional pegging on a core currency within a more general float. That is what happened in Europe during the era of the European Monetary System. The Americas have a natural anchor currency in the dollar. In East Asia, however, no dominant currency exists, with the dollar, renminbi, and yen all important. The likelihood is a shift from targeting of the dollar to targeting of the renminbi. That should happen automatically over the next one or two decades, provided China abolishes exchange controls. A de facto currency area is then likely to emerge in that region, focused on the renminbi. But first the renminbi would need to become more flexible. At present both the yen and the renminbi are instead targeted toward the dollar, making the dollar the region's anchor currency.

Yet another alternative is the adoption of formal currency baskets. A joint float would then be possible if a number of countries chose the same basket. This too seems to be a possible outcome in East Asia, instead of targeting on the renminbi.

One feature is shared by all of these arrangements, which makes movements against other currencies likely: the need to avoid large currency mismatches. Thus whether it is a free float, a managed float, fairly tight pegging to a specific anchor, loose pegging against such an anchor, or pegging against a currency basket, and whether the currency regime is national or regional, it is essential to develop a vibrant domestic financial system in which large-scale borrowing is possible in the domestic currency at long maturities and moderate interest rates. This requirement may be forgone only if monetary autonomy is abandoned altogether in a monetary union or through adoption of another currency. Furthermore, borrowing in the domestic currency must apply to foreign borrowing as much as to domestic borrowing. While that cannot make international finance safe, it can at least make it safer. It is the only imaginable way forward for a world that wants to avoid both the emerging market financial crises of the past and the excessive reliance on borrowing by the United States and a few other high-income countries of the present.

Yet not everything can be achieved domestically. If emerging countries are to receive net capital inflows safely, there should also be global reforms.

CHAPTER 7

Toward Global Reform

Do we need an IMF? Is there a role for a multilateral institution in the management of the international monetary system? If so, what is it?

MERVYN KING, GOVERNOR OF THE BANK OF ENGLAND

CREATING A FINANCIAL SYSTEM that allows the global economy to
function reasonably smoothly is primarily a task for individual countries.
Now that emerging market countries have greatly strengthened themselves after the crises of the 1990s and the United States has reached
its limits as the world's predominant net borrower, the task has become
more urgent. The most critical reforms are those at the country level, as
discussed in Chapter 6, above all the development of domestic-currency-
denominated markets in which foreigners are able to participate.

What changes are required at the international level? The discussion in
this chapter focuses on four areas: the prospects for a global monetary system, reform of global finance, reform of international financial institutions
and above all of the International Monetary Fund, and reform of informal
groups, such as the Group of Seven leading high-income countries (G-7)
and the Group of Twenty (G-20), which includes leading emerging countries and some additional high-income countries. In this discussion the focus is on how to create the conditions for a better-balanced world economy
with fewer financial crises. The dominant theme remains the need to nur-
ture a wider range of domestic currency markets in emerging countries, including bond markets, in which foreigners can invest and there is relative
safety for both the investors and the recipients of the funds.

A Global Monetary System

A fundamental assumption of the discussion in Chapter 6 is that flexible exchange rates and fiat money are here to stay.[1] A return to the gold standard is out of the question in the foreseeable future. So too is the creation of a global monetary union on the model of the European Union. While the present multicurrency era may prove a failure in the long term and the number of currencies may fall, as small countries adopt the currencies of bigger trading partners or form currency unions, the monetary environment is unlikely to be transformed within the next decade or two.

Floating rates among the big currencies are therefore here to stay, at least for a while. This has powerful implications. It means that global finance will continue to operate in a very different monetary context from that of the late nineteenth and early twentieth centuries. It also means that generating a sustained net flow of funds from rich countries to poor countries without a succession of massive financial crises is a significant challenge, for reasons discussed at length in previous chapters. Finally it means that currencies will often fluctuate wildly.

Reform of Global Finance

How then can we act at the global level to improve the workings of the financial system within this monetary context? To indicate how complicated this has become, consider the following list of bodies that have been actively engaged in the development of new codes and standards and in offering technical assistance: the IMF, the World Bank and the regional development banks, the Bank for International Settlements, the Basel Committee on Banking Supervision, the Financial Stability Forum, the International Organization of Securities Commissions on securities regulation, the International Association of Insurance Supervisors on insurance supervision, and the International Accounting Standards Board on accounting oversight. In principle, the promulgation of standards and codes should be a good thing. One can only hope that all of their work has borne some fruit.

Yet even the best-regulated systems can go off track during a mood of euphoria—one need only look at the combination of the so-called subprime crisis and the collapse of securitized lending in the United States. This experience shows that financial crises are inevitable. But it also shows that a crisis can be relatively manageable if both the assets and the liabilities are denominated in the currency of the afflicted country. Thus the most significant lessons of the crisis are the inevitability of financial irresponsibility and the importance of domestic-currency finance.

One interesting idea, promoted by those who endorse the concept of "original sin," is that the World Bank and the regional development banks —the so-called international financial institutions—could accelerate the use of the domestic currencies of emerging countries.[2] They propose the creation of an emerging market currency index, composed of an inflation-indexed basket of the currencies of twenty or so of the world's largest emerging countries. The World Bank and similar international organizations would issue debt denominated in this index. These institutions could achieve the currency matching they need by on-lending to the emerging countries in their own currencies. In the process the international financial institutions would create a market for the domestic-currency-denominated debt of emerging countries on which the private sector could build. The idea is intriguing. It certainly could do no harm to try it out, though the emerging countries do not need to wait for it to come to fruition before borrowing in their own currencies, as many have already begun to do.

Another possibility is to use international regulation to strengthen the development of domestic-currency finance in emerging countries. Anne Krueger, former first deputy managing director of the IMF, has argued that regulation can achieve this end. She has suggested that the G-7 should pass and enforce legislation requiring the financial institutions of its member countries to accept liabilities abroad only in the local currency of the borrower. The resultant foreign-currency risk should be hedged in international markets.[3] The proposal is radical. It is also attractive, even if it probably goes too far. Yet there is no good reason why emerging countries themselves should not enact such legislation for domestic transactions. In general, however, it is important that the regulatory framework for global financial institutions not create an incentive for them to lend only in their domestic currencies, since that is likely to lead to currency mismatches in borrowing countries.[4] This is most likely in the case of banks. Since banks have always proved to be the most dangerous source of cross-border finance, because their lending tends to be both short term and volatile, this is just another reason for borrowing countries to restrict access to international bank lending.

When she was at the IMF, Krueger proposed another idea worth considering: the sovereign debt restructuring mechanism (SDRM), an institutionalized way to restructure sovereign debt in the event of insolvency.[5] The SDRM was essentially to be an international bankruptcy procedure. The idea—which built on previous work by a number of leading economists, including Kenneth Rogoff of Harvard University (former chief economist at the IMF) and Jeffrey Sachs, now at Columbia University—has evident attractions, given the difficulties involved in negotiating debt restructuring where there are many creditors—a situation increasingly common in today's debt-dominated markets.[6] But experience with the Argentine default in the early 2000s has underlined the lesson that a determined sovereign is normally stronger than its creditors: there is little the latter can do to force debt service on a recalcitrant sovereign debtor, unless they have the assistance of a great power.

Walter Wriston, head of Citibank at the time of the Latin American debt crisis of the early 1980s, famously said that countries do not go bust. He was right. But they default: more than ninety have done so over the past two centuries.[7] So their creditors do go bust—again and again and again. What is needed is not to make default easier but to make it less credible, thereby lowering the default-risk premium in sovereign lending. This is where reliance on domestic-currency finance has considerable virtues, since countries usually find it particularly difficult to default outright to their own citizens. Exceptions do exist, of course, notably Russia after its devaluation of 1998. But even then the scale of domestic lending was modest and the default was consequently of minor impact. In retrospect the most valuable outcome of the debate on the SDRM was the move toward so-called collective action clauses in international lending, which facilitate debt negotiations by making it impossible for a small minority of creditors to prevent agreement.

Reform of International Financial Institutions

What can global institutions do? This discussion focuses on the four principal tasks of the IMF: technical assistance, surveillance, coordination, and crisis management. Associated with these are questions of institutional reform and representation.

Technical assistance is the simplest. In principle the availability to developing countries of a body of expertise on fiscal and monetary policy and the financial system is of great value, a classic public good. As officials and outside economists in emerging countries attain an ever-higher standard of professional training and expertise, this function becomes decreasingly important. But even the large emerging countries suffer from a shortage of the relevant skills, and thus technical assistance continues to be a valuable function of the IMF.

The IMF is also the body principally responsible for surveillance of macroeconomic, exchange rate, and financial policies. Rodrigo de Rato, the managing director from June 2004 to October 2007, stressed that improved surveillance was a central function of the IMF not only to avoid the problems we have seen in individual countries but, even more importantly, to address the systemic impact of those policies.[8] Such surveillance is in the form of both country analyses—so-called Article 4 consultations—and reports that examine the overall world economy, particularly the *World Economic Outlooks*. Exchange rate policy, by definition, affects more than one country. It is therefore particularly important for a respected global institution to focus on this topic.

Yet can the IMF be effective at surveillance? One must doubt it. As King notes, the organization needs, first of all, a legitimate managing director—one chosen by all the members, not one selected in a back room by the Europeans, who have a long-standing agreement with the United States that they are allowed to appoint the head of the IMF while the latter appoints the head of the World Bank. The IMF must also suffer less day-to-day interference from its resident board of midlevel officials—an outdated legacy of the days when communication with the field was slow and expensive. Above all, it is dominated by the developed countries who hold more than three-fifths of the votes, with the high-income members of the European Union holding 29.2 percent, the United States 16.8 percent, and Japan 6.0 percent (Figure 7.1). Belgium alone has a bigger voting share than India. Thus the organization is dominated by countries that will never borrow from it. It is inevitable that emerging countries are unwilling to trust themselves to the IMF's tender mercies.

King asks whether the IMF is living up to John Maynard Keynes's injunction that it engage in "ruthless truth-telling." He answers his own question by stating that this phrase does not "conjure up memories of any of the international meetings I have attended."[9] It is inevitable that the fund is unwilling to cross the will of the powerful countries that hold most of the votes. But if the IMF is far from fully effective at surveillance, it cannot do much about coordination of exchange rate and macroeconomic policies either. Its power is, after all, only that of persuasion. The countries that must cooperate cannot be coerced. They are not even inclined to listen to the IMF's feeble bleating.

Finally there is the question of the IMF's role as a crisis lender. At the end of 2007 the IMF had only one large borrower—Turkey—and the amount of outstanding credit on its balance sheet had shrunk to a mere $16.6 billion, down from $82 billion three years before (Figure 7.2). While the collapse in IMF lending is due to the shift in large current account deficits from emerging countries to a few developed countries, as discussed at length in this book, that is unlikely to be the end of the story. Sooner or later, deficits are likely to return to developing countries that do not have the capacity to issue internationally accepted currencies on an enormous scale. That, after all, has been the justification for the huge accumulations of foreign-currency reserves in recent years. For this reason there remains a strong case for pooling of reserves, rather than continued self-insurance

Figure 7.1 Shares of International Monetary Fund Votes

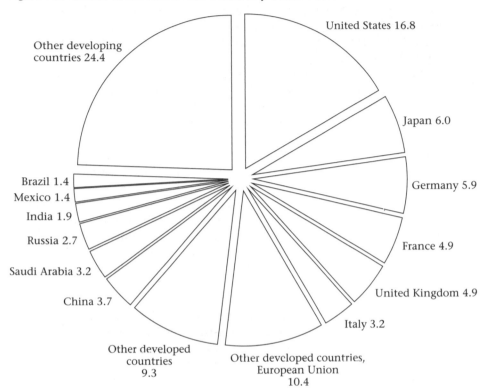

United States 16.8

Other developing countries 24.4

Japan 6.0

Germany 5.9

Brazil 1.4

Mexico 1.4

India 1.9

Russia 2.7

France 4.9

Saudi Arabia 3.2

United Kingdom 4.9

China 3.7

Italy 3.2

Other developed countries 9.3

Other developed countries, European Union 10.4

Source: International Monetary Fund.
Note: Values are percentages as of December 27, 2007.

on the present massive scale. At the end of 2007 countries held almost $6 trillion in reserves, which represents an immense transfer of resources to a few rich economies and predominantly the United States, since roughly two-thirds of all reserves still seem to be held in dollars.

Pooling of reserves would make much more sense, but it would work only if the IMF would lend freely in a crisis, without too much policy conditionality. At present potential borrowers do not trust the IMF to act effectively in this way, particularly given the domination of the institution by the United States and Europe. Furthermore, at about $340 billion at the end of 2007, the IMF's resources are now too small to be relevant in any general crisis—or, in all probability, even in a crisis that affects a large emerging country.

Figure 7.2 Total International Monetary Fund Credit Outstanding

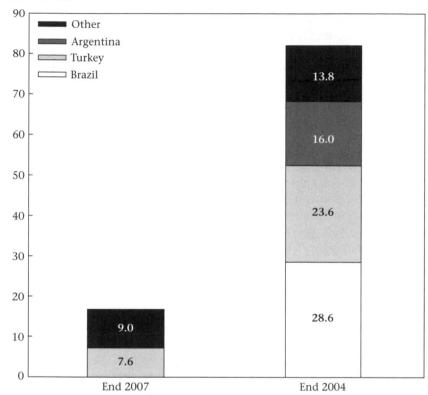

Billions of US$

Source: International Monetary Fund.

The difficulty has always been to distinguish liquidity crises from solvency crises. The latter require debt restructuring, in which the IMF can only offer its good offices, largely by indicating what it considers to be a manageable debt service burden. But in liquidity crises, such as the one that hit South Korea in 1997, it makes good sense to lend. The requirement is simply that the lender of last resort be convinced it will get its money back.

An independent IMF staff, headed by a competent and well-respected management, should be allowed to make such judgments in the event of liquidity crises. If it turns out that the management has judged wrongly, they should be fired. But the resources of the IMF are far too limited for it to be able to play this role effectively. For that reason self-insurance, combined with regional reserve pooling arrangements (of which the Chiang Mai Initiative in Asia is the most important example), seems to be the only plausible solution.[10]

The collapse in IMF lending provides an excellent opportunity to reform the institution. It also makes such reform more urgent, since the IMF is financed by the interest paid on its emergency lending. Thus the absence of international financial crises is itself a crisis—for the IMF. Without crises, there is no lending; without lending, there is no income; and without income, there are no jobs.

How far has the IMF gone toward necessary reforms? Not far enough. Peter Kenen, one of the world's foremost experts on international finance, now working at the Council on Foreign Relations in New York, argues that IMF reform has five elements, closely related to the challenges outlined above: the lack of a revenue model in the absence of crisis lending; the need to make bilateral surveillance more streamlined and effective; the need to make multilateral surveillance more effective; establishing a new facility to provide precautionary financing for countries that have followed prudent policy; and reforming the distribution of IMF quotas. To this I would add the scale of IMF resources and the need to make selection of the managing director the outcome of a legitimate global process.[11]

On the revenue model, a proposal has been made by a committee appointed by the managing director that the fund sell up to four hundred tons of gold and use the proceeds to establish an endowment to finance its activities. The idea is attractive, albeit at an early stage.

On bilateral surveillance, sensible proposals have been made for biennial analysis of small and stable countries. Surveillance will focus particularly on financial and balance sheet vulnerabilities, as recommended in Chapter 6.

Some progress has been made on defining multilateral surveillance more broadly, with new guidelines suggesting that a country may be considered to have violated its obligations under the fund's articles if it is deemed to maintain an undervalued exchange rate. Needless to say, the Chinese executive director opposed this idea. But it is at least a small step in the right direction. So have been the consultations on global imbalances led by the IMF, with the participation of China, the Eurozone, Japan, Saudi Arabia, and the United States. But these discussions have not advanced very far: the big players—China and the United States—merely repeated pledges they had already made on exchange rate and fiscal policies.

As has been the case in the past, the attempt to create a precautionary facility for potential borrowers has proved problematic (which is why I prefer the simpler approach suggested above). But, as Kenen notes, most countries do not consistently meet plausible criteria. The danger is that, by publishing data on the deteriorating performance of countries that had previously qualified, the facility would create crises rather than reduce their likelihood. This idea therefore seems to have little chance of making progress.

Finally there has been much discussion of changing quotas in the fund. The new formula will place more weight on GNP, including it at purchasing power parity. But a projected increase of 10 percent in fund quotas cannot bring about much reweighting of the present votes, even if the twelve countries with the largest quotas all agree to forgo increases.

There is some agreement that Dominique Strauss-Kahn should be the last managing director to be chosen in the old Eurocentric way. There is no agreement at all on the need to make the fund large enough to be relevant in a global crisis. One can only hope that the development of the domestic-currency-based financial system recommended strongly in this book goes so far that international lending largely ceases to be necessary. But that seems unlikely. Even if a country does not suffer a large currency mismatch, it is vulnerable to crisis if it has a large current account deficit and does not possess one of the world's dominant currencies, in which it is always relatively easy to borrow. "Sudden stops" would still be costly under such circumstances. For that reason a larger reserve pool seems highly attractive. But it also seems highly unlikely.

What is going to happen to the IMF? It will no doubt continue to make small improvements. But it is going to remain a marginal institution. Emerging countries are largely on their own. The IMF can advise, warn, and cajole, but it cannot deliver much help. Emerging countries should set their policies accordingly.

Reform of Informal Groups

It is in certain informal bodies that the course of much of the world's economic discussion is charted. Ideally that would occur within a reformed IMF. But that is not going to happen. So what should we do about all of the "Gs"? The G-7 (Canada, France, Germany, Italy, Japan, the United Kingdom, and the United States) is reasonably like-minded but grossly unrepresentative of the world as it exists today. The G-20 (Argentina, Australia, Brazil, Canada, China, the European Union, France, Germany, India, Indonesia, Italy, Japan, Mexico, Russia, Saudi Arabia, South Africa, South Korea, Turkey, the United Kingdom, and the United States) is more complete, but some of its members are not systemically important. It is also surely too large.

What about creating a G-15? Here are the possible candidates for a group of countries that have some significant systemic role in managing the current system, a group that would certainly make more sense than the G-7: Brazil, Canada, China, France, Germany, India, Indonesia, Italy, Japan, Russia, Saudi Arabia, South Korea, the United Kingdom, the United States, and the European Union. If one were being ruthless, one would argue that the members of the Eurozone should all be represented by one set of delegates. Of course, the United Kingdom is not a member of the currency union. So it should have independent representation.

What can be expected of the international system? Not much. Creating a global financial and monetary system that is reasonably stable, allows emerging countries to be net recipients of capital without fearing a devastating crisis at any moment, and does not depend on huge net borrowing by the issuer of the world's key currency would seem a high enough priority. But the efforts to do so have been feeble at best. It would help if the IMF were far better funded for this purpose. It would help too if IMF multilateral surveillance had teeth—perhaps even the capacity to allow trade sanctions against those with inordinately mercantilist currency policies, such as China. But none of this is in the least likely to happen. Emerging countries must look after themselves. The accumulation of massive reserves is an expensive first step. It cannot be the last. Creating a sound domestic-currency-based financial system is even more important. The fate of the emerging countries lies ultimately in their own hands.

CHAPTER 8

Toward a More Stable World

If something cannot go on forever, it will stop.
HERBERT STEIN, FORMER CHAIRMAN OF THE
COUNCIL OF ECONOMIC ADVISERS

STEP BACK A MOMENT. We can see that the so-called subprime crisis in the United States should not have been a surprise. On the contrary, it was what the experience of the previous three decades should have led one to expect.

Countries that run large current account deficits are by definition spending more than their income. What must be the domestic counterparts of such spending? One or more of the significant domestic sectors must also be spending more than their income. This is least disturbing if the excess spending takes the form of corporate investment, particularly in the production of tradable goods and services. More often, however, the domestic counterpart has taken the form of excess spending on consumption, public or private. If it is the former, the domestic counterpart of the external borrowing will take the form of a large fiscal deficit. If it is the latter, it will take the form of credit-fueled household spending. Often there is an associated boom in commercial property, residential property, or both. And a time of easy credit usually means increases in leverage throughout the economy and consequent increases in financial fragility.

The credit squeeze in the United States fits this broad pattern. At the time of writing, it appears that domestic financial fragility will prove a bigger constraint than external solvency on the ability of the United States to run large current account deficits. It is also probable that monetary policy will prove ineffective in sustaining domestic spending: people do not borrow to buy assets that are falling in price; nor do lenders happily lend freely against such collateral. Unless the U.S. government is prepared to run a very large fiscal deficit, a continued decline in the external deficit and at least a sharp slowdown in demand, if not a severe and prolonged recession, seem probable.

Compared with the emerging countries that ran sizable current account deficits in the 1980s and 1990s, the United States has the great advantage of borrowing in its own currency. This means that it has the ability to manage the consequences of its borrowing—though there may still be a bout of inflation and a severe jolt, not just to the economy but also to the credibility of the dollar as the key international currency. The credit expansion was associated with what was, in retrospect, unsound lending of a particularly innovative kind, involving such strategies as securitization and special investment vehicles. As a result, the unwinding of the excess credit is likely to be particularly painful, since it has become difficult to identify the locus of insolvency and, as a result, mistrust permeates the financial system. Financial innovation in the world's most advanced financial system appears to have made it particularly difficult to manage the consequences of credit excess.

One obvious conclusion is that, given free rein, even the most sophisticated financial system is capable of excess. This is hardly surprising in view of the fragility of the system, as discussed in Chapter 2. Crises seem inevitable. The aim can only be to reduce their severity and frequency.

Many blame the United States' predicament on the policies of the Federal Reserve and lax regulation of the financial system. These arguments are not without merit, but they are exaggerated. Given the pattern of global savings and investment, the United States emerged naturally—I would argue, inevitably—as the world's borrower of last resort. That severely constrained the degrees of freedom for Federal Reserve monetary policy, on the plausible presumption that it was loath to permit a sustained recession. Given the scale of the net borrowing by the United States and the lack of corporate demand for outside funding, the aggressive monetary easing, the consequent financial excess, and above all the housing-related excess were almost inevitable.

Thus the United States is at least as much the victim of decisions made by others as the author of its own misfortunes. That is an unpopular view— in the United States, because it is easier for Americans to accept that they are guilty than that they are impotent, and in the rest of the world, because it is far easier for others to accept that the United States is guilty than that they themselves are responsible. But the principal argument of this book is that this is a global predicament explained by decisions—and frailties—

across the globe. Part of the solution to that predicament is to limit the scale of macroeconomic imbalances, since they frequently exacerbate financial fragility. The other part is to operate the financial system in ways that reduce fragility when macroeconomic corrections occur.

Where do we go from here? We need to create a financial and global macroeconomic regime that allows reasonably well-run countries to import at least some capital with a degree of safety, that ends reliance on the United States as the borrower and spender of last resort, and that halts the cycle of financial crises in emerging countries that preceded the ascendance of the United States as borrower of last resort.

It is perfectly feasible to do this:

- Countries running huge current account surpluses need to ask themselves whether they could not better use these resources at home. China certainly could—and should. Its enormous and rapidly rising current account surplus is a massively destabilizing force in the world economy. Indeed, based on present trends, with a current account surplus in 2007 of about 12 percent of GDP and a significant net private capital inflow, China is becoming a gigantic cuckoo in the global economic nest. These policies must change: it simply irrational for China's gross savings to be close to three-fifths of GDP. It is wasteful for China and destabilizing for the rest of the world.
- The U.S. deficit should diminish, but not disappear. At present there are a large number of countries with massive surpluses, like Germany and Japan, the oil exporters, and some emerging economies, notably China. It is helpful for global macroeconomic stability if fundamentally solvent high-income countries absorb some of those excess savings.
- Emerging countries must do more to give themselves the stability they need than accumulate massive foreign-currency reserves. They also need to create financial systems able to cope with integration into the global financial markets, or, failing that, they should decide to stay out of those markets, so far as possible. The necessary steps are to encourage inflows of foreign direct investment and portfolio equity; keep most borrowing in the domestic currency; create a sound financial system, which entails fiscal and monetary discipline and elimination of severe distortions in the financial system; monitor and if necessary regulate the state of the national balance sheet, thereby precluding the emergence of currency mismatches; and make only those exchange rate commitments that they have an excellent chance of keeping.

The performance of the financial system has been the Achilles heel of the era of globalization. A brittle stability was won in the 2000s by simply shifting the world's deficits largely onto the United States. But this was neither a desirable nor, in the long run, a sustainable solution. A different world must now be envisaged, one in which capital flows productively and safely to poor countries. The correction in the U.S. current account deficit now under way makes this both necessary and desirable. Can it be done in safety? Or will another huge round of financial crises take place in the emerging countries at some time within the next decade? That is the question to be addressed. Let us hope that policy makers come up with the right answers.

Notes

Preface

Epigraph: Bagehot, *Essay on Edward Gibbon.*
1. Glyn, *Capitalism Unleashed.*
2. Ibid., xi.
3. Wolf, *Why Globalization Works,* Chap. 8.
4. Triffin, *Gold and the Dollar Crisis.*
5. The Bretton Woods system was named after Bretton Woods, New Hampshire, where the Allies planned the creation of the International Monetary Fund and the World Bank in 1944.
6. Kindleberger and Aliber, *Manias, Panics and Crashes,* 239.
7. Wolf, *Why Globalization Works,* Chap. 13.
8. Wolf, "Fixing Global Finance."
9. Wolf, "Will Asian Mercantilism Meet Its Waterloo?" I also lectured along similar lines in October 2005 for Oxonia, at the Department of Economics, Oxford University. The Oxford lecture turned out to be the dry run for the Snape lecture, which in turn became the kernel of the much bigger series of lectures I delivered at SAIS in 2006.

1 • Learning Lessons

Epigraph: Beattie and Alden, "The U.S. Treasury Secretary."
1. See Stiglitz, *Globalization and Its Discontents,* and Bhagwati, "The Capital Myth."
2. See Soros, *Crisis of Global Capitalism* and *Open Society.*
3. Díaz-Alejandro, "Good-Bye Financial Repression."
4. Sterilization refers to the sale of illiquid assets to commercial banks in order to mop up the money created by intervention in the foreign exchange markets by central banks. The aim is to reverse the monetary impact of such interventions.

2 • Blessings and Perils of Liberal Finance

Epigraph: Summers, "Remarks before the International Monetary Fund."
1. These data are from Board of Governors of the Federal Reserve System, *Flow of Funds Accounts of the United States.*
2. The data on the global capital market are all taken from McKinsey Global Institute, *Mapping the Global Capital Market.*
3. Taleb, *Black Swan.* It used to be thought that all swans were white. But then the black swan was discovered in Australia.
4. Rajan and Zingales, *Saving Capitalism,* 28.
5. Ibid., 33–34.
6. World Bank, *Doing Business in 2006.*
7. Rajan and Zingales, *Saving Capitalism,* 33.
8. Mishkin, *Next Great Globalization,* 29.
9. Douglass C. North won a Nobel Prize in economics for his work on the role of institutions in economic history. See his *Structure and Change in Economic History.* An alternative view, which emphasizes the role of the state in creating competitive manufacturing industry, is advanced by Erik Reinert, a self-professed "heterodox" economist, in *How Rich Countries Got Rich . . . and Why Poor Countries Stay Poor.*
10. See Acemoglu et al., "Institutions as the Fundamental Cause of Long-Term Growth." Jeffrey Sachs argues, however, that environmental constraints play a significant part in explaining underdevelopment, particularly in Africa; see *The End of Poverty.* It is not obvious why these should be mutually exclusive alternatives. One might instead see them as mutually reinforcing. On a vast continent of low-productivity agriculture, low population densities, and shifting populations, certain institutions—those specifying and protecting property in land—were simply unnecessary.
11. In a seminal article, Daron Acemoglu, Simon Johnson, and James A. Robin-

son argue that the history of former colonies can be explained by their original development, or lack of it. Colonial powers set up rent extraction regimes in rich regions and development-promoting regimes in poor ones. As a result, the relative poverty and wealth of these regions reversed. This is shown most clearly in the Americas, where the initially impoverished North succeeded and the initially wealthy South failed; see "The Colonial Origins of Comparative Development."

12. This is a principal theme of Mancur Olson's brilliant posthumously published book *Power and Prosperity.*
13. Smith, *Wealth of Nations,* Book IV, Chap. 5, 349.
14. Macdonald, *A Free Nation Deep in Debt.*
15. Ibid., 7.
16. See Bagehot, *Lombard Street.*
17. While a staunch advocate of financial liberalization, Mishkin justifies government intervention to promote transparency and provide deposit insurance; but this must be offset by prudential regulation, to curb the risks of moral hazard. See *Next Great Globalization,* 32–35.
18. Olson, "Big Bills Left on the Sidewalk."
19. Rajan and Zingales, *Saving Capitalism,* 68–92. On the impact of the revolution in financial theory on markets, see, in particular, Donald MacKenzie, *An Engine, Not a Camera.*
20. Mishkin, *Next Great Globalization,* 36–48, esp. 36–37.
21. King and Levine, "Finance and Growth." Much of the literature of the 1990s on this topic is summarized in World Bank, *Finance for Growth.*
22. Levine et al., "Financial Intermediation and Growth."
23. Mishkin, *Next Great Globalization,* 37, citing Rajan and Zingales, "Financial Dependence and Growth."
24. Levine, "Finance and Growth."
25. The doubting reader should examine Kindleberger and Aliber, *Manias, Panics and Crashes,* esp. 1–20.
26. World Bank, *Finance for Growth,* 19.
27. Kose et al., "How Does Financial Globalization Affect Risk Sharing?"
28. Henry, "Capital Account Liberalization," 95.
29. Forbes, "Microeconomic Evidence on Capital Controls."
30. Prasad et al., *Effects of Financial Globalization;* Kose et al., "Financial Globalization"; and International Monetary Fund, "Reaping the Benefits."
31. Kose et al., "Financial Globalization," 4.
32. International Monetary Fund, "Reaping the Benefits," 7.
33. Kindleberger and Aliber, *Manias, Panics and Crashes,* 107.
34. Calvo, "Capital Flows and Capital-Market Crises."
35. Ibid., 517.
36. International Monetary Fund, "Reaping the Benefits," 27.

3 • Financial Crises in the Era of Globalization

Epigraph: Mohamad, "A Backlash Begins."

1. Kindleberger and Aliber, *Manias, Panics and Crashes,* 241.
2. See, for example, Eichengreen et al., "Original Sin." The term is exaggerated, since it suggests helplessness. But borrowing in one's own currency requires a reputation for probity—which takes decades to build and a month to destroy.
3. This extremely important source of weakness in financial structures is discussed in detail in Goldstein and Turner, *Controlling Currency Mismatches.*
4. World Bank, *Finance for Growth,* 75.
5. Eichengreen and Bordo, "Crises Now and Then."
6. Ibid., 30.
7. Ibid.
8. See Caprio and Klingebiel, "Systemic and Borderline Financial Crises," and Caprio et al., "Banking Crises Database."
9. These losses were estimated in accordance with the IMF's methodology by comparing, in real terms, the precrisis GDP growth rate with that during the crisis years, until the precrisis rate was reached once again. The output loss is defined as the sum of the differences between the actual growth rate and the trend growth rate in all the years, until the trend growth rate is reached once again. This method underestimates the forgone GDP. One could argue that it is only when GDP reaches its trend *level* once again, not its trend rate of *growth,* that the crisis is over, with the trend level in each year defined as the GDP in the year before the crisis multiplied by the trend growth rate over the succeeding period. Then the loss would be the difference in each year between the actual GDP and the trend GDP level, until the economy regains trend GDP (if it ever does so).
10. There is an enormous literature on the financial crises of the 1990s and early 2000s in the emerging market countries. Among the accounts I have found useful are Mishkin, *Next Great Globalization,* 69–126, which discusses Mexico 1994–95, South Korea 1997–98, and Argentina 2001–2; Blustein, *The Chastening,* a splendid account of the crises of 1997–99 in Brazil, East Asia, and Russia, and *And the Money Kept Rolling In,* on the Argentine crisis of 2001–2; Eichengreen, "Understanding Asia's Crisis"; Fischer, "IMF and the Asian Crisis"; and Independent Evaluation Office of the International Monetary Fund, "Report on Capital Account Crises."
11. See Mishkin, *Next Great Globalization,* 49–68.
12. See ibid., 120–21.
13. When banks are owned or controlled by their borrowers, they will have a strong interest in concealing the true state of the banks' balance sheets from their creditors and regulators. Monitoring such conflicts of interest is almost impossible.

14. According to World Bank research, twenty-four of a list of thirty-two countries that suffered systemic crises in the 1980s and 1990s offered unlimited guarantees to the banking sector. See Claessens et al., *Systemic Financial Crises,* Chap. 6, Appendix Table 2.
15. The story of South Korea's financial crisis is told in Mishkin, *Next Great Globalization,* 85–105.
16. A fuller account of the story told below is contained in an excellent study by John Williamson of the Institute for International Economics in Washington, D.C. See *Curbing the Boom-Bust Cycle,* esp. Chap. 2.
17. What is a systemic financial crisis? The World Bank defines such a crisis as one in which much or all of the banks' capital is exhausted (see Caprio and Klingebiel, "Systemic and Borderline Financial Crises," 1). At the level of one country, this is a reasonable description, since a situation in which a substantial proportion of the banking system is insolvent is one in which there will be crisis intervention by the government.
18. The balance of payments is defined as follows. The balance of trade in goods is exports of goods less imports of goods. The balance of trade in nonfactor services (that is, services other than those of labor and capital) is exports of nonfactor services (such as management consulting, legal services, educational services, or tourism) less imports of nonfactor services. The balance of trade in goods and services is the sum of the balance of trade in goods and the balance of trade in nonfactor services. The balance in income receipts is also known as the balance in factor services. Positive factor service income is income earned by residents abroad from their work or from the assets they own (as dividends, interest, or rent on portfolio or direct investment). Negative sources of factor service income are the income earned by foreign residents from factors of production employed in the domestic economy. Current transfers are gifts from foreign residents less gifts to foreign residents. Remittances are included as transfers (gifts), not as income from labor. Gifts from governments (e.g., aid) are also transfers. The current account then is the sum of the balance in goods and services, the balance in factor service income, and the balance in transfers. The current account is financed by net capital flows—foreign residents' purchases of domestic assets (including purchases by foreign governments) less residents' purchases of foreign assets (including purchases by the government). By definition, a current account deficit is equal to a capital account surplus. In much of the analysis here and in subsequent chapters, the capital account drives the current account.
19. The relation between national income and the balance of payments needs to be analyzed briefly, since it is central to any discussion of the macroeconomic consequences of balance of payments adjustment.

    Gross domestic product is a measure of the gross value added, expenditure on gross value added, or income earned by factors of production within a given jurisdiction. Output, expenditure on output, and income earned from production are always equal, by definition. In simple form, GDP is also equal to private consumption plus government consumption plus private gross investment plus government gross investment plus the balance of trade in goods and nonfactor services. Sales to nonresidents (i.e., exports) are a contribution to domestic output, while purchases from nonresidents (i.e., imports) subtract from domestic output. If one adds net factor income to GDP, one obtains gross national product (GNP). Thus GDP is a measure of the output, income, or expenditure on production within a given jurisdiction, while GNP is a measure of the income accruing to residents from economic activity across the entire world. GDP belongs to a location, while GNP belongs to the people who live in a given location. If the current account, rather than the balance of trade in goods and nonfactor services, is added to consumption and investment, one obtains GNP rather than GDP.

Now consider the absorption of resources by an economy, assuming for simplicity's sake that net transfers are zero and that GDP is equal to GNP (i.e., the balance of factor income is zero). Absorption measures the expenditures by residents on all goods and services. An economy's absorption is domestic output (GDP) plus imports less exports. Imports less exports is a measure of the balance of trade (with the sign reversed). Thus absorption exceeds GDP by the size of the trade deficit. The trade deficit (equal in this case, by assumption, to the current account deficit) must be financed by a net inflow of capital or, in other words, a sale of claims on domestic assets (real property, bonds, and equity). It can continue only so long as it is possible to make such sales. It is clear then that if the net capital inflow falls, so must absorption of resources in the economy—people must spend less.

Finally, consider the uses of claims on income. In national accounts, these can be spent on private or government consumption, or saved, and so can be made available to investors at home or abroad. Since the uses of income must equal GDP, the difference between savings and domestic investment is the balance of trade. If residents save more than they invest at home, they accumulate assets abroad (i.e., run a current account surplus) and vice versa. The difference between savings and domestic investment is also equal to the difference between GDP and absorption, and that in turn is the current account balance.

20. The statistics of the Institute for International Finance use a sample of countries, which it defines as the "emerging market economies." The definitions are as follows: Asia / Pacific: China, India, Indonesia, Malaysia, the Philippines, South Korea, and Thailand; Latin America: Argentina, Brazil, Chile, Colombia, Ecuador, Mexico, Peru, Uruguay, and Venezuela; Europe: Bulgaria, the Czech Republic, Hungary, Poland, Romania, Russia, Slovakia, and Turkey; and Africa / Middle East: Algeria, Egypt, Morocco, South Africa, and Tunisia.

The data used in Figure 3.2 come from a privately supplied long series and from Institute for International Finance, "Update on Capital Flows."

21. On absorption, see note 19 above.

22. The source for this and the subsequent figures drawn from data from the Institute for International Finance are the same as that for Figure 3.2, with the addition of Institute for International Finance, "Capital Flows to Emerging Market Economies."

23. Many high-income countries were able to relax monetary policy after abandoning defense of the currency. The United Kingdom in 1992 is a good example.

24. Goldstein and Turner, *Controlling Currency Mismatches*, 45–46. On this topic see also Reinhart et al., "Addicted to Dollars."

25. Eichengreen, "Understanding Asia's Crisis," Table 9.3.

26. More precisely, any country with a net liability position and liabilities denominated in foreign currency must have a currency mismatch, and any country that runs a current account deficit long enough will end up with a net liability position.

4 • From Crises to Imbalances

Epigraphs: Bernanke, "Global Saving Glut"; Greenspan, "Remarks."

1. These data are from International Monetary Fund, *World Economic Outlook*, April 2007, www.imf.org, Statistical Appendix, Table 1. Estimates of growth of the world economy measured at purchasing power parity exchange rates are higher (largely because this approach gives a heavier weight to large, poor developing countries, such as China and India), at 5.3 percent in 2004, 4.9 percent in 2005, 5.4 percent in 2006, and a forecast of 4.9 percent for 2007—an average of 5.1 percent over these years. But for global real interest rates what matters more is actual GDP, since it determines demand for loanable funds.

2. The real interest rate is measured as the GDP-weighted average of the ten-year (or nearest maturity) government bond yields less inflation rates for Canada, France, Germany, Italy, Japan, the United Kingdom, and the United States (excluding Italy prior to 1992). This is not a true measure of the real interest rate, which is a forward-looking measure based on expected, not actual, inflation. In recent years, the "true" real interest rate would have been higher than the estimated real interest rate if expected inflation were lower than the already low actual rates.

3. Catão and Mackenzie, "Perspectives on Low Global Interest Rates."

4. Summers, "Reflections on Global Account Imbalances," 3.

5. Duncan, *Dollar Crisis.*

6. See International Monetary Fund, *World Economic Outlook,* April 2007, Chap. 5.

7. This is probably one of the reasons for the recent activity of private equity in taking public companies private. Where corporate sectors are running a financial surplus (i.e., they are cash positive), heavy leveraging of the balance sheet is a tax-efficient way to extract the surplus. This is also a good way to curb the self-aggrandizement of corporate executives: they are forced to run their companies for cash.

8. The data here and in subsequent figures are taken from International Monetary Fund, *World Economic Outlook,* April 2007, Chap. 1. A more detailed analysis was contained in *World Economic Outlook,* September 2005, Chap. 2. But those data go up only to 2004.

9. This analysis of the sectoral contributions to the savings surplus is derived from International Monetary Fund, *World Economic Outlook,* September 2005, Chap. 2. The data go up only to 2004 and have not been updated on a comparable basis.

10. The implications of Japan's post-bubble debt overhang for the behavior of the economy are explored in Koo, *Balance Sheet Recession.* This debt overhang problem also afflicted most of the emerging economies hit by financial crises, with the difference that much of the debt was denominated in foreign currency.

11. See McKinsey Global Institute, *U.S. Imbalancing Act.*

12. The data are taken from International Monetary Fund, *World Economic Outlook,* various issues.

13. See Corden, "Exchange Rate Protection."

14. Both the influential underlying theory and the label have been proposed by three economists who work together for Deutsche Bank: Michael P. Dooley of the University of California, Santa Cruz, David Folkerts-Landau, and Peter M. Garber. Their theory is explained in a number of papers, including "The Two Crises of International Economics."

15. See note 4 in Chapter 1 for an explanation of sterilization.

16. The numbers do not add up owing to the omission of some capital flows.

17. Guillermo A. Calvo and Carmen M. Reinhard call it "fear of floating"; see their "Fear of Floating."

18. These data are taken from Wooldridge, "Changing Composition of Official Reserves."

19. Summers, "Reflections on Global Account Imbalances."

20. This was known as the N-1 problem. With N countries, only $N-1$ could fix their exchange rates.

21. Bernanke, "Deflation."

22. Analysis of the U.S. predicament in terms of the financial balances in the economy has been a characteristic of the work of Wynne Godley, now a sen-

ior visiting research fellow at the Cambridge Endowment for Research in Finance and, prior to that, a distinguished scholar at the Levy Economics Institute, New York. See, among many other writings, "As the Implosion Begins" (with Alex Izuretia), "Prospects and Policies for the U.S. Economy" (with Alex Izuretia and Gennaro Zezza), "Some Unpleasant American Arithmetic," "The U.S. Economy" (with Marc Lavoie), and "The United States and Her Creditors" (with Dimitri B. Papadimitriou, Claudio H. Dos Santos, and Gennaro Zezza). A similar analysis is applied by Charles Dumas and Diana Choyleva of London's Lombard Street Research in *The Bill from the China Shop.*

23. The personal sector's balance is defined as savings less residential investment, while the balance of the business sector is undistributed profits less all other private investment.

24. Errors are due to rounding.

25. These data are from Organisation for Economic Co-operation and Development, *Economic Outlook,* June 2007, Annex Table 58.

26. I elaborated this view in the discussion of the economists' forum in my column "Villains and Victims of Global Capital Flows." The context was a discussion of the relevance of the IS-LM model of the late Sir John Hicks, in which macroeconomic activity is determined jointly by the level of investment, the propensity to save, the supply of money, and liquidity preference. My remarks were as follows: "First, there has been an increase in the world's (ex ante) propensity to save out of income and a decline in the (ex ante) propensity to invest, partly because of the bursting of the stock market bubble after 2000, partly because of the worldwide rise in profit shares in GDP and partly because of the large shift in global incomes towards high-saving countries (i.e. East Asia and the oil exporters). All this generated a shift in the global IS curve down and to the left. If there had been no monetary policy response there would have been a global recession. But there was such a response in the significant countries. So the LM curve was also shifted downwards to the right. The new equilibrium point kept the world economy close to 'full employment' (itself, of course, a moving point in terms of output, given the expansion in global capacity), but at lower nominal (and real) interest rates than before."

27. Reading, Monthly Review 216.

28. Barry Eichengreen of the University of California, Berkeley, describes the different views on what has happened in terms of the simple identity $S_u - I_u = I_r - S_r$, where S is saving, I is investment, u is the United States, and r is the rest of the world. Those who think the deficits are the result of U.S. profligacy stress the decline in S_u. Those who think the "imbalances" are the result of improved attractiveness of investment in the United States would emphasize a rise in I_u. But since there has been no such rise, it cannot explain the current account deficits. Those who emphasize the savings glut would

point to the rise in S_r. Such a rise has occurred in some countries, notably China and the oil exporters. Finally, those who emphasize the global investment dearth point to declines in I_r. Those have also happened. The argument here is that shifts in the relationship between I_r and S_r that have raised the surplus, partly driven by government decisions in the rest of the world, have led to policy shifts in the United States that, given the exogenous I_u, have generated a fall in S_u. The latter fall is partly the result of an exogenous decision by the U.S. government to raise cyclically adjusted fiscal deficits and partly the result of decisions by the Federal Reserve. The housing bubble was part of the transmission channel from U.S. monetary policy to the decline in S_u. See Eichengreen, "Blind Men and the Elephant."

5 • Calm before a Storm

Epigraphs: Attributed to John Maynard Keynes, in "Down Communism's Sink"; International Monetary Fund, "Money Matters."

1. The remark is often mistakenly attributed to Charles de Gaulle, first president of the Fifth Republic. President de Gaulle no doubt thought exactly the same thing. The remark by d'Estaing was cited by the philosopher and historian Raymond Aron in *Le Figaro*, February 16, 1965 (*Les Articles du Figaro*, 1475). I am indebted for this information to Gourinchas and Rey, "From World Banker to World Venture Capitalist," 2.
2. International Monetary Fund, *World Economic Outlook*, April 2007, Box 3.1, 84–87.
3. The fact that the nominal cost of liabilities was lower than the growth rate of the U.S. economy lowered U.S. net liabilities by only 1.5 percent of GDP. The principal explanation was the difference between the cost of U.S. liabilities and the return on U.S. assets abroad, which lowered the ratio of net liabilities to GDP by 30 percentage points over this period. Specifically the U.S. benefited from the relatively poor performance of the U.S. stock market, from the fall of the U.S. dollar (in which its liabilities are denominated) after 2001, and from the composition of its portfolio: higher-returning equity instruments (including FDI) made up roughly 60 percent of its assets and 40 percent of its liabilities. See International Monetary Fund, *World Economic Outlook*, April 2007.
4. In an important paper on the "exorbitant privilege," Pierre-Olivier Gourinchas of the University of California, Berkeley, and Hélène Rey of the Woodrow Wilson School at Princeton refer to the U.S. role as that of "world venture capitalist." "Hedge fund" seems a broader concept. A hedge fund borrows to invest in relatively risky assets. That is what the United States as a whole does. See Gourinchas and Rey, "From World Banker to World Venture Capitalist."

5. Corden, "Current Account Imbalances."
6. This is roughly the analysis provided by Barry Eichengreen in "Global Imbalances," 2.
7. Among their number are (in alphabetical order by first-named author): Olivier Blanchard of the Massachusetts Institute of Technology, Francesco Giavazzi of Bocconi University, and Filipa Sa of MIT; William Cline of the Peterson Institute for International Economics; Sebastian Edwards of the Anderson Graduate School of Business, University of California, Los Angeles; Barry Eichengreen of the University of California, Berkeley; Matthew Higgins, Thomas Klitgaard, and Cédric Tille of the Federal Reserve Bank of New York; Catherine Mann of Brandeis University and the Peterson Institute; Maurice Obstfeld of the University of California, Berkeley, and Kenneth Rogoff of Harvard; and Nouriel Roubini of the Stern School at New York University and his associate, Brad Setser. See Blanchard et al., "U.S. Current Account and the Dollar"; Cline, *United States as a Debtor Nation;* Edwards, "Is the U.S. Current Account Deficit Sustainable?"; Eichengreen, "Blind Men and the Elephant"; Higgins et al., "Borrowing without Debt?"; Mann, "Managing Exchange Rates"; Obstfeld and Rogoff, "Unsustainable U.S. Current Account Position Revisited" and "Global Current Account Imbalances"; and Roubini and Setser, "U.S. as a Net Debtor."
8. Ahearne et al., "Global Imbalances."
9. Among many others in this camp are Blanchard et al., "U.S. Current Account and the Dollar"; Edwards, "Is the U.S. Current Account Deficit Sustainable?"; and Obstfeld and Rogoff, "Unsustainable U.S. Current Account Position Revisited" and "Global Current Account Imbalances."
10. Ahearne et al., "Global Imbalances."
11. A thorough—and relatively optimistic—analysis of the exchange rate requirements of adjustment is contained in the International Monetary Fund's *World Economic Outlook,* April 2007. It concludes that "Typical estimates from the standard econometric models of the U.S. economy suggest that narrowing the ratio of the current account deficit to GDP by 1 percentage point would require a real depreciation ranging from 10 percent to 20 percent. The evidence on trade elasticities presented in this chapter is consistent with estimates at the lower end of this range." See Chap. 3, 105. This would suggest that a 40 percent real depreciation is needed to bring about a 4-percentage-point swing in the U.S. deficit, without a big shortfall in economic growth.
12. Obstfeld and Rogoff make this point strongly; see "Global Current Account Imbalances."
13. William Cline lays out the hard landing scenario in *The United States as a Debtor Nation,* 174–80. Sebastian Edwards argues that "it is not possible to rule out a scenario where the U.S. current account deficit would shrink abruptly by 3 to 6 percent of GDP. According to the simulations this type of

adjustment would imply an accumulated real depreciation of the trade-weighted dollar in the range of 21 percent [to] 28 percent in the first three years of the adjustment." Furthermore, he argues, this is likely to mean a deep reduction in growth of GDP. See "Is the U.S. Current Account Deficit Sustainable?," 41.

14. I have taken these headings from Eichengreen, "Global Imbalances."
15. See Cooper, "U.S. Deficit," *Living with Global Imbalances,* and "Understanding Global Imbalances."
16. According to the Organisation for Economic Co-operation and Development's *Economic Outlook,* June 2007, in 2006 the current account surplus of Japan was $171.2 billion, of Germany $147.9 billion, of Switzerland $65.3 billion, of the Netherlands $59.6 billion, and of Norway $56.1 billion. According to the International Monetary Fund's *World Economic Outlook,* April 2007, Singapore's current account surplus was $36.3 billion.
17. McKinsey Global Institute, *U.S. Imbalancing Act,* Exhibit 1.10, 26.
18. Clarida, "Japan, China, and the U.S. Current Account Deficit," 112.
19. Caballero et al., "Equilibrium Model."
20. Gourinchas and Rey, "From World Banker to World Venture Capitalist."
21. "U.S. Net International Investment Position at Year End 2007," www.bea.org.
22. In an important paper, Christopher M. Meissner of Cambridge University and Alan M. Taylor of the University of California, Davis, argue that the size of these "other changes" in the valuation adjustments of the U.S. net international investment position makes both understanding what is happening and extrapolation of past favorable outcomes "ill advised." See their "Losing Our Marbles."
23. Gourinchas and Rey, "From World Banker to World Venture Capitalist," 20, and "International Financial Adjustment."
24. See Dooley et al., "Two Crises of International Economics." The idea originated in their "U.S. Current Account Deficit."
25. Corden, "Current Account Imbalances," 367.
26. Hausmann and Sturzenegger, "Why the U.S. Current Account is Sustainable" and "Global Imbalances or Bad Accounting?"
27. Ibid., 238.
28. In 2006 reported U.S. net asset income was $43.1 billion. Capitalized at 5 percent, this becomes an estimated stock of $863.4 billion. The U.S. net liability position at the end of 2006, as computed by the U.S. Bureau of Economic Analysis, was $2.14 trillion. The difference is just over $3 trillion.
29. See Buiter, "Dark Matter or Cold Fusion?," and Gros, "Why the U.S. Current Account Deficit Is Not Sustainable."
30. Willem Buiter also argues that there is no reason to take the foreign income accounts at face value. See "Dark Matter or Cold Fusion?," 11–12.

31. Technically the current cost is the denominator of Tobin's Q, the valuation ratio, and the market value is its numerator.
32. Kitchen, "Sharecroppers or Shrewd Capitalists?," Table 3.
33. See Meissner and Taylor, "Losing Our Marbles," 3.
34. Gros, "Why the U.S. Current Account Deficit Is Not Sustainable," 254–56.
35. Eichengreen, "Global Imbalances."
36. Goldstein and Lardy, "China's Role," 7–8.
37. Duncan, *Dollar Crisis*, esp. Parts 1 and 2.
38. Cooper, *Living with Global Imbalances*, 9.
39. Mann, "Managing Exchange Rates."
40. See Dooley et al., "Two Crises of International Economics," "U.S. Current Account Deficit," and "Essay on the Revived Bretton Woods System."
41. Dooley et al., "Two Crises of International Economics."
42. The Deutsche Bank authors use the concept of a "total return swap," which they define as "a promise by one party to pay the total return (capital gains plus dividends) on the notional amount of an asset such as an equity or equity index for some future interval in exchange for receipt of fixed income on notional principal over the same interval. . . . The interesting aspect of such contracts for our argument is that the less creditworthy party to the contract is required to post collateral for actual or potential mark to market losses." Ibid.
43. This account relies heavily on the excellent discussion in Goldstein and Lardy, "China's Role."
44. Ibid., 15.
45. Eichengreen, "Blind Men and the Elephant," 17.
46. Ibid.
47. McKinnon, "Why China Should Keep Its Dollar Peg," 54. His fullest statement is in *Exchange Rates*.
48. Consider only the U.S. example. In 2006 overall domestic purchases were some 106 percent of GDP; imports were about 17 percent of GDP; and exports were about 11 percent of GDP. Assume that demand for imports falls proportionately with spending: a 1 percent fall in aggregate spending generates a 1 percent decline in spending on imports. Assume no shifts in relative prices and so no increase in the incentive to supply exports or import substitutes. Assume, more restrictively, no ability to shift import substitutes into exports. Assume too that the current account deficit is to fall by 4 percent of GDP. Then imports need to fall from 17 percent to 13 percent of initial GDP. How much does overall spending need to fall to achieve that outcome? The answer, based on these extremely simplified assumptions, is that domestic purchases need to fall by 26 percent and GDP by 21 percent to reduce the current account deficit by a mere 4 percent of GDP.

Assume instead that exports, imports, and import substitutes are perfectly substitutable (and so can be aggregated into the standard broad category of "tradables") and also that spending on tradables is 30 percent of purchases and so 32 percent of GDP and that the supply of tradables is 26 percent of GDP (giving us, again, an external deficit of 6 percent of GDP). To reduce demand for tradables to 28 percent of GDP, domestic purchases must fall by 12.5 percent and GDP by 9.25 percent. Again, the result is a deep recession, though not as deep as in the previous example. This description is not purely theoretical. It is exactly what happened in the Asian financial crisis. It is bound to happen if a deficit must be eliminated quickly.

6 • Toward Adjustment and Domestic Reform

Epigraph: "Act on Volatility, Stiglitz Urges Asia."
1. Fischer, "International Lender of Last Resort," 7.
2. McKinsey Global Institute, *U.S. Imbalancing Act,* Chap. 2.
3. Christopher Meissner and Alan Taylor note that the "yield privilege" of the United States—its ability to earn higher payments than it provides to its creditors—has indeed been related to its net external asset position. U.S. long-term interest rates are already high by the standards of Japan and the Eurozone. See Meissner and Taylor, "Losing Our Marbles."
4. Figure 6.2 shows that prices of tradables have been falling relative to those of nontradables. That is why the rise in the ratio of imports and exports to GDP has been much faster in constant prices than in actual prices. In real terms, since 1980 imports have tripled relative to GDP while exports have only doubled. This is what has to change if the deficit is to stop rising relative to GDP. Given the starting point (with imports more than 50 percent higher than exports), the deficit would rise relative to GDP so long as trade grew faster than GDP, even if imports and exports grew at the same rate in real terms. So reducing the deficit requires exports to grow substantially faster than imports.
5. Obstfeld and Rogoff, "Global Current Account."
6. Cooper, *Living with Global Imbalances.*
7. See International Monetary Fund, "Staff Report on the Multilateral Consultation."
8. McKinsey Global Institute, *U.S. Imbalancing Act,* 66–68.
9. Ibid., 62.
10. One must assume changes in macroeconomic balances in these economies and accompanying policies, to accommodate the impact of such swings in real exchange rates.

11. See Lardy, "China," 1.
12. Ibid.
13. Wolf, "Why Is China Growing So Slowly?"
14. These arguments are drawn from Lardy, "China."
15. Max Corden emphasizes the need to pay attention to the interests of each country in his "Exchange Rate Policies."
16. Lardy spells out the needed policy changes in "China."
17. This point is explained fully in Goldstein and Turner, *Controlling Currency Mismatches.*
18. Bank for International Settlements, *Financial Stability.*
19. Ibid., Annex Table 2B, 117.
20. Eichengreen et al., "Original Sin."
21. Bordo, "Sudden Stops," 26.
22. Bank for International Settlements, *Financial Stability,* Annex Table 8, 129.
23. Goldstein and Turner, *Controlling Currency Mismatches,* 81–82.
24. A full discussion of the range of regulatory possibilities is contained ibid., 89–103.
25. This argument is spelled out in detail by Reinhart et al., "Debt Intolerance."
26. See Calvo and Reinhart, "Fear of Floating."

7 • Toward Global Reform

Epigraph: King, "Reform of the International Monetary Fund."
1. Fiat money is money whose value is determined by its role in government-controlled transactions, such as the payment of taxes.
2. See Eichengreen and Hausmann, "Original Sin."
3. Krueger, "Conflicting Demands."
4. See Goldstein and Turner, *Controlling Currency Mismatches,* 85–87.
5. See Krueger, "International Financial Architecture for 2002" and "Proposals for a Sovereign Debt Restructuring Mechanism."
6. On the history of this idea, see Rogoff and Zettelmeyer, "Early Ideas of Sovereign Debt Reorganization."
7. Krueger, "Countries like Argentina."
8. See, for example, de Rato, "IMF's Medium-Term Strategy."
9. King, "Reform of the International Monetary Fund."
10. The Chiang Mai Initiative was set up in 2000 by the Association of Southeast Asian Nations (ASEAN, consisting of Brunei, Cambodia, Indonesia, Laos, Malaysia, Myanmar, the Philippines, Singapore, Thailand, and Vietnam), plus Japan, China, and South Korea, in response to Asian anger at how the countries of the region had been treaded during the financial crisis of 1997–98. The

initiative allows reserve pooling among the members. But the sums available in agreed swaps are still relatively small.

11. Kenen, "IMF Reform." See also his *Reform of the International Monetary Fund.*

8 • Toward a More Stable World

Epigraph: Stein, "Herb Stein's Unfamiliar Quotations."

References

Acemoglu, Daron, Simon Johnson, and James A. Robinson. "The Colonial Origins of Comparative Development: An Empirical Investigation." *American Economic Review* 91, no. 5 (2001): 1369–1401.

———. "Institutions as the Fundamental Cause of Long-Term Growth." In Philippe Aghion and Steven N. Durlauf, eds., *Handbook of Economic Growth*, vol. 1, part A. Amsterdam: North-Holland, 2005, 385–472.

"Act on Volatility, Stiglitz Urges Asia." *International Herald Tribune*, September 7, 2005. wwwiht.com.

Ahearne, Alan, William R. Cline, Kyung Tae Lee, Yung Chul Park, Jean Pisani-Ferry, and John Williamson. "Global Imbalances: Time for Action." Bruegel Policy Brief 2007/02, March 2007, www.bruegel.org.

Aron, Raymond, ed. *Les Articles du Figaro*, vol. 2. Paris: Fallois.

Bagehot, Walter. *Lombard Street: A Description of the Money Market*. London: Henry S. King and Co., 1873.

———. *Essay on Edward Gibbon,* cited in Charles P. Kindleberger and Robert Z. Aliber, *Manias, Panics and Crashes: A History of Financial Crises,* 5th ed. Basingstoke, UK: Palgrave Macmillan, 2005, inside front cover.

Bank for International Settlements, Committee on the Global Financial System. *Financial Stability and Local Currency Bond Markets*. CGFS Paper 28. Basel: Bank for International Settlements, June 2007.

Beattie, Alan, and Edward Alden. "The U.S. Treasury Secretary Is a Firm Believer in Non-intervention over the Value of the Dollar. . . ." *Financial Times*, May 5, 2002.

Bernanke, Ben. "Deflation: Making Sure 'It' Doesn't Happen Here." November 21, 2002. www.federalreserve.gov.

———. "The Global Saving Glut and the U.S. Current Account Deficit." March 10, 2005. www.federalreserve.gov.

Bhagwati, Jagdish N. "The Capital Myth: The Difference between Trade in Widgets and Dollars." *Foreign Affairs* 77 (May–June 1998): 7–12.

Blanchard, Olivier, Francesco Giavazzi, and Filipa Sa. "The U.S. Current Account and the Dollar." National Bureau of Economic Research Working Paper 11137. February 2005. www.nber.org.

Blustein, Paul. *The Chastening: Inside the Crisis That Rocked the Global Financial System and Humbled the IMF.* New York: Public Affairs, 2001.

———. *And the Money Kept Rolling In (and Out): Wall Street, the IMF and the Bankrupting of Argentina.* New York: Public Affairs, 2005.

Board of Governors of the Federal Reserve System. *Flow of Funds Accounts of the United States: Flows and Outstandings First Quarter 2006.* June 8, 2006. www.federalreserve.gov.

Bordo, Michael. "Sudden Stops, Financial Crises and Original Sin in Emerging Countries: Déja Vu?" National Bureau of Economic Research Working Paper 12393. July 2006. www.nber.org,

Buiter, Willem. "Dark Matter or Cold Fusion?" Goldman Sachs Global Economics Paper No. 136. January 16, 2006. www.nber.org/~wbuiter/dark.pdf.

Caballero, Ricardo J., Emmanuel Farhi and Pierre-Olivier Gourinchas. "An Equilibrium Model of "Global Imbalances" and Low Interest Rates." National Bureau of Economic Research Working Paper 11996. January 2006. www.nber.org.

Calvo, Guillermo A. "Capital Flows and Capital-Market Crises: The Simple Economics of Sudden Stops." In *Emerging Capital Markets in Turmoil: Bad Luck or Bad Policy?* Cambridge, MA: MIT Press, 2005, 227–42.

Calvo, Guillermo A., and Carmen M. Reinhard. "Fear of Floating." In Guillermo A. Calvo, *Emerging Capital Markets in Turmoil: Bad Luck or Bad Policy?* Cambridge, MA: MIT Press, 2005, 431–60.

Caprio, Gerard, and Daniela Klingebiel. "Episodes of Systemic and Borderline Financial Crises." World Bank. January 2003. www.worldbank.org.

Caprio, Gerard, Daniela Klingebiel, Luc Laeven, and Guillermo Noguera. "Banking Crises Database." World Bank. October 2003. www.worldbank.org.

Catão, Luis and George A. (Sandy) Mackenzie. "Perspectives on Low Global Interest Rates." IMF Working Paper WP/06/76. March 2006. www.imf.org.

Claessens, Stijn, Daniela Klingebiel, and Luc Laeven. "Crisis Resolution, Policies, and Institutions: Empirical Evidence." In Patrick Honohan and Luc Laeven, eds., *Systemic Financial Crises: Containment and Resolution.* Cambridge: Cambridge University Press for the World Bank, 2005, Chap. 6.

————. *Emerging Capital Markets in Turmoil: Bad Luck or Bad Policy?* Cambridge, MA: MIT Press, 2005.

Clarida, Richard H. "Japan, China, and the U.S. Current Account Deficit." *CATO Journal* 25, no. 1 (Winter 2005): 111–14. www.cato.org/pubs/journal/cj25n1/cj25n1.html.

Cline, William R. *The United States as a Debtor Nation.* Washington, DC: Institute for International Economics and Center for Global Development, 2005.

Cooper, Richard N. "U.S. Deficit: It Is Not Only Sustainable, It Is Logical." *Financial Times,* October 31, 2004. www.ft.com.

————. *Living with Global Imbalances: A Contrarian View.* Policy Briefs in International Economics. Washington, DC: Institute for International Economics, November 2005.

————. "Understanding Global Imbalances." 2006. www.economics.harvard.edu/faculty/cooper/papers.html.

Corden, W. Max. "Exchange Rate Protection." In Richard N. Cooper, Peter B. Kenen, Jorge Braga de Macedo, and Jacques van Ypersele, eds., *The International Monetary System under Flexible Exchange Rates.* Cambridge, MA: Ballinger, 1982.

————. "Those Current Account Imbalances: A Sceptical View." *The World Economy* 30, no. 3 (2007): 363–82.

————. "Exchange Rate Policies and the Global Imbalances." Paper for Meade Conference, Bank of England, July 2007. Unpublished.

De Rato, Rodrigo. "The IMF's Medium-Term Strategy." February 9, 2006. www.imf.org.

Díaz-Alejandro, Carlos. "Good-Bye Financial Repression, Hello Financial Crash." *Journal of Development Economics* 19, no. 1–2 (1985): 1–24.

Dooley, Michael P., David Folkerts-Landau, and Peter M. Garber. "An Essay on the Revived Bretton Woods System." National Bureau of Economic Research Working Paper 9971. September 2003. www.nber.org.

————. "The U.S. Current Account Deficit and Economic Development: Collateral for a Total Return Swap." National Bureau of Economic Research Working Paper 10727. September 2004. www.nber.org.

————. "The Two Crises of International Economics." National Bureau of Economic Research Working Paper 13197. June 2007. www.nber.org.

"Down Communism's Sink," *The Economist,* February 13, 1982, 11.

Dumas, Charles and Diana Choyleva. *The Bill from the China Shop.* London: Profile Books, 2006.

Duncan, Richard. *The Dollar Crisis: Causes, Consequences, Cures.* Singapore: Wiley, 2003.

Edwards, Sebastian. "Is the U.S. Current Account Deficit Sustainable? And if Not How Costly Is Adjustment Likely to Be?" National Bureau of Economic Research Working Paper 11541. August 2005. www.nber.org. [*Brookings Papers on Economic Activity* 1 (2005).]

Eichengreen, Barry. "Understanding Asia's Crisis." In *Capital Flows and Crises*. Cambridge, MA: MIT Press, 2004, Chap. 9.

———. "The Blind Men and the Elephant." Brookings Institution, Issues in Economic Policy 1. January 2006. www.brookings.edu.

———. "Global Imbalances: The New Economy, the Dark Matter, the Savvy Investor, and the Standard Analysis." *Journal of Policy Modeling* 28, no. 6 (2006), 645–52.

Eichengreen, Barry, and Michael D. Bordo. "Crises Now and Then: What Lessons from the Last Era of Financial Globalization?" National Bureau of Economic Research Working Paper 8716. January 2002. www.nber.org.

Eichengreen, Barry, and Ricardo Hausmann. "Original Sin: The Road to Redemption." University of California, Berkeley; Harvard University; and Inter-American Development Bank. August 2003. www.econ.berkeley.edu/~eichengr/research/osroadaug21- 03.pdf.

Eichengreen, Barry, Ricardo Hausmann, and Ugo Panizza. "Original Sin: The Pain, the Mystery, and the Road to Redemption." Paper presented at a conference on "Currency and Maturity Matchmaking: Redeeming Debts from Original Sin." Washington, DC, Inter-American Development Bank, November 21–22, 2002.

Fischer, Stanley. "On the Need for an International Lender of Last Resort." In Stanley Fischer, *IMF Essays from a Time of Crisis: The International Financial System, Stabilization, and Development*. Cambridge, MA: MIT Press, 2004, Chap. 1.

———. "The IMF and the Asian Crisis." In Stanley Fischer, *IMF Essays from a Time of Crisis*. Cambridge, MA: MIT Press, 2004, Chap. 3.

Forbes, Kristin J. "The Microeconomic Evidence on Capital Controls: No Free Lunch." National Bureau of Economic Research Working Paper 11372. May 2005. www.nber.org.

Glyn, Andrew. *Capitalism Unleashed: Finance, Globalization and Welfare*. Oxford: Oxford University Press, 2006.

Godley, Wynne, with Alex Izuretia. "As the Implosion Begins . . .? Prospects and Policies for the U.S. Economy: A Strategic View." Levy Economics Institute, Strategic Analysis. August 2001. www.levy.org.

Godley, Wynne, with Alex Izuretia and Gennaro Zezza. "Prospects and Policies for the U.S. Economy: Why Net Exports Must Now Be the Motor for U.S. Growth." Levy Economics Institute, Strategic Analysis. August 2004. www.levy.org.

———. "Some Unpleasant American Arithmetic." Levy Economics Institute Policy Note 2005/5. June 2005. www.levy.org.

Godley, Wynne, with Marc Lavoie. "The U.S. Economy: What's Next?" Levy Economics Institute, Strategic Analysis. March 2007. www.levy.org.

Godley, Wynne, with Dimitri B. Papadimitriou, Claudio H. Dos Santos, and Gennaro Zezza. "The United States and Her Creditors: Can the Symbiosis Last?" Levy Economics Institute, Strategic Analysis. September 2005. www .levy.org.

Goldstein, Morris, and Nicholas R. Lardy. "China's Role in the Revived Bretton Woods System: A Case of Mistaken Identity." Peterson Institute for International Economics, WP 05-02. March 2005. www.iie.com.

Goldstein, Morris, and Philip Turner. *Controlling Currency Mismatches in Emerging Markets*. Washington, DC: Institute for International Economics, 2004.

Gourinchas, Pierre-Olivier, and Hélène Rey. "International Financial Adjustment." National Bureau of Economic Research Working Paper 11563. August 2005. www.nber.org.

———. "From World Banker to World Venture Capitalist: U.S. External Adjustment and the Exorbitant Privilege." National Bureau of Economic Research Working Paper 11563. August 2005. www.nber.org.

Greenspan, Alan. "Remarks by Chairman Alan Greenspan to the International Monetary Conference, Beijing, People's Republic of China." June 6, 2005. www.federalreserve.gov.

Gros, Daniel. "Why the U.S. Current Account Deficit Is Not Sustainable." *International Finance* 9, no. 2 (Summer 2006): 241–60.

Hausmann, Ricardo, and Federico Sturzenegger. "Global Imbalances or Bad Accounting? The Missing Dark Matter in the Wealth of Nations." Harvard University CID Working Paper 124. 2006. www.cid.harvard.edu/cidwp/pdf/ 124.pdf.

———. "Why the U.S. Current Account Is Sustainable." *International Finance* 9, no. 2 (Summer 2006): 223–40.

Henry, Peter Blair. "Capital Account Liberalization, the Cost of Capital and Economic Growth." *American Economic Review* 93, no. 2 (2003): 91–96.

Higgins, Matthew, Thomas Klitgaard, and Cédric Tille. "Borrowing without Debt? Understanding the U.S. International Investment Position." Federal Reserve Bank of New York Staff Report 271. December 2006. www.newyorkfed.org/ research/staff_reports/sr271.pdf.

Honohan, Patrick, and Luc Laeven, eds. *Systemic Financial Crises: Containment and Resolution*. Cambridge: Cambridge University Press for the World Bank, 2005.

Independent Evaluation Office of the International Monetary Fund. "Report on Capital Account Crises in Brazil, Indonesia and South Korea." August 2003. www.imf.org.

Institute for International Finance. "Update on Capital Flows." March 30, 2006. www.iif.com.

———. "Capital Flows to Emerging Market Economies," May 31, 2007. www .iif.com.

International Monetary Fund. "Proposals for a Sovereign Debt Restructuring Mechanism." January 2003. www.imf.org.

———. *World Economic Outlook,* September 2005. www.imf.org.

———. *World Economic Outlook,* April 2006. www.imf.org.

———. *World Economic Outlook,* April 2007. www.imf.org.

———. "Reaping the Benefits of Financial Globalization." Staff Discussion Paper. May 29, 2007. www.imf.org

———. "Staff Report on the Multilateral Consultation on Global Imbalances with China, the Euro Area, Japan, Saudi Arabia, and the United States." June 29, 2007. www.imf.org.

———. "Money Matters: An IMF Exhibit—The Importance of Global Cooperation: Debt and Transition (1981–1989)." July 2008. www.imf.org.

Kenen, Peter B. *Reform of the International Monetary Fund.* Council Special Report 29. New York: Council on Foreign Relations, May 2007.

———. "IMF Reform: A Marathon, Not a Sprint." Vox. October 30, 2007. www.voxeu.org.

Kindleberger, Charles P., and Robert Z. Aliber. *Manias, Panics and Crashes: A History of Financial Crises,* 5th ed. Basingstoke: Palgrave Macmillan, 2005.

King, Mervyn. "Reform of the International Monetary Fund." Speech delivered in New Delhi, February 20, 2006. www.bankofengland.co.uk.

King, Robert, and Ross Levine. "Finance and Growth: Schumpeter Might Be Right." *Quarterly Journal of Economics* 108, no. 3 (1993): 717–37.

Kitchen, John. "Sharecroppers or Shrewd Capitalists? Projections of the U.S. Current Account, International Income Flows, and Net International Debt." March 2007. http://users.starpower.net/kitch/ShareShrewd.pdf.

Koo, Richard C. *Balance Sheet Recession: Japan's Struggle with Uncharted Economics and Its Global Implications.* Singapore: Wiley, 2003.

Kose, M. Ayhan, Eswar S. Prasad, Kenneth Rogoff, and Shang-Jin Wei. "Financial Globalization: A Reappraisal." IMF Working Paper 06/189. Washington, DC: International Monetary Fund, 2006.

Kose, M. Ayhan, Eswar S. Prasad, and Marco E. Terrones. "How Does Financial Globalization Affect Risk Sharing? Patterns and Channels." IMF Working Paper 07/238. Washington, DC: International Monetary Fund, November 2007.

Krueger, Anne. "Conflicting Demands on the International Monetary Fund." *American Economic Review* 90, no. 2 (2000): 38–42.

———. "International Financial Architecture for 2002: A New Approach to Sovereign Debt Restructuring." November 26, 2001. www.imf.org.

———. "Should Countries like Argentina Be Able to Declare Themselves Bankrupt?" January 18, 2002. www.imf.org.

———. "Proposals for a Sovereign Debt Restructuring Mechanism." January 2003. www.imf.org.

Lardy, Nicholas R. "China: Rebalancing Economic Growth." In *The China Balance Sheet in 2007 and Beyond.* Washington, DC: Center for Strategic and International Studies and Peterson Institute for International Economics, 2008, Chap. 1. www.iie.com.

Levine, Ross. "Finance and Growth." National Bureau of Economic Research Working Paper 10779. September 2004. www.nber.org.

Levine, Ross, Norman Loayza, and Thorsten Beck. "Financial Intermediation and Growth: Causality and Causes." *Journal of Monetary Economics* 46, no. 1 (2000): 31–77.

Macdonald, James. *A Free Nation Deep in Debt: The Financial Roots of Democracy.* Princeton, NJ: Princeton University Press, 2006.

MacKenzie, Donald. *An Engine, Not a Camera: How Financial Models Shape Markets.* Cambridge, MA: MIT Press, 2006.

Mann, Catherine. "Managing Exchange Rates: Achievement of Global Rebalancing or Evidence of Global Co-dependency?" *Business Economics* 29, no. 3 (July 2004).

McKinnon, Ronald I. *Exchange Rates under the East Asian Dollar Standard: Living with Conflicted Virtue.* Cambridge, MA: MIT Press, 2005.

———. "Why China Should Keep Its Dollar Peg." *International Finance* 10, no. 1 (Spring 2007): 43–70.

McKinsey Global Institute. *Mapping the Global Capital Market.* January 2007. www.mckinsey.com.

———. *The U.S. Imbalancing Act: Can the Current Account Deficit Continue?* June 2007. www.mckinsey.com.

Meissner, Christopher M., and Alan M. Taylor. "Losing Our Marbles in the New Century? The Great Rebalancing in Historical Perspective." National Bureau of Economic Research Working Paper 12580. October 2006. www.nber.org.

Mishkin, Frederic S. *The Next Great Globalization: How Disadvantaged Nations Can Harness Their Financial Systems to Get Rich.* Princeton, NJ: Princeton University Press, 2006.

Mohamad, Mahathir. "A Backlash Begins." *Financial Times,* September 4, 1998.

North, Douglass C. *Structure and Change in Economic History.* New York: W. W. Norton, 1981.

Obstfeld, Maurice, and Kenneth Rogoff. "The Unsustainable U.S. Current Account Position Revisited." National Bureau of Economic Research Working Paper 10869. October 2004. www.nber.org.

———. "Global Current Account Imbalances and Exchange Rate Adjustments." *Brookings Papers on Economic Activity* 1 (2005). www.economics.harvard.edu/faculty/rogoff/papers/BPEA2005.pdf.

Olson, Mancur. "Big Bills Left on the Sidewalk: Why Some Countries Are Rich and Others Poor." *Journal of Economic Perspectives* 10 (Spring 1996): 3–24.

———. *Power and Prosperity: Outgrowing Communist and Capitalist Dictatorships.* New York: Basic Books, 2000.

Organisation for Economic Co-operation and Development. *Economic Outlook,* June 2007. Paris.

Prasad, Eswar S., Kenneth Rogoff, Shang-Jin Wei, and M. Ayhan Kose. *Effects of Financial Globalization on Developing Countries: Some Empirical Evidence.* IMF Occasional Paper 220. Washington, DC: International Monetary Fund, 2003.

Rajan, Raghuram, and Luigi Zingales. "Financial Dependence and Growth." *American Economic Review* 88, no. 3 (1998): 559–86.

———. *Saving Capitalism from the Capitalists: Unleashing the Power of Financial Markets to Create Wealth and Spread Opportunity.* New York: Crown, 2003.

Reading, Brian. "Monthly Review 216." Lombard Street Research, London. June 2007. www.lombardstreetresearch.com (subscribers only).

Reinert, Erik S. *How Rich Countries Got Rich . . . and Why Poor Countries Stay Poor.* London: Constable and Robinson, 2007.

Reinhart, Carmen, Kenneth Rogoff, and Michael Savastano. "Addicted to Dollars." National Bureau of Economic Research Working Paper 10015. October 2003. www.nber.org.

———. "Debt Intolerance." *Brookings Papers on Economic Activity* 1 (2003): 1–62.

Rogoff, Kenneth, and Jerome Zettelmeyer. "Early Ideas of Sovereign Debt Reorganization: A Survey." IMF Working Paper 02/57. March 2002. www.imf.org.

Roubini, Nouriel, and Brad Setser. "The U.S. as a Net Debtor: The Sustainability of the U.S. External Imbalances. Roubini Global Economics. November 2004. www.rgemonitor.com/Roubini-Setser-US-External-Imbalances.pdf.

Sachs, Jeffrey. *The End of Poverty: Economic Possibilities of Our Time.* New York: Penguin, 2005.

Smith, Adam. *An Inquiry into the Nature and Causes of the Wealth of Nations,* first published 1776, with an introduction and notes by Jonathan B. Wright. London: Harriman House, 2007.

Soros, George. *The Crisis of Global Capitalism.* New York: Little, Brown, 1999.

———. *Open Society: Reforming Global Capitalism.* New York: Public Affairs, 2000.

Stein, Herbert. "Herb Stein's Unfamiliar Quotations: On Money, Madness, and Making Mistakes." *Slate,* May 16, 1997. www.slate.com.

Stiglitz, Joseph E. *Globalization and Its Discontents.* New York: W. W. Norton, 2002.

Summers, Lawrence H. "Remarks before the International Monetary Fund." March 9, 1998. www.ustreas.gov.

———. "Reflections on Global Account Imbalances and Emerging Markets Reserve Accumulation." L. K. Jha Memorial Lecture, Reserve Bank of India, March 24, 2006. www.president/harvard.edu/speeches/2006/0324_rbi.html.

Taleb, Nassim Nicholas. *The Black Swan.* London: Penguin, 2007.

Triffin, Robert. *Gold and the Dollar Crisis.* New Haven, CT: Yale University Press, 1960.

Williamson, John. *Curbing the Boom-Bust Cycle: Stabilizing Capital Flows to Emerging Markets*. Policy Analyses in International Economics. Washington, DC: Institute for International Economics, July 2005.

Wolf, Martin. *Why Globalization Works*. New Haven, CT: Yale University Press, 2004.

———. "Why Is China Growing So Slowly?" *Foreign Policy,* January–February 2005. www.foreignpolicy.com.

———. "Will Asian Mercantilism Meet Its Waterloo?" Richard Snape Lecture, Melbourne, Australian Government Productivity Commission, November 14, 2005. www.pc.gov.au/lectures/snape/wolf/wolf/pdf.

———. "Fixing Global Finance": Lecture 1: "Hopes Unfulfilled: Capital Flows and the Emerging Market Crises"; Lecture 2: "Capital Flows Upstream: The Emergence of the Global Imbalances"; Lecture 3: "Task Unfinished: Making Global Finance Work." Bernard L. Schwartz Forum on Constructive Capitalism, School of Advanced International Studies of the Johns Hopkins University, Washington, DC, March 28–30, 2006. www.sais-jhu.edu/mediastream/video Ondemand/martinwolf20006.html.

———. "Villains and Victims of Global Capital Flows." *Financial Times,* June 12, 2007. www.ft.com.

Wooldridge, Philip D. "The Changing Composition of Official Reserves." *BIS Quarterly Review,* September 2006, 25–38.

World Bank. *Finance for Growth: Policy Choices in a Volatile World*. Washington, DC, 2001.

———. *Doing Business in 2006: Creating Jobs*. Washington, DC, 2006. www.doing business.org.

Index

adverse selection, 13, 22, 35–36, 45
Aliber, Robert, 28
Argentina: crises in, 31, 33, 34, 37, 45, 49; default by, 186; exchange rate policies of, 171, 181
Asia: Chiang Mai Initiative, 190, 211–12n10; domestic-currency bonds in, 175; export-led growth in, 57, 141; foreign direct investment in, 84, 145; reserve accumulations in, 84, 87, 92, 141; savings rates in, 69. *See also* current account surpluses, in Asia; emerging economies; *individual countries*
Asian financial crisis (1997–98), 27, 37, 39, 41, 49, 57. *See also* South Korea
asymmetric information problems, 13–14, 22

Bagehot, Walter, 19
balance of payments, 77, 201n18, 201–2n19; of emerging economies, 37–39; global, 4–5, 77–78, 81. *See also* current account balances; trade balances
Bangladesh, microfinance in, 14
Bank for International Settlements, 95, 172, 184
banking crises, 31, 32. *See also* financial crises

banks, 15–16; deposit insurance, 19–20; deposits, 11, 26–27; in emerging economies, 21, 23; as financial intermediaries, 15–16; foreign-currency deposits, 26–27; foreign-currency loans, 26–27, 48; loans, 15–16, 19, 41, 44; regulation of, 20, 23, 82, 194; risks, 15–16; stability of system, 19–20, 34–35
Beck, Thorsten, 21
Bernanke, Ben, 58, 75, 100, 119
Bhagwati, Jagdish, 2
"black swans," 13
bonds. *See* debt securities
Bordo, Michael, 31, 174
Brazil, 37, 92
Bretton Woods system, 17, 81–82, 98
"Bretton Woods Two," 81–82, 100, 140, 141–46, 167
Bruegel, 115, 116
Buiter, Willem, 132, 134–35
Bureau of Economic Analysis, U.S., 124, 126, 136

Caballero, Ricardo J., 122, 128
Calvo, Guillermo, 25, 26
capital, efficiency of, 21, 142